NIETZSCHE
AS
CULTURAL
PHYSICIAN

NIETZSCHE AS CULTURAL PHYSICIAN

DANIEL R. AHERN

THE PENNSYLVANIA STATE UNIVERSITY PRESS
UNIVERSITY PARK, PENNSYLVANIA

Library of Congress Cataloging-in-Publication Data

Ahern, Daniel R., 1952–
   Nietzsche as cultural physician / Daniel R. Ahern.
      p.   cm.
   Includes bibliographical references and index.
   ISBN 0-271-01425-3 (alk. paper)
   1. Nietzsche, Friedrich Wilhelm, 1844–1900.   I. Title.
B3317.A37   1995
193—dc20   94-31510
                                                                                          CIP

Copyright © 1995 The Pennsylvania State University
All rights reserved.
Printed in the United States of America
Published by The Pennsylvania State University Press,
University Park, PA 16802-1003

It is the policy of The Pennsylvania State University Press to use acid-free paper for the first printing of all clothbound books. Publications on uncoated stock satisfy the minimum requirements of American National Standard for Information Sciences—Permanence of Paper for Printed Library Materials, ANSI Z39.48–1992.

Contents

Acknowledgments vii
Key to Abbreviations ix
Introduction 1
Chapter 1 The Philosophical Physician: Life as Will to Power 9
Chapter 2 The Physiology of Spirit 27
Chapter 3 Philosophy as Will to Power and the Case of Socrates 51
Chapter 4 Jesus Christ and the Origins of Christianity 85
Chapter 5 Visions of Innocence 123
Conclusion 187
Bibliography 201
Index 205

For Brendan

Acknowledgments

I wish to express my thanks to Dr. Jakob Amstutz, of the University of Guelph, for his help and confidence from the very beginning. Thanks also go to Dr. Jean-Marc Lemilin, of the Memorial University of Newfoundland, Dr. Frank Cronin, of St. Thomas University, and Dr. John van Buren, of Fordham University, for their interest, encouragement, and friendship. I am also very grateful to Sanford G. Thatcher, director of the Pennsylvania State University Press, for his patience and interest in this work, and to Lionel Gadoury for his generosity and care in designing and illustrating the jacket of this book.

I cannot even begin to thank my best friend, Dr. Annette Ahern, for her love, criticism, patience, and support throughout. Finally, thanks go to my son, Brendan, for sleeping through the nights and for his understanding of promises.

Key to Abbreviations

Listed below are the abbreviations I use for all references to Nietzsche's published and unpublished works as well as his correspondence.

I. Translations of Nietzsche's Published Works

A	*The Anti-Christ*
B	*Beyond Good and Evil*
BT	*The Birth of Tragedy*
C	*The Case of Wagner*
D	*Daybreak*
E	*Ecce Homo*
G	*On the Genealogy of Morals*
GS	*The Gay Science*
HH	*Human, All Too Human*
T	*Twilight of the Idols*
U	*Untimely Meditations*
Z	*Thus Spoke Zarathustra*

II. Translations of Nietzsche's Unpublished Works

HC	"Homer's Contest"
P	"The Last Philosopher; the Philosopher; Reflections on the Struggle Between Art and Knowledge"
PAC	"The Philosopher as Cultural Physician"
PH	"Thoughts on the Meditation: Philosophy in Hard Times"
PTA	"Philosophy in the Tragic Age of the Greeks"
SSW	"The Struggle Between Science and Wisdom"

TL   "On Truth and Lies in a Nonmoral Sense"
WP   "The Will to Power"

III. Nietzsche's Collected Works

BKG   *Nietzsche Briefwechsel: Kritische Gesamtausgabe*
M   *Friedrich Nietzsche Gesammelte Werke: Musarionausgabe*
WKG   *Nietzsche Werke: Kritische Gesamtausgabe*

IV. Translations of Nietzsche's Letters and Early Notebooks

SPL   *Nietzsche: A Self-Portrait from His Letters*
SLN   *Selected Letters of Friedrich Nietzsche*
PT   *Philosophy and Truth: Selections from Nietzsche's Notebooks of the Early 1870's*
PN   *The Portable Nietzsche*

All references to Nietzsche's published works are found in parentheses in the body of the text. These parentheses contain the abbreviation of the work referred to (see part I of the list above), the essay number or abbreviation (when applicable), and the section number from which the reference is taken. The translations I have used for the published works, unless indicated otherwise, are Walter Kaufmann's and R. J. Hollingdale's and are found in the Bibliography.

The majority of my references to Nietzsche's unpublished works are to his notes between 1883 and 1888, the translations of which are from *The Will To Power*. For the purposes of brevity, my references to these notes are also in parentheses in the body of the text and contain the abbreviation WP along with the section number from which the reference is taken. The section numbers are identical to those found in *Friedrich Nietzsche Gesammelte Werke: Musarionausgabe*.

References to Nietzsche's notebooks between 1872 and 1876, also found in parentheses in the text, contain, first, the source of the translation (an abbreviation from part II above and the relevant page or section numbers) and, second, the source for the German original (an abbreviation from part III above and the relevant page numbers). I have used Marianne Cowan's translation of "Philosophy in the Tragic Age of the Greeks." References to this work are found in parentheses in the text, containing, first, the source of the translation (the abbreviation PTA followed by both the section and page numbers) and, second, the source of the German original (an abbreviation from part III above and the relevant volume and page numbers). Translations of "The Last Philosopher; the Philosopher; Reflections on the Struggle Between Art and Knowledge," "The Philosopher as Cultural Physician," "Thoughts on the Meditation: Philosophy in Hard Times," "The Struggle Between Science and Wisdom," and "On Truth and Lies in a Nonmoral Sense" are from *Philosophy and Truth: Selections from Nietzsche's Notebooks of the Early 1870's*, translated by Daniel Breazeale. I have used Walter Kaufmann's translation of "Homer's Contest."

Unless indicated otherwise, the German text for my references to Nietzsche's correspondence is *Nietzsche Briefwechsel: Kritische Gesamtausgabe*. All references to the letters are found in footnotes, indicating the recipient, the date (when indicated), the source for the translation (an abbreviation from part IV above and the relevant page or pages), and, in parentheses, the source for the German original (the abbreviation BKG and the relevant volume and page numbers).

All italics in quotations from Nietzsche's texts are Nietzsche's unless indicated otherwise. Finally, my editorial omissions of Nietzsche's words or phrases are indicated by ellipsis points. Wherever the ellipsis points are Nietzsche's, this is indicated in a footnote.

I am still waiting for a philosophical *physician* in the exceptional sense of that word—one who has to pursue the problem of the total health of a people, time, race or of humanity—to muster the courage to push my suspicion to its limits and to risk the proposition: what was at stake in all philosophizing hitherto was not at all "truth" but something else—let us say, health, future, growth, power, life.

—Nietzsche

Introduction

When we read Nietzsche's texts, we find that he was familiar with quiet, delicate things. Sometimes it seems his descriptions of cultures blooming into genius and death were possible only because he overheard flowers in conversation. He speaks of our world in the gentle tone of a whispered secret, while somehow, and at the same time, with the cold conviction of an ancient warrior king. And his is always the language of life: instincts, perspectives, power, blood, suspicion, and, most notably, sickness and health. Sickness and health serve as a standard for Nietzsche, one through which he judges the value of everything from individuals and cultures to philosophy and political ideologies, according to what he called an order of rank.

This book explores the significance of Nietzsche's conception of sickness and health, for, as I hope to show, he approaches virtually everything he speaks of in the manner of a physician of culture. As is appropriate to such a physician, he possesses what I call a clinical standpoint. This standpoint plays a pivotal role in the dominating themes in his thinking: namely, the will to power, the revaluation of all values, the eternal recurrence, the overman, and the symbol of Dionysus.

It is fairly common knowledge that Nietzsche emphasizes the body as a philosophical point of departure. And it is also common for commentators to refer to Nietzsche's tendency to pursue medical, biological, naturalistic, and physiological themes. But what Nietzsche called "my physiological turn of mind" has not been pursued to any great length.[1] Martin Heidegger sees the "physiology" embedded in

---

1. Nietzsche to Franz Overbeck, February 11, 1883, SPL 70–71 (BKG III¹:324).

Nietzsche's philosophy as a serious inadequacy. He rightly says that Nietzsche's philosophy is "thought absolutely in terms of the physiology of the will to power."[2] But for Heidegger, this "physiology" bars Nietzsche from asking the essential question of Being. Karl Jaspers says Nietzsche's references to the body "allow a biological way of speaking [to] constantly . . . pass for insight."[3] Walter Kaufmann, on the other hand, is so concerned with attacking those who identify Nietzsche with the aspirations of Nazi Germany that he is rendered incapable of looking at the pervasive theme of physiology. Indeed, the very word "physiology" is a red flag to Kaufmann, particularly in its connotation of selective breeding.[4]

There are many paths through Nietzsche's texts, and the "physiology" I pursue here is by no means "definitive." My excavation of this theme in Nietzsche's published and unpublished works is based merely on my own curiosity about how he could, with such ringing conviction, refer to various individuals or entire epochs as "healthy" or "sick." Hence, my study is limited to articulating Nietzsche's thinking in terms of the body's physiological dynamics and is not particularly concerned with deconstructing, demythologizing, or defending his physiological turn of mind. Every interpretive path, including that taken here, opens up possibilities for others; and when, now and then, we find ourselves on the verge of a "conclusion," we always seem to have more questions than answers. Aside from the questions we ask ourselves, we also ask them of others. In light of the physiology explored here, I have found myself wondering if Heidegger's insistence on the "question of Being" might not itself be an expression of will to power? Is his demand for the essence of Being peculiar to the perspective of that multifaceted instinct Nietzsche called self-preservation? Is what Jaspers called Nietzsche's biological way of speaking really so devoid of genuine insight into everything Nietzsche took seriously?

Kaufmann is quite justified in his antagonism to the Nazi propagandists' exploitation of Nietzsche's observations on breeding. But does the ugliness of the Third Reich justify ignoring Nietzsche's comments on the possibility of breeding certain types of human beings? Kaufmann is right to attack the perception of Nietzsche as an anti-Semite. But had he

---

2. Martin Heidegger, *Nietzsche*, vol. 4, *Nihilism*, ed. David F. Krell, trans. Frank A. Capuzzi (San Francisco: Harper & Row, 1982), 134.

3. Karl Jaspers, *Nietzsche: An Introduction to the Understanding of His Philosophical Activity*, trans. Charles F. Wallraff and Frederick J. Schmitz (South Bend, Ind.: Regnery/Gateway, 1979), 315n.

4. Walter Kaufmann, *Nietzsche: Philosopher, Psychologist, Antichrist*, 3d ed. (New York: Vintage, 1968), 304–5.

looked at the theme of physiology in Nietzsche's texts, he would have recognized why Nietzsche saw the Jews as "the strongest, toughest, and purest race now living in Europe" (B 251) and how the Jews—unlike the Greeks—avoided cultural decadence.[5]

Nietzsche's diagnosis of nihilism as the disease reserved for modernity has, in many respects, radically changed the face of philosophy. Some, of course, will find my idea of Nietzsche as a cultural physician too limited, since it relies too heavily on his interpretations of nature and physiology. It is suggested that since cultural values and morality are somehow "unnatural," we cannot understand Nietzsche's perception of these by concentrating on his depiction of the role of nature and the dynamics of the organic realm. As one commentator says, the choice of morality is, for Nietzsche, "made on aesthetic grounds."[6] There can be little doubt that, indeed, morality and values are embraced according to a certain "aesthetics" in Nietzsche's thinking. But I hope to show that this "aesthetics" can also be understood in terms of the organic necessity for "deception" as a condition of life.

The human ability to create deceptions, the illusions essential for survival and growth, is characteristic of that realm in Nietzsche's philosophy generally referred to as perspectivism. It is here that he is seemingly irresistible to contemporary deconstruction. Though this is not the place to consider the problems and merits of deconstruction, Nietzsche's influence on it is evident. By eroding the conviction that via interpretations of eternal Truth, Justice, and Beauty we had an intimate connection to the transcendent foundations of existence, he was instrumental in undermining the tradition of metaphysics. The works of Jacques Derrida have pushed this erosion further. With Derrida, the coherent structure of language does not stand in accord with or represent the structures of "reality." Hence the meaning of any interpretation bears within itself the seeds of its own dissolution because, as Derrida says, "meaning . . . is already, and thoroughly, constituted by a tissue of differences . . . the presumed interiority of meaning is already worked upon by its own exteriority."[7] If I understand Derrida correctly,

---

5. In this regard, one should also look at Nietzsche's conception of a mixed European race in HH 1:475. I have seen only one approach to Nietzsche's work that bears a powerful resemblance to my investigation of physiology: Claudia Crawford's "Nietzsche's Physiology of Ideological Criticism," in *Nietzsche as Postmodernist: Essays Pro and Contra*, ed. Clayton Koelb (Albany: State University of New York Press, 1990), 161–86.

6. Allan Megill, *Prophets of Extremity: Nietzsche, Heidegger, Foucault, Derrida* (Berkeley and Los Angeles: University of California Press, 1985), 31.

7. Jacques Derrida, *Positions*, trans. Alan Blas (Chicago: University of Chicago Press, 1981), 33.

he is telling us that the meaning of an interpretation is not to be regarded as something corresponding to reality. On the contrary, his idea of *différance* indicates that every interpretation possesses a "meaning,"—that is, its interiority—only through a web of (what Nietzsche would call) "resistances" to other perspectives embedded in the very fabric of language. The meaning of an interpretation is "maintained" *via* a cluster of other possible interpretations that have been, as it were, "sealed off" and kept "external" to the original within its very construction. Hence, any interpretation, any text, is deconstructed through an examination of how its construction has "silenced" a plethora of interpretive possibilities. By allowing even one of these to "speak," the "integrity" of the text dissolves into a multiplicity of interpretations that were "repressed" in the construction of the text.

Nietzsche certainly sees that an interpretation is a "perspective" with its particular agenda. For him, each interpretation not only proceeds via a blindness to and silencing of multiple perspectives but also cannot "function" without resisting other perspectives. What distinguishes Nietzsche's thinking from deconstruction, however, is that in spite of his pointing to the multiplicity of interpretations, he sees them all betray the symptomatic codes of sickness and health. For him, interpretation is the sign language, not of the eternal truths of metaphysics, but of the concrete events of the body as will to power.

Generally speaking, deconstructionists see each of what Nietzsche would consider multiple perspectives as somehow possessing an equal status within any interpretation. But again, what separates Nietzsche from deconstruction is his inclination to rank interpretations according to the standard mentioned above: sickness and health. For this reason, Nietzsche does not see an egalitarian or democratic relation between the perspectives embedded in any interpretation. On the contrary, it seems quite clear that, at least as far as he is concerned, the inclination to embrace egalitarian or democratic interpretations is itself symptomatic of mediocrity at best, or profound illness at worst.

Whether or not deconstruction is an exercise in mediocrity or characteristic of the illness of our epoch is not my concern here. My examination of Nietzsche's thinking makes no pretense of representing a deconstructionist approach. But my look at Nietzsche shows that he is one of its foremost precursors insofar as he locates the dynamics of interpretation within the hieroglyphs of a multiplicity of instincts, all of which are locked in the combat essential to the preservation and growth of every living thing.

Derrida has pointed out the lack of "protocols" to determine which interpretations are "good" or "bad."⁸ And here again, Nietzsche can be separated from deconstruction insofar as his standard of sickness and health, or "ascending and descending" instincts, does, whether or not we accept this standard, provide him with these protocols. For example, Socrates' interpretation of morality certainly bears a multiplicity of perspectives, but each perspective stands in an order of rank determined by the *strength* of an "infection" peculiar to Socrates. Hence, Nietzsche sees Socratic morality as bad, to say the least, and says that our only chance for "goodness" rests in being "immoral" at all times.

Beginning with Nietzsche, the means to determine "good and bad" interpretations started to dissolve. But this does not mean that he was indifferent to creating new standards. His conception of physiology is possibly a metaphor for the activity of interpretation. But integral to this activity, for Nietzsche, is a means to decide when to say yes and when to say no. The standard he embraces hinges, not on the transcendent "Truths" of metaphysics, but rather on the absence of these in a future promising, not metaphorical, but quite certain death, pain, and suffering.⁹

When Nietzsche set out to annihilate metaphysics, he saw the simultaneous destruction of "everything men have heretofore respected and loved."¹⁰ Inherent to this destruction is the confrontation of the human animal with the impossibility of deceiving itself with the security of absolute, eternal Truth. In this wilderness, the absence of Truth is only the occasion for the genuine tragedy of cultivating the metaphors vital to everything Nietzsche considered essential to any healthy culture: sacrifice, respect, love, honor, and, of course, courage. In short, despite his attempt to obliterate the foundations of Western values, he sought new foundations, new standards, indeed, a new "virtue." In this, he remained within the spirit of the metaphysics he sought to destroy and was as concerned with the question of values as was Plato.

Like the deconstructive analyses he anticipated, Nietzsche could dissolve any interpretation that attempted to speak according to some secret code of Truth. But unlike deconstruction, Nietzsche exploded interpretations, not for interpretation's sake, but rather to expose the

---

8. Ibid., 63.
9. For the purposes of clarity, I use the term "Truth" in reference to what Nietzsche considered a fiction contingent upon will to power, but a fiction that falls within his understanding of decadence and sickness. In contrast, I use the term "truth," again, in reference to a fiction contingent upon will to power, but a fiction that falls within his understanding of vitality and health.
10. Nietzsche to Reinhardt von Seydlitz, February 12, 1988, SPL 106 (BKG III⁵:248).

multifaceted codes of "sickness" that undermine the capacity of the human animal to decide what is worth destroying, what is worth preserving, and what is worth dying for. The question remains whether deconstruction can, or even should, provide the interpretations that allow for these decisions. But from Nietzsche's "clinical" point of view, the death of metaphysics only galvanizes the necessity to make them. In this sense, an openness to a multiplicity of interpretive perspectives can be symptomatic of the "strength" to decide on moral questions or of a "paralysis" before them.

The first two chapters of my study investigate Nietzsche's clinical standpoint per se. In this vein, the dynamics of the will to power are explored in terms of his unique understanding of physiology. This physiology is the foundation of the criterion used by Nietzsche to determine health, sickness, weakness, exhaustion, and decadence. I describe this criterion via both the individual (Chapter 1) and culture (Chapter 2) as organic structures of life as will to power.

Chapter 3 consists of three separate yet simultaneous enterprises: examinations of (*a*) Socrates as an example of physiological decadence, (*b*) his decadence as symptomatic of the sickness of his culture as a whole, and (*c*) this illness as a factor in the sickness of modernity. This chapter constitutes an *application* of the clinical standpoint delineated in the first two chapters. It exemplifies how Nietzsche diagnoses decadence within both the philosophical type and the culture wherein this type flourishes. Here "decadent" is "a word . . . meant not to condemn but only to describe."[11]

Chapter 4 has approximately the same goals as Chapter 3, but is concerned with Christ and Christianity. Here the physiological decadence of Christ and Christianity is considered in relation to the relative health of the ancient Hebrew culture. In light of Nietzsche's clinical treatment of the ancient Greek and Hebrew cultures, considered in Chapters 3 and 4 respectively, his comparison of ancient and Christian cultures raises problems of historical accuracy. His physiological approach to Greek metaphysics and Christianity is so predominant that his adherence "to the facts" is questionable at best. My primary concern, however, is to demonstrate the pervasive clinical standpoint of the physician of culture and not to assess Nietzsche's qualifications as a historian.

The fifth and final chapter again consists of several simultaneous considerations: (*a*) of nihilism as the disease peculiar to modernity, (*b*)

---

11. Nietzsche to Carl Fuchs, suspected to have been written around the middle of April 1886, SPL 83 (BKG III³:177).

of Nietzsche himself as infected with this disease, and (c) of Nietzsche's proposal for a cure. In pursuing these matters, I explore the physiological basis of the revaluation of all values, the doctrine of eternal recurrence, the overman, and the symbol of Dionysus. My investigation concludes with critical observations in regard to the foregoing.

1
The Philosophical Physician: Life as Will to Power

> The path to my fixed purpose is laid with iron rails, whereon my soul is grooved to run. Over unsounded gorges, through the rifled hearts of mountains, under torrents' beds, unerringly I rush! Naught's an obstacle, naught's an angle to the iron way!
>
> —Herman Melville, *Moby Dick*

There is nothing ordinary about Nietzsche's texts. Kazantzakis called them a "jungle full of famished beasts and dizzying orchids,"[1] and he is right. Therein pythons wind through drunken flowers, grim laughter spites death on smoking battlefields, and a hush lies over temple ruins wherein Nietzsche would linger but soon would leave behind. Rilke said, "[W]e live our lives, forever taking leave,"[2] and I think Nietzsche, both in life and thought, was always moving on to a place he could call his own.

Having never found that place, his spiritual homeland, he became one of the few "to call themselves homeless in a distinctive and honorable sense" (GS 377). Far, far into the future Nietzsche envisioned epochs greater and healthier than his own. But this vision hinges on a

---

1. Nikos Kazantzakis, *Report to Greco*, trans. P. A. Bien (New York: Bantam Books, 1971), 306.
2. Rainer Maria Rilke, *Duino Elegies*, trans. J. B. Leishman and Stephen Spender (New York: W. W. Norton, 1939), 71.

fascinating expedition to the sources of modernity's spiritual illness. This voyage is his critique of the *history* of Western values. Here, with the calm and sensitivity of those no longer shocked at unexpected grandeur or the macabre, he leads us through the palaces, as well as the sewers, of Greek philosophy and Christianity.

Convinced that Western values are bled of their once overflowing vitality, Nietzsche foresees an inevitable encounter with another quite different traveler. This refined visitor, with the subtle odor of decay, only calls on cultures that have lost all sense of identity and direction. And Western culture, steeped in the values of a dying Greek culture and Christianity, is well prepared for this "uncanniest of all guests" (WP 1)—nihilism.

Within the dissolution of Western culture's unity of purpose, nihilism has found a home, and so the West flies toward "catastrophe, with a tortured tension that is growing from decade to decade" (WP pref.:2). For Nietzsche, nihilism is the secret death wish of a culture. In the haunted soul of a coward contemplating suicide, killing another human being, taking another's life "with" one into death, may be an easy step. Within the ravages of nihilism, Nietzsche sees us seeking not only our own destruction but, in despairing rage, that of the very cosmos itself.

But he also sees another path for the human spirit, one in which all the suffering in history is justified in creating the hero, whose soul, forged within the calamities and victories of the human race, constitutes "the first of a new nobility . . . [and] a happiness . . . humanity has not known so far" (GS 337). Here is a vision of humanity that, liberated from history and an attendant weariness with life, exploits its history toward a future of spiritual nobility. Finding *this* tomorrow is Nietzsche's philosophical project.

The Will to Power as Cosmological Doctrine

Physiology

The more Nietzsche regarded his age as sick, the more he identified himself as a cultural physician. He became the philosophical doctor for an ailing Western culture whose illness required stern diagnosis. Then, as he said, "with a responsibility for all millennia after me" (E 2:10), he proposed a cure that for some is incomprehensible and for others is terrifying. But the "diagnosis" (exemplified in the cases of Socrates and Jesus Christ) and the "cure" (a facet of which is embodied by the overman) are inaccessible without close exegesis of his idea of will to power. Clearly, such a task must take seriously and clarify not only Nietzsche's innumerable references to sickness and health but also, and more important, the highly mobile framework within which he uses these terms: specifically, the conception of physiology intrinsic to his articulation of will to power.

Nietzsche's view of physiology bears little resemblance to the specialized science recognized today. Nietzsche spoke of "physiology" in terms of its meaning within the all-encompassing doctrine of will to power. This cosmological frame of reference is lacking in the modern science of physiology, but it permeates Nietzsche's view of physiology as he weaves it into observations on history, culture, science, and, intimately related to these, the question of values. Just as the pre-Socratics interpreted the totality of being as the *archē* of water, fire, and so forth, so Nietzsche interprets the totality of being as will to power. To understand physiology as he did, we must consider (*a*) will to power as a cosmological principle, (*b*) the will to power manifest in organic life forms, and (*c*) the physiology of the human animal within the context of this cosmology.[3]

Caution is required in referring to the will to power as metaphysics, because of Nietzsche's well-known antagonism to the tradition *after* Socrates. Yet in saying "the innermost essence of being is will to power" (WP 693), Nietzsche makes what is generally considered a metaphysical claim. However, since he held philosophy after Socrates in such contempt, I hesitate to assert his desire to philosophize within a tradition he despised. To Nietzsche, Socrates is an "infection" pervading all philosophy, that is, "metaphysics, theology, psychology, epistemology" (T 4:3). On the other hand, the old cosmological tradition is prodigiously healthy, and it is his identification of health with cosmology and sickness with metaphysics that constitutes for Nietzsche their radical difference.

Cosmology

When a young man, Nietzsche embraced the pre-Socratic quest for an articulation of the unity of all things. In 1872 he found philosophy's *"highest worth"* in the pre-Socratic interpretation of the *archē*, which takes the cosmos *"and subdues it to unity"* (P 9; M 6:11). In 1888, the final

---

3. The descriptions of sickness and health provided in this chapter are general. They are developed further in the following chapter and are *applied* to the cases of Socrates and Jesus Christ.

year of his intellectual life, he maintained that the pre-Socratics forge "the great conceptions of things . . . represent these conceptions," and articulate "the great possibilities of the philosophical ideal" (WP 437). Even if its systems are completely erroneous, Greek cosmology remained a path to "reconstruct[ing] the philosophic image . . . and therefore a possibility" (PTA pref.:23; M 4:151).

Nietzsche seized this possibility and affirmed the will to power: a grand cosmological scheme, nearly two thousand years after Socrates. From out of the vortex of this strange *archē*, Nietzsche approached anew the ancient question, "Why is there something rather than nothing?" and dissolved the world into a

> magnitude of force . . . [that] transforms itself . . . at the same time one and many . . . eternally changing, eternally flooding back . . . a becoming that knows no . . . weariness: this [is] my *Dionysian* world of the eternally self-creating . . . [and] self-destroying . . . do you want a *name* for this world? . . . *This world is the will to power—and nothing besides*! And you yourselves are also this will to power—and nothing besides! (WP 1067)

This passage, with its drunken bravado and insolent challenge to death itself, echoes the laughter of Dionysus but lacks a *human-centered* metaphysics with a built-in moral code. The conception of will to power is devoid of "the *hyperbolic naiveté* of man: positing himself as the meaning and measure of the value of things" (WP 12).[4] The self-absorbed character of post-Socratic thought is typical of metaphysics. "Beginning with Socrates," Nietzsche says, "the individual all at once began to take himself too seriously" (SSW 132; M 6:103). A certain "anxiety concerning oneself becomes the soul of philosophy" (SSW 135; M 6:107), culminating in morbid concerns over "the 'salvation of the soul' or . . . 'what is happiness?' " (SSW 144; M 6:117). As philosophy became more *self*-centered, there developed an inclination to negate the value of life via an attempt to escape the world. For Nietzsche, pre-Socratic cosmology may moralize, but it neither denies the value of existence nor attempts to escape it.

The world, Nietzsche says, "is the will to power—and nothing besides"; as such, our world is devoid of ultimate goals, duties, or

---

4. Nietzsche denies man as "the measure of all things." Heidegger, on the other hand, sees the conception of the overman as Nietzsche's "fall" toward a "subjectivism" that Heidegger traces back through Descartes and Plato to Protagoras. My investigation reveals that the overman is by no means the "measure of all things." See note 7 to Chapter 2.

"progress." Nor is there the consolation that our existence has an a priori, transcendent value, because every living thing "is only a *means* to something; it is the expression of forms of the growth of power" (WP 706). Humanity is not an end in itself; we are simply another organic structure; and it is "quite arbitrary to assert that everything strives to enter into *this* form of the will to power" (WP 692). From this standpoint, it is naive to see "spirituality or morality or any other particular of the sphere of consciousness as the highest value . . . [or to] justify 'the world' by means of this" (WP 707).

The universe is the child of chaos; nothing is stable; nothing remains. Assertions of "reality" and "truth" are the attempts of one form of power to realize stability within cosmic anarchy. As will to power, everything is swept up into the hurricane of becoming, the womb of all things. How do we capture in words precisely what allows us to speak at all? How can we give voice to the silence at the heart of things natural or produced by human hands? This is exactly what Nietzsche tried to do with his idea of will to power: a terrifying, mesmerizing chaos, the primal lightning of creation and destruction, an immaterial force heaving throughout the cosmos, and the law of the possibility and inevitable obliteration of all things. The will to power is the name for the unity of being and nothingness. It is Nietzsche's vision of ourselves and infinite worlds, flung upon the shores of contingency, innocent and forever mauled by the waves of becoming, each exploding with "the lust to dig up treasures . . . [until] nothing remains of the world but green twilight and . . . lightning" (GS 310).

Within this flux and flow of being and nonbeing, Nietzsche creates a standpoint that holds fast and echoes the dynamics of the *arche* of the cosmos. From there, he feels the tempo of will to power in everything from the edifice of culture to a butterfly balanced on a wildflower.

The Physiology of the Will to Power

Organic Life

Just as the pre-Socratics "bring *themselves* into a system" (WP 437; emphasis added) and thereby recognize human beings as unified with the cosmos, so does Nietzsche's conception of will to power. He saw the dynamics of power as constituting the being of all living things.

Every organism reveals becoming, that spontaneous and blind ignition to growth, transition, and transformation. Among living things, humans are just "one particular line of the total living organic world" (WP 678). Life is "defined as an enduring form of processes of the establishment of force, in which the different contenders grow unequally." This inequality pervades all organic life, including our own, and extends into the inorganic realm as well. What binds the organic and the inorganic together *as* will to power is "the repelling force exercised by every atom of force" (WP 642). The river and the mountain, for example, are power quanta repelling each other insofar as the river cannot wash away the mountain and the mountain cannot bury the river. They exist as what they "are" only through mutual resistance and opposition.

The organic realm is also a plethora of power quanta, but here a capacity for *deception* reveals a "rising order of rank of creatures. It seems to be lacking in the inorganic world . . . cunning begins in the organic world; plants are already masters of it" (WP 544). It seems odd to think of plants as masters of deception. But what Nietzsche saw in them was an uncanny ability to subjugate and exploit organic and inorganic compounds in order to enhance themselves. This blind and mysterious "force that through the green fuse drives the flower" is will to power.[5] The organic realm is "higher" than the inorganic insofar as the former reveals *dynamic* displays of power, while "in the domain of the inorganic . . . distant forces balance each other" (WP 637).

The will to power, Nietzsche says, "can manifest itself only against resistances; therefore it seeks that which resists it" (WP 656). Inorganic things are, of course, power quanta, but these lack the exploitative subtlety of the organic realm. Strictly speaking, Nietzsche sees the inorganic deadlocked through the mutual resistance of inertia: "power against power, quite crudely" (WP 544). On the other hand, every *living* thing is "an incarnate will to power . . . striv[ing] to grow . . . [and] become predominant" (B 259). Deception, cunning, a certain shrewdness, and a wonderful proficiency in self-enhancement and growth, beyond mere survival, constitute the domain of organic life.

Self-Preservation

Nietzsche's understanding of the instinct for self-preservation and of its place in the primitive organic realm is basic to his views on: (*a*) will to

---

5. Dylan Thomas, "The force that through the green fuse," in *Dylan Thomas Collected Poems: 1934–1953*, ed. W. Davies and R. Maud (London: J. M. Dent & Sons, 1988), 13.

power, (*b*) humanity as one of its organic forms, and (*c*) the fundamental distinction between pre- and post-Socratic thought.⁶

Zarathustra says the "living creature values many things higher than life itself; yet out of this evaluation itself speaks—the will to power" (Z 2:12). In short, life is not primarily self-preservative; enhanced strength is the secret of every living thing. Each reaches "as far from itself with its force as it can, and overwhelms what is weaker" (WP 769). When the protoplasm "extends pseudopodia and feels about," this is not, Nietzsche says, merely a self-preservative search for food. As will to power, this primitive organism seeks whatever resists it. Success in this search stimulates the "desire to overwhelm" until the obstacle is absorbed "into the power domain of the aggressor and has increased the same" (WP 656).

The *archē* of life is revealed in the mutual resistance of all organic entities, in the contest within which the victor wins, not the prize of bare survival, but enhanced strength. It is important to bear in mind that within this "contest" an organism as will to power may destroy itself in the attempt "to become *more*" (WP 688). Hence, Nietzsche insists that when it comes to living things, we cannot "take hunger as the *primum mobile*, any more than self-preservation" (WP 652). Self-preservation is only a consequence of "the original will to become stronger" (WP 702). Predictably, Nietzsche says physiologists "should think before . . . [naming] self-preservation as the cardinal instinct of an organic being" and should "beware of *superfluous* teleological principles" (B 13).

The Human Body

I think Camus was right in saying Nietzsche adopted the attitude of a clinician toward the problem of nihilism.⁷ But Nietzsche's diagnosis of nihilism is only one feature of the clinical standpoint that grounds virtually all the central tenets of his thought.

Nietzsche says any investigation into the origin of values requires, first, "a *physiological* investigation and interpretation." The creation of values and, therewith, culture is an activity peculiar to humans and needs, he says, "a critique on the part of medical science." It is therefore essential to engage "the interest of physiologists and doctors in these

---

6. It seems strange that a feature of even the most primitive life-forms is essential to the division of two epochs of Greek philosophy. Yet this basic characteristic of will to power—that is, that self-preservation is not the goal of life—pervades virtually every facet of Nietzsche's thought.

7. Albert Camus, *The Rebel*, trans. Anthony Bower (New York: Vintage, 1956), 65–66.

problems" (G 1:17).[8] Why? Because the organic activity integral to the creation, maintenance, and growth of culture has become seriously debilitated. Nihilism is the name of this degeneration—promoted by a philosophical tradition that has neglected the human as a living organism. Seeing this negligence as a symptom of the serious biological problem of nihilism, Nietzsche sets out to destroy the "quack-doctoring with which . . . mankind has hitherto been accustomed to treat the illnesses of its soul" (D 52).

Combat and the Order of Rank

For the cultural physician, the "body and physiology [is] the starting point" because these provide "the correct idea of the nature of our subject-unity . . . [as] an order of rank and division of labour . . . [that make] possible the whole and its parts." The body displays a physiological order of rank between different organic functions, and hence life as will to power. Within the chain of command constituting the body, Nietzsche sees resistance and struggle among its multiple functions. This opposition reveals "obeying and commanding, and that a fluctuating assessment of the limits of power is part of life" (WP 492). As an exquisite manifestation of will to power, Nietzsche insists that the human body be "discussed first, methodologically" (WP 489).

Even the "subject," or personal "identity," he says is a concept generated and determined by the dynamics of the body. Western philosophy has, "thanks to Socrates" (SSW 136; M 6:108), asserted that Truth is possible only through knowledge of the "self"—a knowledge that demands a radical separation of consciousness from the body. With this separation, the *unity* of the human animal with the cosmos is shattered and becomes a primary source of modern nihilism. It comes as no surprise then, that Nietzsche denies not only the radical schism between consciousness and the body but also the traditional high estimation of consciousness. He sees consciousness as yet another, and one of the weakest, of the body's physiological activities (GS 11). Whatever is in the sphere of conscious thought—from subjectivity and knowledge to truth and logic—is just the pale shadow of the fluctuating order of rank among "basic animal functions" (WP 674).

---

8. Nietzsche enthusiastically endorsed the creation of academic prizes for essays that help transform the "mistrustful relations between philosophy, physiology and medicine into . . . [an] amicable and fruitful exchange" (G 1:17).

Instinctive Interpretation: Perspectivism

These functions are that "tremendous quantum of *power*" (WP 704) he calls the instincts, all of which are "contained in a powerful unity" (B 36).[9] We are a multiplicity of instincts, all of which demand gratification. Each is a center of force seeking domination over the others. When one drive subdues another, the strength of the weaker is harnessed by the stronger. This produces, says Nietzsche, an "affect," or sensation of power, that is felt throughout the body and derived "from the one will to power" (WP 786).

The affects are a synthetic unity of sensations permeating the entire organism, including consciousness. These sensations of the power struggle among the drives are reflected in and constitute all conscious activity. Our interpretations of the world and the "self" are based, therefore, not on the sovereignty of self-consciousness, but on a "natural expediency in the organic" (WP 676). Ultimately, our instincts interpret everything, since "thinking is merely a relation" of the drives (B 36). For Nietzsche, when it comes to the "meaning of 'knowledge' . . . the concept is to be regarded in a strict and narrow anthropocentric and biological sense" (WP 480).

The primary role of the drives in all interpretation constitutes the physiological dynamics of Nietzsche's famous "perspectivism." Every drive, he says, "is a kind of lust to rule; each . . . has its perspective that it would like to compel all the other drives to accept as a norm" (WP 481). Each is a "center of force [that] adopts a perspective . . . i.e., its own particular valuation, mode of action, and mode of resistance." What occurs to consciousness "is a specific mode of action on the world, emanating from a center . . . and the 'world' is only a word for the totality of these actions" (WP 567). Before any articulation of the "world" becomes possible, Nietzsche says the perspectives of "our drives . . . their For and Against" (WP 481), is determined within "the fight" among "these onesided views . . . [until] there is a kind of justice and contract" between them (GS 333).

In short, among the drives an order of rank is established wherein they "maintain their existence and assert their rights against each other." This "contract" constitutes the overall perspective of the chain of command among the instincts. And it is this "contract," this overall affect, that, after the "last scenes of reconciliation . . . rise[s] to consciousness" (GS 333).

9. Nietzsche uses the terms "instinct," "passion," "drive," "need," and "desire" equivocally, as do I.

Since what appear to consciousness are the final "scenes" wherein an order of rank among the drives is established, we have traditionally believed consciousness imposes the "treaty" among our warring instincts. But this assumes consciousness is an active agent independent of and "essentially opposed to the instincts." But on the contrary, for Nietzsche, consciousness passively reflects and is itself "nothing but a *certain behaviour of the instincts toward one another*" (GS 333).

This is the underworld conflict Nietzsche saw within every human being: we are the combat of our instincts and their perspectives, each of which seeks power over the others. And even the canniest explorer in the realm of self-knowledge has a very incomplete image of the drives that "constitute his being . . . their number and strength, their ebb and flood, their play and counterplay among one another" (D 119).

What appears to consciousness is "based on a physiological process unknown to us" (D 119). We are conscious only of the affects, the sensations of power inherent to the struggle among the instincts, all of which strive to be "the highest courts of value in general, indeed as creative and ruling powers" (WP 677). Each is a self-centered, self-affirming perspective, through which the world is "seen, felt, interpreted as thus and thus so that organic life may preserve itself in this perspective of interpretation" (WP 678).

Such observations hint at Nietzsche's clinical standpoint on the whole of Western intellectual history, which consists of the hieroglyphs of the body, the "perspective valuations by virtue of which we can survive in life, i.e., in the will to power." History has never shown—nor will the future ever see—an individual or a culture grow in strength, Nietzsche says, unless the order of rank among the instincts "opens up new perspectives and . . . [thereby] new horizons—this idea permeates my writings" (WP 616).

An example of such "new horizons" is the possibility for radical transformation of what is called "human." *Der Übermensch* (the overman), that "metaphor" promising terror and spiritual supremacy for the future of humanity, is impossible without the power-perspectives of countless instincts all unified as flesh and blood (see WP 866). Every function of the body repeats "in miniature . . . the tendency of the whole" toward growth. Here Nietzsche sees "a diminutive formula for the total tendency" (WP 617) revealed in all living things as will to power. If we could learn to exploit this "formula," we would "stand in the service" of the power dynamics inherent to what he calls the "economics" of the body (WP 866). The possibility of manipulating this "economy" leads Nietzsche to say, "Not 'mankind' but *overman* is the goal!" (WP 1001). This idea of drive-perspectives unified to "the coordination of physiological forces and systems" (WP 229) is not only basic to Nietzsche's views on interpretation but also essential to both his articulation of Western history *and* that of a radical transformation of humanity. But to appreciate the tremendous cost (WP 867) Nietzsche recognized in his terrifying and inspired conception of the overman,[10] further discussion of the instincts is necessary.

The Order of Rank: Physiological Dynamics

Health

For Nietzsche, our instincts are a plethora of perspectives and strictly self-seeking centers of force that, as an organic mesh of will to power, are essential to our preservation and growth potential. Nietzsche's remarks on the ever-shifting chain of command among the drives opens the door to two basic themes in his thought: health and sickness. All the variations on these themes encountered throughout my study presuppose the flux in the order of rank among the instincts.

The human animal, like any other, evaluates or interprets the world according to the "definite perspective" of whichever instinct is dominant.[11] However, the instincts of animals other than ourselves answer, Nietzsche says, "to quite definite tasks." They possess, therefore, a harmony we humans do not share, since we are the combat of "a vast confusion of contradictory valuations and consequently of contradictory drives" (WP 259). Within this struggle, our instincts "oppose or subject each other (join synthetically or alternate in dominating)" (WP 677) and "are constantly increasing or losing their power" (WP 715).

There is no doubt that our instincts are our greatest sources of strength and most exquisitely manifest the cosmological law of life. The healthy individual must have these instincts, and it is essential that "one possesses them to the highest degree" (WP 928). But possession of powerful drives alone is not enough. Within the genuinely healthy type, one drive must establish its dominance and exploit the combined power of all the others in the *service of one goal*. The goal is, of course, the perspective of this overarching drive.

10. This region of Nietzsche's thought is given direct consideration in Chapter 5.
11. In this vein, Nietzsche also speaks, not of just one dominating instinct, but of several of them—an "oligarchy" of drives that share power to the extent that they are incapable of eclipsing one another's strength.

This "dominating passion" is the mark of "the supremest form of health," since "here the co-ordination of the inner systems and their operation in the service of one end is best achieved" (WP 778). When one drive, by its very intensity, overwhelms the others, it does not negate them; it synchronizes them. To this extent, it harmonizes the other instincts so as to allow them *all* gratification within *its* predominant perspective. Thus, the " 'great man' is great owing to the free play and scope of his desires and to the yet greater power that knows how to press these magnificent monsters into service" (WP 933). The cumulative affect, that sensation reflected in consciousness, is "the power of understanding with only the least assistance . . . 'intelligent' *sensuality.*" One's "thought" is a reflection of "strength as a feeling of dominion in the muscles . . . pleasure in movement, as dance . . . and *presto*" (WP 800). For now, the above may stand as a general sketch of "health." It serves as an outline to be expanded in this chapter and those that follow.

Weakness

The more complicated and, for Nietzsche, more "instructive" phenomenon of sickness, as a physiological dynamic, is not only a manifestation of will to power but also the sine qua non for all living things. To begin what is here again only a preliminary sketch, we have to outline the physiological conditions that make sickness possible. The first is weakness.

The weak individual, like the healthy, is saddled with multiple, competing drives. It is even possible that the former possesses instincts far superior in strength to the latter. The problem is, no one drive can harness the power of the others to establish the integrity characteristic of health. Instead, a constant "antagonism of the passions" prevails, which, Nietzsche says, is "very unhealthy" because synchronicity is lacking. Unless "one passion at last becomes master" (WP 778), the individual has, as it were, no priorities, no *telos*. Without a dominant instinct that gives rein to the other drives within the bounds of its perspective, the weak individual will attempt to satisfy the demands of all the drives. He or she is physiologically incapable of not *reacting* to them. There is no choice here, moral or otherwise; weakness is a lack of discipline based on physiological dynamics.

To ascribe an equal value to all human beings qua human beings independent of the conditions of the body is, for Nietzsche, not only a contradiction of the law of life but also a symptom of sickness. A "strong" or a "weak" physiological constitution is not essentially a matter of choice; like the color of one's skin or eyes, this depends, so to speak, on the luck of the draw. If we walk in a garden, through a field, or by a river shore, we see that everything is dominating or dominated, reflecting an order of rank throughout all species—there is no equality—whether we speak of birds, insects, blades of grass, or human beings. One's capacity to accommodate the instincts toward health, or the incapacity that renders one mediocre, hinges on a multiplicity of conditions. Nietzsche's emphasis on the body as "the richer . . . more tangible phenomenon" (WP 489) of will to power necessitates his denial of equalitarian values. As he said, "What determines your rank is the quantum of power you are" (WP 858). According to this standard, the value of the individual, including that of the overman, is, within the cosmology of will to power, virtually negligible.

Exhaustion

In the condition of weakness, the affects can be "the source of . . . terrible and irrevocable fatality" (WP 931). They are, remember, those sensations inherent to the chain of command among the drives that are passively reflected in consciousness. But when the drives are in a state of constant combat, uncoordinated by a dominating instinct, their affects are a "multitude and disgregation of impulses . . . lack[ing] . . . systematic order among them." And the power of the drives, so lacking in "precision and clarity" (WP 46), is squandered in all directions. Weakness is this "inner ruin . . . and anarchism" (WP 778), and the cumulative affect that, as Nietzsche puts it, "rise[s] to our consciousness" (GS 333), is exhaustion.

Nietzsche portrays the exhausted type as a person in a state of "constant irritability . . . as it were, a kind of itching" (GS 305). This itch is a psychological turbulence, or restlessness, that, when scratched, only gets worse. In short, this person is scattered. The condition is one of psychological fragmentation as the physiological affect of disparate, unharnessed instincts.

The "consequence of . . . [this] excessive excitement" (WP 231) is that this type of person does not act so much as "merely react to stimuli from outside" (WP 71). Without the perspective, the "interpretation," of a dominating instinct, the perspectives of all the drives run riot. The individual lacks a "feeling of distance" (E 3:1); that is, the individual has no standard or sense of direction, and priorities are scrambled within a whirligig of interpretations, all of which are equally valid or invalid.

Decadence

Exhaustion is, physiologically, extremely important because it provides the essential condition within which sickness makes its debut. The sketch of the exhausted individual above depicts an individual in a state of emergency. Nietzsche makes the telling observation that in this condition individuals begin *instinctively* to resist "taking anything deeply . . . spend[ing] their strength partly in assimilating things, partly in defense, partly in opposition" (WP 71). Constantly provoked by whatever both attracts and repels him, this type always feels "as if his self-control were endangered" (GS 305). Within this hyperdefensive posture the instinct of self-preservation, one of our oldest and strongest drives, is stimulated. It makes its power play in reaction to the individual's general state of siege, and precisely this reaction marks the beginning of physiological decadence.

We might think the instinct of preservation should help the physiologically exhausted rather than promote further decay. However, weakness and exhaustion are the conditions within which this drive has emerged. It cannot be separated, even in the case of health, from the physiology wherein it functions. In the context of weakness and exhaustion this drive displays the overall fatigue of the organism as a whole. Yet, as an instinct, it is still will to power and therefore attracted to precisely the *resistance* to *its* perspective. Weakness and exhaustion are leading to disintegration, and in the face of this threat the instinct of preservation, cultivated and honed in the human animal for thousands of years, is stimulated into a bid for power.

That the human race is still here proves the strength of this ancient and multifaceted instinct—even in the weakest individuals. How, then, does it actually aid in the process of decay? In the condition of exhaustion the organism is threatened by the anarchy of its drives. Clearly, if it is to survive, this anarchy must cease. The drive of preservation sets out to fight the other instincts to bring them under its control. It tries to impose "stability" at all costs and, and here, in the *necessity* "to combat one's instincts," we find "the formula for *décadence*" (T 3:11).

This may seem strange because, insofar as each drive manifests will to power, its combat is predictable. Moreover, the health of the individual described above hinges on the battle through which a dominating drive harnesses the combined strength of the others within its perspective— including that of preservation. Hence, the necessity to fight one's instincts as the "formula for decadence" must have a character peculiar to the physiologically unstable. Nevertheless, this does not explain how the instinct of preservation fights the other drives so as to provide the formula for decadence. Nietzsche claims that preservation is the oldest, strongest, and most unconquerable of all the drives because it "constitutes *the essence* of our species, our herd" (GS 1). How is it possible, then, that in the case of health this "all-powerful" drive can actually be surpassed in strength to the point of exploitation by even more powerful ones?

The goal of life as will to power is *not* preservation but growth in power. In the physiologically strong individual, the battle with preservation reveals "the organic process" through which the most potent drives "continually extend the bounds of their power . . . the imperative grows" (WP 644). The dominant drives of the strong individual are not inclined to annihilate the instinct of preservation. On the contrary, perhaps "contest" or "seduction" is a term more appropriate here than "combat."

Since the organism is will to *power*, destroying one of its most vital sources of strength would be a physiological contradiction. Preservation must be compelled to yield to these other vigorous instincts and in a way that convinces it of *profit*. Preservation is a greedy, insatiable craving for life at all costs. And since the more powerful drives are the path to growth, then not only is preservation "acknowledged," but there is also the possibility that this appetite for life will itself be enhanced. This is the irresistible point, and for the sake of life, the instinct of preservation submits while simultaneously asserting its rights.

There is here, as Nietzsche says, "a kind of justice and contract" the affect of which is the pleasure of overall enhanced strength for the individual. Those of this type are not dominated by the desire to preserve themselves. More powerful, creative drives have ascended to rule them, and, as Nietzsche points out, their "preservation" is only a derivative phenomenon (B 13).

In contrast to the genuinely healthy type above, the weak person is already displaying the symptoms of fatigue when the drive of preservation emerges. The irritated and reactionary traits of the weak person also characterize the instinct of preservation's mode of combat with the other drives. Stimulated by the chaos within and without, this ancient drive emerges within a state of physiological emergency; the strength of the organism as a whole is being drained by the constant combat of the other drives. This ebbing of vitality is manifest also within the drive of preservation in two respects. First, its impulse is not toward future growth via the other drives but toward an immediate stop to the hemorrhage of the body's strength. In short, its perspective is limited to mere stability. Second, it strives for stability through negating the most powerful drives.

The urge toward negation of these drives as dangerous threats reveals preservation's enervated condition *and* the formula for decadence because the desire to nullify the most powerful drives in order to achieve stability is simultaneously the desire to cancel precisely the source of the body's greatest strength. The very attempt to "preserve" itself promises, therefore, the degeneration of the organism as a whole. This constitutes a "physiological defect" that, with its own "practice and procedure" (C 7), devitalizes the entire organism. However, the instinct of preservation is, even if encysted within a weak organism, still a comparatively potent drive. Its initial move toward equilibrium consists in harnessing and gaining ascendancy over the lesser drives. Having established this power base through which its perspective is enhanced, it is, as it were, armed for the fight with more powerful ones.

The warlike, independent drives with which preservation does battle are, predictably, only stimulated to further effort, and this plays into the hands of preservation. In alliance with the weakest instincts, preservation keeps up a fairly consistent campaign while the more independent creative drives fight on against preservation and each other. The outcome holds no surprises; the mavericks dissipate themselves to the point where preservation easily overrides and levels off their affects.[12] This suspension of hostilities as the negation of the most powerful drives in the organism is decadence. It is the warfare of the weakest drives against the most powerful ones and allows weak and exhausted organisms to at least maintain themselves.

Sickness: A Morphological Death Wish

The cumulative affect is an individual who cannot trust "any instinct or free wingbeat; he stands . . . armed against himself" (GS 305), thinking the "inner anarchy . . . between those opposing value drives, is at last put an end to" (WP 351). This "maintenance," however, is an illusion. The instinct of preservation is siphoning the power of already weak

---

12. Looking at the larger organism of culture in Chapter 2, I show that Nietzsche identifies the instinct of preservation with what he calls the "herd instinct" (WP 315). Just as the most powerful drives of the healthy *individual* keep the instinct of preservation in its place, so does the aristocratic *class* keep "the herd" at a distance. And just as the dominance of the instinct of preservation over the more powerful drives of the body marks the beginning of decadence, so does the dominance of the herd point to the decline of culture.

drives to repress the body's most potent sources of growth. It is a no-win situation. Abandoning this repression invites degenerative chaos; maintaining it continually drains what little vitality remains. "We stand before a problem of economics" (WP 864). The instinct of preservation seeks life at all costs, at a cost the organism cannot afford. But as will to power this drive does all it can to keep its position of dominance, producing an organism that "*prefers* what is harmful to it" (A 6); this is sickness in the strict physiological sense. The preference for "preservation" is the path to further debility. This "physiological self-contradiction" (T 10:41) eventually leads to the affect of a thoroughly burnt-out instinct of preservation. Sinking deeper into torpor, the instinct desires the ultimate stability of death, that perfect stasis wherein all combat ceases.

Clearly, for Nietzsche, self-preservation is not the "*primum mobile*" of life as will to power (WP 652). When the imperative "to the accumulation of force" becomes flawed (WP 689), the law of life is affirmed through the power dynamics required for destruction of the organism. Decadence and sickness go hand in hand as a necessary *physiological revaluation* of the values required for ascending life. They are the natural means through which life as will to power weeds out whatever degenerates.

2 The Physiology of Spirit

> For every age is fed on illusions, lest men should renounce life too early and the human race come to an end.
> —Joseph Conrad, *Victory*

Appreciating Nietzsche's perception of "spirit"[1] requires development of three main concerns: first, "spirit" as an organic function determined by the law of life, the will to power; second, the dynamics of this function within the individual and the larger organism of culture; third, philosophy as a manifestation of the function of "spirit" within the physiology of culture. In delineating these concerns, I explore Nietzsche's portrait of ancient Greek culture. This exploration reveals Nietzsche's use of physiological principles in describing a healthy culture and sets the stage for the case of Socrates, whose philosophizing is symptomatic of the Greek culture's "spiritual" decline.

This chapter expands upon the central themes of Chapter 1 and leads to the threshold, as it were, of philosophy. My primary concern here is with the physiological dynamics that make philosophy possible. How

---

1. I place "spirit" in quotation marks throughout this study to indicate that it is meant in the specifically Nietzschean sense of its *physiological* foundation.

these bear on Nietzsche's view of the history of philosophy is reserved for Chapter 3.

Culture as a Social Organism

The Politics of the Body

Philosophy, Nietzsche says, is "the most spiritual will to power" (B 9). But if "spirit" is seen in terms of the physiology of organic life, what is the relation between this physiology and philosophy? Clues to answering this question lie in the botanical metaphors Nietzsche uses when speaking of philosophy and philosophers. The pre-Socratic systems, he says, let us "reconstruct the philosophic image, just as one may guess at the nature of the soil . . . by studying a plant that grows there" (PTA pref.:23; M 4:151). Elsewhere, he says that every philosophy reveals "the real germ of life from which the whole plant had grown" (B 6).

Here, within the cycles of decay, growth, light, and sun, Nietzsche notes the signs of sickness and health as he goes "among men as a naturalist does among plants" (HH 1:254). The genuine philosopher is, he says, "a rare plant" rooted in the rich or impoverished soil of culture (WP 420). But any appreciation of the violent and mysterious birth of the philosophical type requires an understanding of Nietzsche's view of the dark origins of culture itself.

Again the body is the point of departure because it displays a certain "political" structure. The very "struggle between cells and tissues" reveals, he says, an "aristocracy in the body" (WP 660). We saw that the drives of an individual can be harnessed by one or perhaps a few potent instincts. This is the formula for genuine health insofar as an order of rank among the drives is established toward a dominating perspective. For Nietzsche, this "aristocracy," together with all the conflict required for the generation of a truly *healthy* individual, is a blueprint for the power-dynamics inherent to a healthy culture.

Since life is will to power, it is natural that the strongest, most healthy individuals live accordingly. In short, they become the original "commanding forces [who] continually extend the bounds of their power and . . . simplify within these bounds" (WP 644). "The ego," says Nietzsche, "operates like an organic cell: it is a robber and violent. It wants to regenerate itself . . . and see all mankind at its feet (WP 768). To realize more power, the strong enslave the weak, thereby "embed[ding] themselves in great communities" in order to impose "a single form to the multifarious and disordered; chaos stimulates them" (WP 964).

All "events in the organic world," Nietzsche says, "are a subduing, a *becoming master*" (G 2:12). Now the "grandiose prototype: man in nature," emerges to make "himself master, [by] subjugating stupider forces" (WP 856). This struggle is "a consequence of the will to power" (B 259) manifest throughout the organic realm. To speak of justice in this domain is, Nietzsche says, "quite senseless . . . since life operates *essentially* . . . in its basic functions, through injury, assault, exploitation, destruction" (G 2:11). Violence is typical of growth, typical, that is of the will to power as "the *primordial fact* of all history" (B 259). And the origins of an aristocratic order of rank are, "like the beginnings of everything great on earth, soaked in blood thoroughly and for a long time" (G 2:6).

The order of rank among the drives of the strongest, most dangerous individuals is imposed upon the weak, who serve the interests of the former. Obviously, enslaving and exploiting weaker individuals enhances the power of the strongest. Here, in accordance with the law of life, the latter are the means to "creating *greater* units of power (G 2:11).

Just as, for Plato, the individual is the microcosm for his Republic, so, for Nietzsche, is the physiology of the individual represented in the larger organism of culture. Every person "transports the order of which he is the physiological representative into his relations with other human beings and with things" (T 7:2). The body is, says Nietzsche, "a social structure composed of many souls" (B 19). This "social structure" is the order of rank among the drives of the individual organism. The structure of any healthy culture reveals this same order of rank wherein each class manifests the instincts of those who compose it. Powerful, warlike drives are expressed in the form of a ruling caste, and they exploit the strength of the weaker drives as represented in lower castes. Every healthy culture possesses a natural order of rank, and when this order is lacking, a culture is ripe for decadence.

Nietzsche posits, "without trying to be considerate," the cruel origins of every "higher culture." History, he says, is fraught with thoroughgoing barbarians who "in possession of [an] unbroken . . . lust for power, hurled themselves upon weaker . . . races." In "the beginning, the noble caste was always the barbarian caste" (B 257). The constant threat to their own existence taught them the qualities to which "they owe the fact that, despite gods and men, they are still there." The roots of an aristocracy are savages who enslave the weak in the teeth of their own destruction. In this situation, whatever allows them to survive and grow in strength "they call virtues, these virtues alone they cultivate." The cultivation of these virtues allows the growth of "a type with few but very strong traits, a species of severe, warlike . . . men, close-mouthed and closely linked." Since the will to power is manifest only in situations of resistance, the consolidation of a warrior elite demands the same resistance insofar as it requires "the long fight with essentially constant *unfavorable* conditions" (B 262).

Physio-Economics

Upon this treacherous background Nietzsche sees "an arrangement, whether voluntary or involuntary, for *breeding*" self-reliant human beings who "want their species to prevail" in the face of annihilation (B 262). In short, the progeny of the barbarian caste must *inherit* the instincts essential to ruling other human beings.

Adversity, for instance—the "constant fight with . . . neighbors or with the oppressed who . . . threaten rebellion" (B 262)—hones the instincts of command. These "are acquired laboriously . . . through . . . self-constraint . . . [and] obstinate . . . repetition of the same labours, the same renunciations" (WP 995). This austere self-discipline indicates a firm order of rank among the drives of the warrior elite, "that economy in the law of life" (T 6:6) that forbids an organism's squandering of strength in a multiplicity of directions. Nietzsche sees these physiological economics being bred into succeeding generations, since it is impossible "that a human being should *not* have the qualities and preferences of his parents and ancestors in his body" (B 264).

Those born to command are "the heirs and masters of this slowly-acquired manifold treasure of virtue and efficiency" (WP 995). The inherited efficiency of an order of rank among the noble's drives is the microcosm for that imposed by the nobility upon weaker individuals. Just as the exploitation of weaker drives by stronger ones is the sign of a healthy person, so is the exploitation of the weak by the strong characteristic of a healthy culture. Through the noble type, the physiological dynamics of health are generated in the creation of culture.

" 'Exploitation,' " Nietzsche says, is not the mark of "a corrupt or . . . primitive society"; it is "a basic organic function . . . of the will to power, which is after all the will of life" (B 259). The strong exploit the energy of the weak, who derive their "value" in terms of how well they serve. These observations leave no doubt that the "right of altruism cannot be derived from physiology; nor can the right to help and to an equality of lots" (WP 52).

The nobility "have left behind . . . the concept 'barbarian' wherever they have gone . . . their highest culture betrays a . . . pride in it" (G 1:11). Its instincts of command are preserved and nurtured "through fortunate and reasonable marriages." By these means "and also through fortunate accidents, the acquired and stored-up energies of many generations have not been squandered . . . but linked together by a firm ring and by will" (WP 995). The significance of this "economy" to the physiological fortunes of generations of nobility, as well as to the future of culture, cannot, in Nietzsche's view, be overestimated. He says that marriage, in the old aristocratic sense of the word, "was a question of the breeding of a race . . . of the maintenance of a fixed, definite type of ruling man." Clearly, "love was not the first consideration here." The priority was "the interest of a family, and beyond that—the class." The clarity of this "noble concept of marriage" is in perfect accord with life as will to power, and "has ruled in every healthy aristocracy" (WP 732).

The nobility, as the physiological heirs to generations of accumulated strength, possess profound reverence for "age and tradition" and the conviction of their right to rule other human beings. This type "experiences *itself* as determining values . . . as *value-creating* . . . and respects all severity and hardness" (B 260). Just as their own self-discipline keeps their drives in check and is the mark of rank, so the nobility keep those not of their class at a distance according to rank. Nietzsche saw the noble individual as commanding and, at the same time, as identifying "himself with the executor of the order." In short, "*L'effet c'est moi*: what happens here is . . . the governing class identifies itself with the successes of the commonwealth" (B 19).

As a living thing, a culture follows the will of life permeating every function of its body. Hence, it will attack weaker cultures because it "is part of the concept of the living that it must grow—that it must extend its power and consequently incorporate alien forces." People speak, Nietzsche says, "of the right of the individual to *defend* himself," but from the standpoint of will to power, "whether one has in view an individual or a living body, an aspiring 'society,' " a culture, can "designate as a right its need to conquer . . . the right to growth, perhaps." In short, a "society that definitely and *instinctively* gives up war and conquest is in decline" (WP 728).

Thus far I have only outlined some of the most important physiological dynamics in Nietzsche's perception of the cultural organism. I want now to explore the following "proposition" found in *Beyond Good and Evil*: "[A]lmost everything we call 'higher culture' is based on the spiritualization of *cruelty*, on its becoming more profound" (B 229). For Nietzsche, cruelty is necessary to the organic process of growth. But the clinical standpoint of the physician requires our seeing this "fatality of life" (WP 728) as essential to "spirit" and culture. Therefore, "let us look around for the highest authority for what we may term cultural health," and study the "truly healthy culture" of the Greeks (PTA 1:28; M 4:154).

The Children of Night

The ancient Hellenes, who for Nietzsche epitomize the most powerful instincts of life, provide him a standard by which he judges other cultures. The "greater and more terrible the passions are that an age, a people, an individual can permit themselves, because they are capable of employing them as *means, the higher stands their culture*" (WP 1025). Through their capacity to harness the strength of their own drives, the Greeks "press everything terrible into *service*" (WP 1025) and create the "best turned out, most beautiful, most envied type of humanity to date" (BT S:1).

Predictably, when "we stride back into the pre-Homeric world" (HC 34; WKG 3:278–79), we do not find, Nietzsche says, "cheerful sensates . . . reverberating with heavy breathings and deep feelings, as the unscholarly . . . like to assume" (PTA 1:29; M 4:154). On the contrary, we find "barbarians in every terrible sense of the word" (B 257) and a "life ruled only by the children of Night: strife, lust, deceit, old age, and death." These are individuals with imaginations "accustomed to the horrible" and for whom "combat is salvation; the cruelty of victory is the pinnacle of life's jubilation" (HC 34; WKG 3:278–79). Theirs is an age when "men were unwilling to refrain from *making* suffer and saw in it an enchantment of the first order, a genuine seduction *to* life" (G 2:7).

Cruelty is so seductive because it provides the "highest gratification of the feeling of power" (D 18). Torture is a celebration of victory and, as "one of the oldest festive joys of mankind" (D 18), has a narcotic effect to the point of intoxication (WP 801). Of course, only the strongest, most dangerous individuals determined who and to what extent others can indulge in this "drug" as a mark of rank (see G 2:5–6).

The will to power is manifest only in the face of resistance; in its human form, "an application of the original will to become *stronger*" (WP 702) is manifest when "great danger challenges our curiosity about the degree of our strength and courage" (WP 949). The creation of Greek culture hinged on the victory of the strongest over the greatest threats to themselves. This "need to conquer" (WP 728) is "a consequence of the will to power, which . . . [as] the *primordial fact* of all history" (B 259), involves not only cruelty but also a desire for and the willingness to suffer. For Nietzsche, the early Hellenes embraced suffering and pain with a "sharp-eyed courage . . . that *craves* the frightful as the . . . worthy enemy, against whom one can test one's strength . . . [and] learn what it means 'to be frightened' " (BT S:1).

With a certain *"craving for the ugly,"* these ancients sought the darkest faces of existence and everything "evil, a riddle, destructive, fatal" (BT S:4). The "good severe will of the older Greeks," Nietzsche says, revealed a "pessimism of *strength"* (BT S:l) that anticipated grim battle with life the destroyer, against which no

> weary mind may stand . . .
> nor a wrecked will work new hope;
> wherefore . . . those most eager for fame
> bind the dark mood fast in their breasts.[2]

To meet such a foe, one had to be well acquainted with both cruelty and suffering as the path to survival and victory, and the capacity to endure both was a mark of distinction. The "continual fight against ever constant *unfavorable* conditions is . . . the cause that fixes and hardens a type" (B 262). Hence, "the 'noble Greek' of the old stamp" (WP 435) was severe, suspicious, ever wary, rarely trusting. An austere ruthlessness in maintaining discipline over themselves and those they ruled is the dominant characteristic Nietzsche attributes to the ancient, warlike Hellenes. The hard and fast rules of a warrior caste dominating a rigorously maintained order of rank enabled this elite to endure and grow in power. We can readily imagine their motto as "What determines your rank is the quantum of power you are: the rest is cowardice" (WP 858).

The Ladder of Cruelty

Today, "when suffering is . . . brought forward as the principle argument *against* existence," one should recall, Nietzsche says, "the ages in which the opposite opinion prevailed" (G 2:7). In those ages pain, suffering, and cruelty determined the measure of one's capacity to endure and meet the exigencies of the most dangerous contests with life. The love of battle indicated "the agonal instinct of the Hellenes" (T 3:8). The instinctive love of *contest*, so fundamental to Nietzsche's perception of the Greeks, reveals a physiological phenomenon central to his thought, namely, that of "overcoming."

---

2. "The Wanderer," from *The Earliest English Poems*, trans. Michael Alexander (Harmondsworth, Middlesex: Penguin, 1977), 70.

A central characteristic of the prodigious health Nietzsche attributes to the Greeks is their tendency to find the greatest threats as irresistible tests of strength.[3] What deserves particular emphasis is that this tendency involves the risk of self-destruction. The Greek desire for combat shows an organic form of will to power striving for victory over a primary fact of life itself, namely, the elimination or enslavement of life's weakest forms. In short, the possibility of wholesale destruction, as will to power, is essential to the creation of the strongest organisms. The "plant 'man,' " Nietzsche says, has "grown most vigorously to a height . . . [when] the dangerousness of his situation . . . grow[s] to the point of enormity" (B 44).

The overcoming of impossible odds has always served "the enhancement of the species 'man' " (B 44). The human being, like any other organism, is the *experiment* of life. All must overcome potential destruction on the path to the creation of new forms of life. All creation seeks to overcome itself as power toward the victory of a transformation of itself *as power*. "I am," says Life to Zarathustra, "*that which must overcome itself* . . . where there is perishing and the falling of leaves, behold, there life sacrifices itself—for the sake of power." And the experiment is endless because whatever Life creates, "soon I have to oppose it . . . thus will my will have it" (Z 2:12).

The Greek desire for suffering, cruelty, and destruction as essential to the contest with life is the physiological key to the creation of their culture. This passion reveals to Nietzsche, not a concern with self-preservation, but an intoxicating affirmation of life and the instinctive knowledge that "the secret for harvesting from existence the greatest fruitfulness and the greatest enjoyment is—to *live dangerously!*" (GS 283).

Spirit

Physiological Reiteration

The origins of culture seen so far are, for the most part, hideous. There is something unspeakably grotesque in the idea of profound cruelty to celebrate victorious slaughter. But from Nietzsche's point of view, there is more to the story of these origins than mere brutality. The magnificent

---

3. Again, "health" is understood here as the capacity to harness the accumulated strength of powerful drives.

culture of Greek antiquity would have been impossible without the "spiritualization of cruelty."

I have shown that in Nietzsche's thought a multiplicity of wholly self-centered *interpretive perspectives*, called the instincts, do battle for supremacy within the individual until the stronger drives extort the energy of the weak and establish themselves at the top of an order of rank. Similarly, Nietzsche recognized that in any healthy culture, the strongest enslave the weak and establish the order of rank Nietzsche recognized as essential to any healthy culture. "Spirit" goes hand in hand with this organic phenomenon since it reveals, Nietzsche says, the same needs and capacities "as those which physiologists posit for everything that lives, grows, and multiplies" (B 230).

Physiological Dogmatics

To appreciate the physiology of "spirit" we must see how each drive within the individual embellishes or "interprets" the world according to whatever affirms its perspective. That is, the perspective of any instinct is *selective*. The "basic will of the spirit," Nietzsche says, is a constant "striv[ing] for the apparent and superficial" (B 229). Whatever is foreign to a drive's perspective is ignored or embellished in a manner that suits it. And the more its perspective is denied, the more a drive's capacity for the artificial is stimulated. Precisely this embellishing of the world within the perspective of each drive is what Nietzsche means by "spirit." As a perspective, each drive is an *interpretation* that, being thoroughly self-absorbed, *insists* on itself as "truth." The instincts are our "spiritual" tendency to "assimilate the new to the old, to simplify the manifold, and to overlook or repulse whatever is totally contradictory" (B 230). In short, starvation can "falsify" the most appalling filth into a banquet, the sex drive can paint anyone as desirable, and a multiplicity of self-seeking motives can justify murder.

Some might say this idea of "spirit" is what most of us call the imagination. But this imagination is *not* a product of reflection. Nor is it something that, by definition, is somehow unhinged from "reality." The "greatest part of our spirit's activity," Nietzsche says, "remains unconscious and unfelt" (GS 333). In Chapter 3 I show how "spirit" functions below the rim of reflection and that instead of being somehow disconnected from "the real world," it determines all interpretations of truth and reality. For now I only want to emphasize that "spirit" is an instinctive capacity to embellish the world according to the cumulative perspective of the hierarchy among the drives. Embellishing enables the connections to Nietzsche's ideas of art and artists. However, as a basic physiological phenomenon, this "spiritual" capacity is not peculiar to artists. Here, at least, Nietzsche has to acknowledge a certain equality among human beings—even those with no imagination.

The process of "spiritualizing" is a constant interpreting of "every piece of the 'external world,' retouching and falsifying the whole to suit itself." This is not a conscious activity; this is a power quantum attempting to overcome what resists it. Predictably, the intent is "growth, in a word—or, more precisely, the *feeling* of growth, the feeling of increased power" (B 230). What is particularly important is that "spirit," as an organic process of falsification essential to growth, is the basis for Nietzsche's vision of "untruth as a condition of life" (B 4).

Self-Preservation Reiterated

There would be "no life at all," Nietzsche says, "if not on the basis of perspective estimates and appearances" (B 34). But why are these estimates, these "falsifications," so necessary for growth? He answers by telling us that "the first instinct of spirituality, [is] *the spirit's instinct for self-preservation*" (T 9:2). Self-preservation is the primary instinct of "spirit." Why, then, would the strong, noble type, the one seemingly the least concerned with self-preservation, need to falsify the world? In short, what does "spirit" preserve the noble from? It preserves them from too lucid a perception of how terrifying their situation really is. Through "spirit" all of us are shielded from the most horrifying faces of existence, since "those who would know it completely would perish." Ultimately, the question is "to what degree one would *require* it to be thinned down, shrouded, sweetened, blunted, falsified" (B 39).

The instinct of preservation is one of the most powerful drives of the human species (GS 1). In Nietzsche's texts it goes by another name—the herd instinct. As the primal drive of "spirit," it fabricates the "world" in whatever way allows our survival. Its "defective" function is the phenomenon of sickness, where the compelling power of preservation subjugates weaker drives and extorts their energy to suspend the affects of the body's more powerful instincts. But if "spirituality" reveals the instinct of preservation, then in the case of sickness its falsifications of the world will betray the symptoms thereof. The falsifications and deceptions typical of a healthy instinct of preservation reveal symptoms of health.

"Spirit" always reveals what, if any, order of rank exists among the drives. Among the healthy, the instinct of preservation is exploited to enhance the strength of the organism as a whole. Here the instinct of preservation is kept at a distance and in its proper place. In the healthy organism preservation is not the dominating drive. Yet it "has its say," or influence, on the powerful instincts of combat and command, such that the organism survives, which is, after all, *its* perspective. But the influence of its perspective depends on its rank among the drives.

For the noble, whose command of their drives is the key to that over other people, preservation has little direct influence. The passions for cruelty, battle, conquest, and ruling others reveal the will "to become *more*" (WP 688) and are hardly conducive to one's personal safety or survival. The fictions required by these individuals allow risk, combat, courage, and all the values essential to a ruling warrior elite. Here "spirit" falsifies the world so that one's survival "is one of the indirect and most frequent *results*" (B 13). Hence, in these people, the organic process of "spiritualizing" the world enables them to survive and, more important, grow in power. In contrast, the values of *liberté, égalité, fraternité* are those of the herd, which, by definition, is dominated by the instinct of preservation.

The Greek Spirit

Nietzsche thinks the greatest cultures, the ones that *"became* worth something, never became so under liberal institutions." Thanks to the law of life, "it was *great danger* which made of them something deserving reverence," because danger "first teaches us to know . . . our *spirit*— which *compels* us to be strong" (T 10:38). The formation of Greek culture contains ample evidence of ugliness and violence. But the physiological dynamics inherent to the "spiritualization" of ugliness and violence provided what was essential to creating the "most envied type of humanity to date" (BT S:1).

For the ancient Hellenes, pain and suffering were not barriers to growth; on the contrary, these only stimulated their agonal instinct.[4] In situations "where the greatest resistance is constantly being overcome" (T 10:38), they exploited the discipline "of *great* suffering" and cultivated their capacity for "profundity, secret, mask, spirit" (B 225). If physical pain and suffering cannot scare or intimidate, what can? Nietzsche says the Greeks endured a suffering far worse than physical: the paralyzing suspicion that a life of battle and victory, with all of its terrors, is *meaningless*. If existence is, at bottom, "in vain" (G 3:28), then all that death, toil, family, and blood become a pathetic joke. A fascination with this suspicion can lead a culture, no matter how promising its origins, into the vortex of a "spiritual" poisoning and "sickness unto death."

---

4. See note 3 above and related text.

The Greek curiosity for the darkest faces of life promised this fascination, but their predictable *nausea* at existence (BT 7) was defeated with the "shield and spear" (T 10:38) of "spiritual" strength.

The Dialectics of Resistance

The capacity to fictionalize the world as the Greeks did is due not only to profound health but also, and perhaps more importantly, to their profound illness. These are not mutually exclusive. When Nietzsche speaks of "spirit," he always bears in mind that within any individual or culture, health "and sickness are not essentially different, as the ancient physicians and some practitioners even today suppose" (WP 47). Moreover, from his clinical standpoint, "sickness is instructive, we have no doubt of that, even more instructive than health" (G 3:9). The question is *why*.

First, there is no getting rid of illness, because it is *necessary* to life. And it is enlightening to the extent that it allows the physician to judge the overall strength of living things. Sickness is a constant threat, a built-in *resistance* that the organism must always keep in check. As a demand upon its strength, illness "restores energy to the slack fibers and toughness to the will to live" (WP 912). Through illness, an organism's vitality is both taxed and kept at a peak; life as will to power provides yet another unfavorable condition to the realization of itself as power. Potent sickness brings terrible suffering, but a living thing reveals its position on an order of rank depending on how, or if, it survives. "That of which more delicate men would perish belongs to the stimulants of *great* health" (WP 1013).

The human animal is part of the constant experiment of life as will to power. Sickness is a means of creating transformations of power within any organism because it feeds off our strength while *forcing* us to develop new sources of vigor. In turn, these new sources are required for other forms of sickness that will flourish within the strength newly attained. Hence, regarding health and sickness, "there are only differences in degree between these two kinds of existence" (WP 47). Within the interplay of these interdependent forces, life persists as the experiment through which "the unique and incomparable [seeks] to raise its head" (GS 120). Not surprisingly, Nietzsche denies that health or sickness can be seen as uniform across the human spectrum. The "more we abjure," he says, "the dogma of the 'equality of men,' " the quicker "the concept of a *normal* health . . . normal diet and the normal course of an illness, [must] be abandoned by medical men" (GS 120).

Every level of health requires its particular form of sickness as its unique adversary threatening the well-being of the organism as a whole. The organism is tested with the threat of destruction and thereby forced to overcome previous levels of sickness and health or be destroyed. When the absurdity of existence occurred to the Greeks, a shudder of nausea went throughout the body of their culture. But they did not go into decline; they had the strength to master this illness. Yet to the extent that they were ill, the conditions for this illness had to be present, especially since, as just seen, sickness needs a certain level of vitality and vice versa. What physiological conditions allowed for this "momentary" illness?

The Physiology of Tragic Art

If the *threat* of sickness could have a face, it would be that of exhaustion. For Nietzsche, it is natural that upon release of a certain amount of energy, exhaustion quickly follows (WP 864). And in this condition of exhaustion the weakest instincts rally around "preservation" as an essential step in the dynamic of decadence. Why, then, did the Greek culture not collapse into decadence? Nietzsche would say that when it comes to judging health and sickness, "one should be careful" because the "standard remains the efflorescence of the body . . . how much of the sickly it can . . . overcome—how much it can make healthy" (WP 1013). The Greeks were in the fortunate position to meet this standard favorably. Through the order of rank among the instincts of this culture—embodied in the discipline of its warrior elite, a reservoir of strength had been preserved. This is typical of the *"large-scale economy"* (WP 852) of life that forbids the squandering of strength. If the order of rank is not maintained, a release of strength, for example, a war or even a celebration of victory, can bring on the exhaustion essential to decadence and sickness.

Great strength had been spent on the formation and maintenance of the ancient Greek culture. True, the suspicion that existence is absurd betrayed a cultural exhaustion that was quickly exploited by the instincts of decadence. But even when exhausted, Greek culture's reserved strength, accumulated over generations of a firmly maintained order of rank, enabled the Greeks to avoid a collapse into anarchy. Fundamental to this escape was the "spiritual" ability to embellish the world according to their most powerful drives. And the grandeur of the deceptions the Greeks used indicated to Nietzsche "where the big question mark concerning the value of existence has thus been raised" (BT S:1).

Through the organic function of "spirit," the Greeks avoided an irreversible negation of life. They maintained, Nietzsche says, the strength that made them "ready with yet another answer to the question, 'What is a life of struggle and victory for?' and . . . gave that answer through the whole breadth of Greek history" (HC 34–35; WKG 3:279). The kind of falsification that allowed this ancient culture to conquer a paralyzing vision of the absurd "selected" a counterbalancing vision of beauty. This deception, so necessary to the survival and growth of Greek culture, constitutes for Nietzsche the origin of tragic art.[5]

Before considering these origins, however, I have to emphasize that I am considering only the *origins* of tragedy. What follows below is limited to Nietzsche's views of "spirit" as a physiological dynamic of culture. The significance of this dynamic for "the still more delicate problems of the *physiology of aesthetics*" (G 3:8) is considered only to the extent that it facilitates access to the "spirit" of Greek philosophy in Chapter 3. What I have to say about "tragedy" below does not even begin to consider the myriad facets of Nietzsche's perception of the artist type in terms of ascending and descending life. How this particular feature of his clinical standpoint casts light on "spirituality," not to mention his observations on this type as healthy and ill, would take me too far afield.[6]

Nietzsche says, " 'Hellenism and Pessimism' would have been a less ambiguous title" for his *Birth of Tragedy* precisely because "their tragedies prove that the Greeks were *not* pessimists" (E BT:1). Tragedy did not originate "in order to get rid of terror and pity . . . [as] Aristotle

---

5. In *The Birth of Tragedy* the physiological origin of tragedy is articulated in terms of its destruction by Socrates. Though he does not speak of Greek tragedy as "spirit," Nietzsche sees the drives as fundamental to its creation, since "in all productive men it is instinct that is the creative-affirmative force." Socrates is the "instinct-disintegrating influence" that destroyed tragedy as an art form (BT 13). Only later does "spirit," as I have described it, become more pronounced in Nietzsche's philosophy. Fourteen years later, in his "Attempt at a Self-Criticism," the standpoint of the cultural physician is clear. He now identifies the age of Socrates and the destruction of Greek art with "symptoms of a decline of strength, of impending old age, and of physiological weariness" (BT 4). The expressions of "physiology" throughout the Nietzsche corpus portray "the birth of tragedy" as an essentially physiological phenomenon of Greek culture.

6. Nietzsche wanted to say a lot more about the "practically untouched and unexplored" (G 3:8) physiological dynamics of aesthetics. And it would be interesting to pursue these dynamics in the direction of his views on art. But to do so now would narrow the scope of the wider implications of his views on "spirit" that I want to explore. However, it is worth mentioning that "spirit," in the case of art and artists, points to the significance of a chapter entitled "Toward a Physiology of Art" (C 7), which was planned for his unfinished book *The Will to Power*. A detailed look at *The Case of Wagner* reveals such a physiology insofar as this "case" discloses art as "an expression of physiological degeneration" (C 7).

misunderstood it" (E BT:3). On the contrary, it was the path to an affirmation and joy in "the *terrifying,* the *evil,* [and] the *questionable"* faces of existence (WP 852). The sacrifice and destruction life requires for growth is beautiful and *perfect;* and the path to one's own beauty and perfection not only lies in the joy of creation but "includes even joy in destroying" (E BT:3). This, for Nietzsche, was the *tragic wisdom* of the Greeks.

The Hellene stared into the vortex of destruction permeating all becoming and saw "everywhere only the horror or absurdity of existence." But "when the danger to his will [was] greatest," the organic function of "spirit" was a "saving sorceress [and] expert at healing" (BT 7). Through the art of tragedy the Greek culture turned "the horror or absurdity of existence into notions with which one can live" (BT 7). The ability to fictionalize the world, *preserved* the Greeks from the greatest threat to their culture. In short, "spirit" as self-deception, or what Nietzsche calls a *"genius in lying"* (WP 853), allowed Greek culture to overcome "the nausea of absurdity" (BT 7).

Tragedy, Nietzsche says, "is a *tonic"* (WP 851). For the Greeks, it was a restorative "fiction" that, as the cumulative perspective of disciplined, vital instincts, "shrouded, sweetened, [and] blunted" (B 39) the paralyzing effect of the absurd. Life is not absurd; tragedy provides an awe-inspiring vision of its beauty and perfection. Here is a spectacle of human beings who are radiant with innocence and, for absolutely no reason at all, are destined for destruction. In the age of the earliest tragic myths (BT SC:4), this "lack of reason" was the key to feeling a perfect unity with the fate of all living things and, more important, to the belief in being worthy of this perfection. In "the age of Socrates, among men of fatigued instincts" (B 212), this "lack of reason" was repugnant and was condemned as "immoral."

The tragic wisdom of the Greeks shows how "spirit" not only reconciled them to the ugliness of life but provided an avenue to the love of even its darkest faces. The tragic insight into the necessity of death and destruction is the passion behind Nietzsche's *Amor Fati.* "[L]et that be my love henceforth! I do not want to wage war against what is ugly. . . . *Looking away* shall be my only negation. And . . . some day I wish to be only a Yes-sayer" (GS 276). "Spirit" is a kind of "looking away," a negation of what seems too necessary, too ugly, but a negation that enables a healthy organism to flourish through thinning down the ugly just enough to assimilate and exploit it for growth. It was the ancient Hellenes who provided for Nietzsche the most exquisite example of how, as "an aesthetic phenomenon existence is still *bearable* for us" (GS 107). The capacity for creating the illusions essential to seeing life's inherent cruelty and destruction as beautiful remained throughout the transition from barbarism to the formation of an aristocracy.

The severity of the ancient warrior type toward itself and the enslaved reveals no easygoing optimism regarding what life required. Life was neither gentle nor kind; it destroyed the weak, the lame, and the sick. Hence, the old nobility, like their ancestors, affirmed life by means of the sword and an unconscious "spiritualizing" process that kept pace according to a *proper* function of the instinct of preservation. Had they been too ill, they would have sought "mere preservation," longed "for a Buddhistic negation of the will" (BT 7), and sunk into slavery and decay. But with more-potent instincts in command, that of preservation did not dominate but was exploited toward deceptions required for growth in power.

Unlike "the more recent and decadent Hellenism," which denied life's cruelty and terror as immoral and irrational, "the older Hellenism" was inspired to identify with its cruelty and terror (SSW 131; M 6:102–3). Hence, the nobility adorned themselves with the terror-inspiring characteristics of life itself. The more they saw themselves as fearless, destructive and frightening, the more beautiful and awe inspiring they became for themselves. By identifying with the most intimidating aspects of life, the values of the strongest, their conviction that they were born to rule was expressed in images of strength, courage, and heroic combat.

Through artistic expressions of death and destruction in the midst of battle, the "virtues" of the nobility were reflected throughout the body of the social organism. This is why "the whole Greek world exult[ed] over the combat scenes of the *Iliad*" (HC 33; WKG 3:278). The warrior elite required cruelty and terror and were "protected by the hand of Homer" (HC 34; WKG 3: 278–79), who, with an "artistic deception," glorified to the point of deification the unspeakable ugliness of war. The illusions generated by "spirit" provided joy in innumerable artistic expressions of "distended human bodies, their sinews tense with hatred or with the arrogance of triumph; writhing bodies, wounded [and] dying" (HC 33; WKG 3:278).

Thus, simple brutality and the search for the most dangerous enemies is, as noted earlier, just one side of the story. For Nietzsche, the "spiritualization" of cruelty is essential to the creation of any high culture, since it provides the falsifications and deceptions necessary to coping with life's cruel faces. In the case of the Greeks, this essential organic function seduced them to life again and again.

The Physiology of "Truth"

The Greek "spiritualization" of cruelty, however, does not reduce to Nietzsche's views on Greek art. "Spirit" is the source of multiple deceptions, and whether or not we call existence beautiful, meaningful, or holy, all of these "fictions" presuppose our need to feel at home in the world, feel that the world is *ours*. The instinct of preservation is, again, "the first instinct of spirituality" (T 9:2). Nevertheless, when preservation is dominated and exploited by more-powerful drives, its affect is indirect. If the situation is otherwise, the organism will only be concerned with preservation—not growth—and "that is the formula for *décadence*" (T 3:12).

Yet even in the case of health, without the initial *fiction* of stability, peculiar to the drive for preservation, the life-enhancing "aesthetics" of more-powerful drive-perspectives would have, as it were, nothing to attack and destabilize. To use the language of deconstruction, the instinct of preservation provides the initial "text," that is, a particular interpretation of "stability" that metaphysics has traditionally called Truth and Being. More-potent, life-affirming drives constitute precisely those perspectives, those interpretations, that are suppressed in order for the text to maintain itself. The struggle of these life-enhancing drives against the interpretation of stability allows the organism to exploit this perspective toward the growth of the organism overall. Just as deconstruction requires a text for a multiplicity of trajectory interpretations, so do the life-enhancing instincts of growth require the essential perspective of stability. The illusion of stability denies other interpretations as a threat and is therefore simultaneously a stimulant to other life-affirming perspectives. Through the instinct of preservation's fable of stability, we "impose upon chaos as much regularity and form as our practical needs require" (WP 595). This fiction allows for a sense of equilibrium within the wilderness of becoming; it negates becoming and allows the human being to take possession of the world. Before we can dance, we have to establish and make the floor our own.

Within becoming, whatever fictions allow us to live and grow become our "truths." Again, "we find here . . . the *hyperbolic naiveté* of man: positing himself as the meaning and measure of the value of things" (WP 12).[7] Thanks to this naiveté, we flourish according to "various

---

7. Heidegger, who was so familiar with Nietzsche's texts and even insisted that Nietzsche's "philosophy proper was left behind as posthumous, unpublished work" (Martin Heidegger, *Nietzsche*, vol. 1, *The Will to Power as Art*, ed. and trans. David F. Krell [San Francisco: Harper & Row, 1979], 8–9), did not consider the note just quoted. This section of "The Will to Power" articulates Nietzsche's view that man is naive for viewing himself as the measure of all things. Heidegger thought Nietzsche's philosophy (insofar as it was dominated by "physiology") led to "subjectivism," evidenced in Nietzsche's overman, who, as the personification of "absolute will to power," is the last echo of Protagoras's dictum: man is the measure of all things (see Heidegger's *Nietzsche*, vol. 4, *Nihilism*, ed. David F. Krell, trans. Frank A. Capuzzi [San Francisco: Harper & Row, 1982], 91–138). But one gets the impression here that Heidegger's view of the will to power is

errors in relation to one another," and without it "an organic entity of our species could not live" (WP 535). Our judgments of value, truth, beauty, and so forth, indicate that the "organic process constantly presupposes interpretations" (WP 643).

Ultimately, "[t]he will to power *interprets*" (WP 643) insofar as multiple drives insist on whatever affirms the perspective of each. The embellishment of the world according to these drives is, therefore, an "organic process by virtue of which dominant, shaping, commanding forces continually extend the bounds of their power and continually simplify within these bounds." The self-centered simplification of the world by each instinct according to its perspective is the activity of "spirit." And for precisely this reason, Nietzsche says spirit "is only a means and tool in the service of higher life, of the enhancement of life" (WP 644).

Thanks to the activity of "spirit," the "world with which we are concerned is false, i.e., is not a fact but a fable . . . it is 'in flux,' as something in a state of becoming, as a falsehood always changing but never getting near the truth: for—there is no 'truth' " (WP 616). Ultimately, "spirit" imposes "upon becoming the character of being— that is the supreme will to power" (WP 617). It is in this sense that Nietzsche speaks of error and deception as the necessary conditions of life. We need the fable of "being" against the threat of chaos in order "to preserve a world of that which is, which abides" (WP 617), for "duration is a first-rate value on earth" (GS 356).

Greek culture, as the healthiest ever seen on earth, possessed a "spirit" that not only preserved the culture but also opened up wider interpretations for the growth of life. This was no accident. Discipline

---

already determined by his unshakable conviction that unless one is concerned with the Truth of Being, then one is merely a metaphysician. That is, one attempts to locate "Truth" either in the "subjective" or in the "objective" pole of traditional epistemology. Heidegger clearly wants to locate Nietzsche within the subjective, voluntaristic tradition of the will. By now it should be apparent that Nietzsche's conception of will to power is not reducible to its articulation by human beings. On the contrary, for Nietzsche, it is precisely because we are confronted with a total lack of solid ground for any interpretation that, as will to power, we preserve ourselves through interpretations of "Being." Even if something like the overman occurs on the face of the earth, the dynamics of "spirit"—as the seat for a multiplicity of deceptions essential for preservation and growth—do not disappear. The existence of the overman is itself something that must also be *surpassed* according to the law of life. To suggest that the infinity of possibilities for growth and destruction inherent to the concept will to power can be reduced to man or even overman indicates (*a*) that Nietzsche's idea of will to power is misinterpreted if seen within the locus of traditional metaphysics, (*b*) that to reduce it to its *human* physiology is a very narrow interpretation, and (*c*) that given Nietzsche's clinical standpoint seen thus far, the Truth of Being is itself subject to a radical critique as soon as it seeks to preserve itself.

provides a kind of capital of energy that is stored up, accumulated, and passed on to succeeding generations. The same may be said for the larger social organism. Generations of a firmly maintained order of rank allow a culture (like that of the Greeks) to store up vast reserves of energy, and from "the pressure of plenitude, from the tension of forces that continually increase . . . there arises a condition like that preceding a storm." Thanks to its order of rank, this strength is "compressed and dammed to the point of torment" until finally "the accumulated forces are shown a way, a whither, so they explode into lightning flashes and deeds" (WP 1022).

Nietzsche sees something extraordinary and unique about the Greeks, since they realized a culture in the genuine sense of the word. Their great accumulated strength exploded into a "splendid fireworks of the spirit" (B 257), bringing forth a multiplicity of "spiritual" types.

Autumn

Abundance

Through "spirit" the Greeks felt themselves to be the rulers of the world. Their culture created the deceptions essential to "the will from multiplicity to simplicity, a will that ties up, tames, and is domineering and truly masterful" (B 230).

Generations of stored-up vitality enabled the Greek culture to explode into the "*affirmative affects*: pride, joy, health, love of the sexes, enmity and war." This reservoir of strength was created through "the discipline of high spirituality" as the path to "the whole force of *transfiguring* virtues, everything that declares good and affirms in word and deed" (WP 1033).

The affects, those sensations of power that vibrate throughout the body, were transformed into those felt throughout the social body and bestowed a confidence peculiar to genuine health, which, out of strength, says yes to life in myriad ways.[8] Integral to this confidence was the disclosure of an essential characteristic of life as will to power—experiment. Such a culture, Nietzsche says, becomes "a hothouse for the luxury cultivation of the exception, the experiment, of danger, of the nuance:—this is the tendency of every aristocratic culture" (WP

---

8. In the chapters to come, I show that the affects can also be those of exhaustion and torpor within individuals and within entire cultures as well.

933). Such a culture displays a certain willingness to play with fire. The cultural organism, like any other, seeks resistance; but now, confident in its strength, it is fascinated and wants to play and experiment with what threatens and contradicts it. It wants to familiarize itself with and pursue what is foreign and stands as an exception and denial of its "truths." But this fascination with other manifestations of "spirit," with contradictory interpretations of the world, only stimulates its will to power. In short, the cultural organism seeks to incorporate these contradictions and exceptions and unify them within itself.

This is the sign of the healthiest and most "spiritual" cultures and individuals. Here the organism's "spiritual" power is challenged as it seeks to absorb a multiplicity of contradictions within its interpretation of the world. Thus, foreign manifestations of "spirit" are cultivated and experimented with so that the selective process of falsification can proceed. Nietzsche describes the exploitative power of "spirit" as giving style to one's character. This "great and rare art" is practiced, he says, by those who, surveying "the strengths and weaknesses of their nature," can "fit them into an artistic plan." What is ugly may be concealed or "reinterpreted and made sublime. Much that . . . resisted shaping . . . [is] saved and exploited for distant views." In the end "a single taste governed and formed everything. . . . Whether this taste was good or bad is less important than one might suppose, if only it was a single taste!" (GS 290). Regarding this "spiritual" blending and artifice, it makes little difference whether one speaks of an individual or a culture, because the "spiritual" dynamics within an individual "bear the strongest resemblance to the cultural structure of entire epochs." Ultimately, the "finest discoveries concerning culture are made by the individual man within himself" (HH 1:276), and he will understand "culture in the sense of a unity of style which characterizes all its life" (PTA 2:37; M 4:161).

For Nietzsche, the Greek culture attained "the highest peak of the spirit" (WP 898) so far and thus "the highest world-affirmation and transfiguration of existence that has yet been attained on earth" (WP 1051). They were a model for his idea of a master race possessing "an excess of strength for beauty, bravery, culture . . . an affirming race . . . beyond good and evil; a hothouse for strange and choice plants" (WP 898).

The First Frost

Within the Greek culture the finest example of delight in experiment is certainly the *sanction* to cultivate what in earlier times would have posed too great a threat but now is allowed to grow. Such a "strange and choice plant" is the philosopher.

The philosopher was a threat to culture in its earlier stages because precisely this independent and critical species attacks the traditions and authority inherent to the order of rank.[9] But now, confident in its ability to meet this threat, the culture exploits philosophy as a source of yet more alternative interpretations of the world diametrically opposed to its traditions. Initially, the philosopher is an exotic curiosity, an interesting distraction. Nevertheless, the philosopher, as innocuous as he or she may seem at the time, is an absolutely essential growth on the tree of culture because the "spirituality" typical of the philosophical type provides the possibility for growth beyond the destruction of the culture. The philosopher's vision carries the seeds for the possibility of life into the future because every culture, no matter how advanced, and indeed because it is "advancing," is preparing the path to its demise.

Within the individual, sickness is a threat essential as a resistance the body must overcome and exploit toward new levels of strength. And for every level of strength, there is a level of sickness that advances parasitically, upon every gain in vitality. The same physiological dynamic pertains within the cultural organism. In any supremely healthy culture, "[w]aste, decay, elimination need not be condemned: they are necessary consequences of life, of the growth of life." The "phenomenon of decadence," Nietzsche says, "is as necessary as any increase and advance of life: one is in no position to abolish it." Hence, no society or culture is "free to remain young . . . even at the height of its strength it has to form refuse and waste materials." And the "more energetically and boldly it advances, the richer it will be in failures and deformities, the closer to decline" (WP 40).

In short, and not surprising, a culture is subject to the fate of all living things: in the very creation of itself it is simultaneously advancing toward its destruction. No matter how the Greek culture "spiritualized" and spun the fables necessary for its growth, the cosmic law of becoming would not be denied. Like fruit that ripens to the point where its skin splits open, the vast reserves of excess strength that accumulated in the Greek culture owing to generations of a severely maintained order of rank could no longer be contained. Every organism, because it is living "seeks above all to *discharge* its strength" (B 13). The Greek culture became pregnant, as it were, with a vitality it could no longer suppress.

The will to power is, on the one hand, essential to the creation of the

---

9. A description of the physiological dynamics characteristic of the philosopher's independence and critical attitude is provided in Chapter 3.

order of rank. On the other hand, this very order, which through its discipline "economically" saves up and creates a huge reserve of excess strength, is ultimately destroyed by precisely what it cherishes most—its vitality, strength, power. This is the path to transformation. The old order of rank, which repressed this excess vitality and "dammed [it] to the point of torment" (WP 1022), is itself obliterated.

The Celebration

This obliteration constitutes the zenith of culture and simultaneously the first step toward decay. The demolition of the old order allows for a frenzy of creativity in all directions, and predictably, the forces of decadence, held in check for so long, make their power play. Aberrations abound; "[l]unatics [and] criminals . . . are increasing: sign of a growing culture rushing on precipitately—i.e., the refuse, the waste, gain importance—the decline keeps pace" (WP 864). The discharge of strength is exploited by all the forces in the organism: it is a free-for-all.

Those rich in strength squander it in lavish experiments, cultivating hybrids of all kinds. The "old ways" are no longer interesting, and the lowest forces in the cultural organism take advantage of this. These are the high points of culture, but in squandering its strength the old capacity to keep decadence and sickness at a distance is also weakened. And with this lapse in discipline comes the beginning of the end.

At such times, and from the point of view of the fading "old nobility," things become slack. It "is obvious," Nietzsche says, that the "pleasure[s] in war diminish, while the comforts of life" are pursued "as ardently as warlike and athletic honors were formerly." But in these ages, which are generally "accused of exhaustion," the "national energies," once so "gloriously visible in war," are now "transmuted into . . . private passions and . . . become less visible." Precisely at these times, the strengths of the culture "are probably greater than ever and the individual squanders them as lavishly as he could not have formerly when he was simply not yet rich enough." The old, gross rituals of torture now "offend the new taste," which prefers even more "spiritualized" expressions of cruelty; and hence, "*malice* and the delight in malice are born." During these "corrupt" ages "tragedy runs through houses and streets . . . great love and hatred are born, and . . . the flame of knowledge flares up to the sky" (GS 23).

These great ages of corruption are a state of anarchy within individuals and cultures. Bribery "and treason reach their peak" (GS 23); drives long suppressed now make their bid for power; jealousy, envy, and vendettas are the order of the day. And unless some other order of rank is quickly established, the energy of the organism is lost on petty squabbles and infighting. Just as one dominating drive, or a handful of them, must emerge to establish an order of rank in the individual, so it is with a culture. Some power must consolidate the others in order to regain stability and put an end to anarchy.

The Harvest

But when the dammed-up strength of a culture is unleashed, no force seems sufficient to bring the others to heel. The great discharge of strength constituting the bloom of the culture marks the beginning of its disintegration. It has gone through its cycle of growth, but in expending its strength, the tree of culture also brings forth its finest fruit; "and the tree existed," Nietzsche says, "only for the sake of these." Now "men emerge whom one calls tyrants," to take advantage of the general chaos and therewith political power. These would-be despots are the forerunners of other, less visible tyrants. The latter are secretive, backdoor men, who will flatter any autocrat because "in truth they . . . need peace from outside" in order to confront the "work inside themselves" (GS 23). These deceptive individuals, so dedicated to the "work inside themselves," are the philosophers. They can live or die on the whim of a dictator, but if they are not murdered and instead "achieve some security from the terrifying ups and downs" of the age (GS 23), one or two may emerge as "tyrants of the spirit" (HH 1:261) to "carry the seeds of the future and are the authors of the spiritual colonization and origin of new states and communities" (GS 23).

In the end, the dissolution of a culture, its "corruption," is only "a nasty word for the autumn of a people" (GS 23). But it is in autumn that the possibilities for the future are harvested. One such possibility is the philosophical type, who will provide another interpretation, another possibility, for life in the soil of decay.

All life as will to power seeks higher forms, and the most "spiritual" individuals, the philosophers, grow "from the tree of a people" (GS 23) as the seeds and promise of new deceptions for the transfiguration of life. But they are only a promise; anything can happen in the garden of life; and these seeds may sprout or die. It is strictly chance that rules here: "Nature propels the philosopher into mankind like an arrow; it takes no aim but hopes the arrow will stick somewhere" (U 3:7).

The philosopher is the product of the long growing season of a genuine culture such as that possessed by the Greeks. For Nietzsche, among "the Greeks alone" the philosopher "is not an accident." The task of the philosopher as a possibility for the future growth of culture is impossible to grasp within "our own circumstances . . . for we have no genuine culture." There is, says Nietzsche "a steely necessity which binds a philosopher to a genuine culture" (PTA 1:33–34; M 4:158–59). This necessity is determined by the law of life permeating the growth of culture, which, if it is healthy, will harvest the possibilities for new interpretations, which, like seeds, will take root within cultural decay.

The ages of "corruption" are "the expression of a threatening anarchy among the instincts" (B 258). And though the philosophical type stands, says Nietzsche, in a necessary relation to culture, how life as will to power exploits this type as the means to higher forms of growth in power is somewhat mysterious.

Regarding the ancient Greek philosophers, specifically the pre-Socratics, Nietzsche says that "though they were quite unconscious of it . . . [they] tended toward the healing and the purification of the whole." The "terrible dangers" that lay in the path of the future of Greek culture had to be "cleared away: thus did the philosopher protect and defend his native land" (PTA 2:35: M 4:160).

Hence, in the blooming of the Greek culture, philosophy emerged when this culture was on the verge of going into decline. The old mores or "spiritual" expressions no longer bound the culture together. But life as will to power provided the philosopher to create a new "spiritual" paradigm. The Greek philosophers, including Socrates, are seen by Nietzsche as *"tyrants of the spirit"* (HH 1:261) bearing the seeds of the future.[10]

---

10. Nietzsche's perception of the distinctions and similarities between Socrates and the pre-Socratics is looked at in greater detail in the next chapter.

3 Philosophy as Will to Power and the Case of Socrates

> Then Socrates resumed the discourse; now you have all, said he, declared your opinions as to what you value yourselves most upon; it remains that you prove it.
>
> —Xenophon

For Nietzsche, the instincts of decadence and therewith the power of sickness find a philosophical voice in Socrates. But this does not make Socrates less than a "great philosopher" in Nietzsche's eyes. On the contrary, it is essential to Nietzsche's admiration for him. To make sense of this seemingly enigmatic view of Socrates, I consider, first, who Nietzsche believed stood on a higher rank than Socrates, the truly "*great Greeks in philosophy, those of the two centuries before Socrates*" (E BT:3), and, second, the role of consciousness within physiology. The latter is essential to an understanding of Socratic "dialectics" as "pathologically conditioned" (T 3:10).

The Pre-Socratics

The Origins of the Philosophical Type

Chapter 2 closed on the threshold of Greek philosophy: when the first signs of decline appear in the great ages of corruption, the philosopher falls from the tree of culture. In the case of Greek culture these ripe apples (GS 23) are the pre-Socratics.

When the old order of rank breaks down within the social organism, all the old fictions provided by "spirit," namely the organism's customs and traditions, lose authority. Every manner of curiosity, every exotic and deformed creature, becomes "interesting." Generations of stored-up strength can no longer be contained; discipline and distance between ruler and ruled become lax, and people grow sick "of the old, used-up 'fatherland,' which has been touted to death" (GS 23).

In this volatile situation, the philosopher emerges as a tool of the will to power, as a possibility for new "spiritual" frontiers within the destruction of the old. The philosopher cultivates a deception that, if it can dominate, exploits the collapse of the old order to harness the power of the culture toward a new interpretation of itself—toward a new goal.

For Nietzsche, the best, most healthy philosophical types to date were the pre-Socratics. These exemplified philosophers as "power-hungry hermits." The "philosophic spirit," Nietzsche says, "always had to use as a mask and cocoon the *previously established* types of the contemplative man" (G 3:10). In short, the earliest disguises of the philosophical type were those of "priest, sorcerer, soothsayer, and in any case a religious type—in order to be able to *exist at all*" (G 3:10).

Just as cruelty, suffering, and "unfavorable conditions" were requisite to the cultivation of the warrior type, so they were of the philosopher. The "earliest race of contemplative men," Nietzsche says, "were despised" for their "inactive, brooding, unwarlike . . . instincts." For these individuals, the forbidding path to survival and growth lay in arousing "a decided *fear* of oneself." They were "men of frightful ages"; to be terrifying was to be respected—even if hated. Making oneself fearsome was done "by using frightful means: cruelty towards themselves, inventive self-castigation."[1] Cruelty "was the principal means these power-hungry . . . innovators of ideas required to overcome the gods and tradition in themselves, so as to be able to *believe* in their own innovations" (G 3:10). Through their capacity to endure self-inflicted torture, the earliest contemplative types fascinated and terrified the warlike members of the community. Thus, says Nietzsche, "did contemplation first appear on earth, at once weak and fearsome, secretly despised and publicly loaded with superstitious reference" (D 42).

In this way the early ancestors of the philosophical type managed to

---

1. This is the origin of *"the ascetic ideal"* Nietzsche identifies in both the religious and philosophical types. What is "unnatural" inspires fear.

survive. In time, those individuals "whose lives were melancholy and poor in deeds" were called "poets or thinkers or priests or medicinemen." Nietzsche tells us they were despised because "they were so inactive." And they would have been ejected from their communities, "but there was some danger attached to that" because it was "never doubted that they commanded unknown sources of power" (D 42).

This pseudo-religious type was the caterpillar that transformed itself and, when "released into the light," became "that many-colored and dangerous winged creature, the 'spirit' " of philosophy (G 3:10). Now the philosophical types, in conditions of relative safety, could stand by their *own* "innovations," that is, their visions of the world, against the religious-mythical visions held by their countrymen. Therefore, in reference to Greek culture and to the pre-Socratics in particular, Nietzsche says that the brilliance of Greek life is evident only under "the radiance of the myth . . . the Greek philosophers deprived themselves of precisely this myth . . . as if they wanted to move out of the sunshine." But no plant, he says, "avoids the light; fundamentally these philosophers were only seeking a *brighter* sun, the myth was not . . . lucid enough for them." In the end, they "discovered this light in their knowledge, in that which each of them called his 'truth' " (HH 1:261).

Tyrants of the Spirit

I have discussed the "spiritualizing" role of the instinct of preservation in the warrior type. In the philosopher this drive certainly functions, but, as with the warrior, preservation is exploited by an even stronger instinct toward *its* interpretation of the world. In other words, self-preservation does not dominate the healthy philosophical type. Those of this type want more than mere survival or even the preservation of culture; they want power, and will exploit all possibilities to get it.

The drive, in the philosophical type, that is strong enough to harness the power of all the others toward its perspective Nietzsche describes as a lust for insight and knowledge that "ruthlessly disposes of all other stores and accumulations of energy, of animal vigour." This "greater energy . . . *uses up* the lesser." When this drive's demands prevail "against those of all the other instincts" (G 3:8), it establishes an order of rank and exploits the strength of the philosopher's other passions.

For the pre-Socratics, power lay in solving the riddle, the "why" of all that is; their passion for knowledge revealed the law of life. The will to power in the drive for knowledge was nothing less than a desire to conquer the world. This passion for knowledge was the basis of Nietzsche's admiration of the pre-Socratics.

The will to power was absolutely unique in the pre-Socratics. Challenged by life as the great mystery, they wanted to "solve everything . . . and to settle all questions with a *single* answer." This passion for "being the 'unriddler of the world' " constituted the thinker's secret dream of *victory*. Such "boundless ambition" made philosophy a "supreme struggle to possess the tyrannical rule of the spirit." And that some lucky individual could attain the goal "was doubted by none, and several . . . fancied themselves to be that one" (D 547).

The pre-Socratics wanted to solve the riddle of the universe and render all former interpretations subject to their own. For this reason Nietzsche calls them the *"tyrants of the spirit."* They wanted to establish their "spiritual" supremacy by reaching "the midpoint of being with a single leap" (HH 1:261). It is precisely because Nietzsche sees philosophy as "this tyrannical drive . . . [as] the most spiritual will to power, to the 'creation of the world,' to the *causa prima*" (B 9), that the pre-Socratics are the embodiment of the pure philosophical type.

This "most spiritual will to power," "to the *causa prima*," is cosmology. And when Nietzsche asks, "[D]o you want a *name* for this world? A *solution* for all its riddles?" and responds, "[W]ill to power—and nothing besides" (WP 1067), he is trying to awaken the ancient voice of Greek cosmology. Heidegger writes, in *An Introduction to Metaphysics*, "A beginning can never directly preserve its full momentum; the only possible way to preserve its force is to repeat, to draw once again (wieder-holen) more deeply than ever from its source. And it is only by repetitive thinking (denkende Wieder-holung) that we can deal appropriately with the beginning and the breakdown of the truth."[2] In Nietzsche's call to return to the source of Western philosophy in pre-Socratic thought, he is practicing what Heidegger would later call *denkende Wieder-holung*. Heidegger says that the task of understanding Being "consists first of all . . . in bringing [Nietzsche's] . . . accomplishment to a full unfolding."[3] He certainly does not follow Nietzsche's interpretation of pre-Socratic thought. Indeed, he says Nietzsche establishes "a vibrant rapport with the personalities of the Preplatonic philosophers; but his interpretations of the texts are commonplace, if not entirely superficial, throughout."[4]

Heidegger never forgave Nietzsche for saying "being is an empty fiction" (T 4:2), but in Nietzsche's call to return to the health of pre-

2. Martin Heidegger, *An Introduction to Metaphysics*, trans. Ralph Mannheim (New Haven: Yale University Press, 1980), 191.
3. Ibid., 36.
4. Martin Heidegger, "The Anaximander Fragment," in *Early Greek Thinking*, trans. David F. Krell and Frank A. Capuzzi (New York: Harper & Row, 1975) 14.

Socratic thought, he foreshadows Heidegger's effort to draw "more deeply than ever" from this source. It is in their return to this "source" that both Heidegger and Nietzsche carry out the program of destroying the tradition of metaphysics. Heidegger finds the forgetfulness of Being at this very source, whereas Nietzsche finds the possibility for destroying the question of Being—so dear to Heidegger, in the *archē* of will to power.

Nietzsche believes the future of philosophy lies in "the digging up of ancient philosophy, above all of the pre-Socratics—the most deeply buried of all Greek temples." Here one finds access "to all those fundamental forms of world interpretation devised by the Greek spirit through Anaximander, Heraclitus, Parmenides, Empedocles, Democritus, and Anaxagoras" (WP 419). These cosmologists reveal the great vitality among the Greek instincts—the passion to rule the world: "[I]t has been the proper task of all great thinkers to be lawgivers as to the measure, stamp and weight of things" (U 3:3). Hence, their " 'knowing' is *creating*, their creating is a legislation, their will to truth is—*will to power*" (B 211).

That there existed individuals convinced they held the key to understanding the cosmos had a profound impact on Nietzsche. To him this conviction expressed an extraordinary unity with the law of life. The pre-Socratic had the "calm conviction that he is the only rewarded wooer of truth." Such conviction carries with it a great pride. "Such men live inside their own solar system; only there can we look for them" (PTA 8:66; M 4:186–87). This pride is typical of what Nietzsche calls the "agonal instinct of the Hellenes" (T 3:8). The pre-Socratics, he says, were hostile "toward others with similar gifts" (PTA 8:66; M 4:186–87), and in matters of wisdom, "each of them was a warlike brutal *tyrant*" (HH 1:261).

While entertaining *The Philosopher as Cultural Physician* as a title for his book on Greek philosophy,[5] Nietzsche said the philosopher "is most useful when there is *a lot to be destroyed*, in times of chaos or degeneration" (PAC 72; M 6:68). To appreciate this observation, we should not be distracted by the pre-Socratic arrogance of believing "that one was in possession of the truth" (HH 1:261). The intoxicated disdain and hubris of this belief is appropriate to the flush of victory. And "the severity, arrogance . . . and evil in such a belief" (HH 1:261) allowed the pre-

---

5. The title he eventually used was "Philosophy in the Tragic Age of the Greeks." This is the best-known and most "complete" work Nietzsche wrote on the pre-Socratics. For more detail on the history of this unpublished text, including Nietzsche's speculations on possible titles, see the introduction to PT, xviii–xxiii.

Socratics to pass judgment "on the whole fate of man . . . on the highest fate that can befall individual men or entire nations" (U 3:3). In so doing, they decided what had merit and what did not. In short, with their "truths" they had a standard by which to judge what deserved to live and what deserved to die.

The philosophical type emerges at the apex and bloom of a healthy culture. This is when philosophers are "most useful," in that within the chaos marking the zenith of a culture, its stored-up strength is now unleashed and squandered in multiple directions. Unless some new "spiritual" frontier, some new deception, can emerge as dominant, the power of the culture is dissipated. The philosopher's function within the cultural organism is to create this deception. And when any "organ in an organism fails . . . to enforce with complete assurance its self-preservation . . . [and the] restitution of its energies—the whole degenerates" (E D:2). Philosophers are an instrument of life as will to power within the cultural organism. They combat whatever is parasitical on the strength of the culture, and exploit whatever remains healthy toward their own ends. For this reason Nietzsche states that in relation to their culture the pre-Socratics "(though they were quite unconscious of it) tended toward the healing and the purification of the whole . . . thus did the philosopher protect and defend his native land" (PTA 2:35; M 4:160). In this way, these "power-hungry hermits" revealed the "steely necessity which binds a philosopher to a genuine culture" (PTA 1:33–34; M 4:159).

The pre-Socratics, convinced of their "truths," were "unconscious" of themselves as the first cultural physicians. For Nietzsche, Socrates was quite "conscious" of himself in this role. But the naive willingness of the pre-Socratics to pass judgment on what deserved to live and to die in their culture led Nietzsche to "conceive of them as the *forerunners of a reformation of the Greeks*, but not as the forerunners of Socrates" (SSW 134; M 6:106). The "sixth and fifth centuries," Nietzsche says, promised more "than they actually brought forth," but "it remained only a promise and proclamation" (HH 1:261). In the end, the pre-Socratics never did bring off a reformation; "all they managed to found were sects" (GS 149). And since "their reformation never occurred" (SSW 134; M 6:106), the "*excision* of the degenerating part" (E D:2) of Greek culture never took place, and "all that remained was Socrates" (SSW 134; M 6:106).

The Failure of Greek Cosmology

Nietzsche says that in "general, the rule that tyrants are usually murdered and that their posterity has but a brief existence also applies to the tyrants of the spirit." "Their history," he says, "is brief and violent, their posthumous influence ceases abruptly" (HH 1:261). The strange fate of the pre-Socratics, their colossal failure, is explicable in light of the chaos typical of the apex of any healthy culture. At such a time there is "a kind of *tropical* tempo in the competition to grow . . . savage egoisms . . . wrestle 'for sun and light.' " Within this explosion of cultural strength, there are all "sorts of new what-fors and wherewithals . . . misunderstanding allied with disrespect; decay . . . and the highest desires [are] gruesomely entangled." Here is "the genius of the race overflowing . . . [in that] calamitous simultaneity of spring and fall" so typical of young, "unwearied corruption" (B 262).

Such turning points in history, Nietzsche says, are "rich in marvels and monstrosities" (B 262), and "every great thinker, in the belief that he was the possessor of absolute truth," provided this point in Greek intellectual history "the same violent, precipitate and perilous character as does their political history." None of these violent and combative tyrants seems actually to have vanquished his "spiritual" adversaries. Nietzsche says, "[I]t seems as though these glorious philosophers had lived in vain" (HH 1:261) to harness the power of such a prodigious "junglelike growth" (B 262). Nietzsche is in the dark at this point. He concedes that here "there is a gap, a breach in evolution" and that "some great disaster must have occurred." But whatever happened, "the only statue from which we could have perceived" the direction "of that great preparatory exercise . . . [must] have miscarried or been shattered." In the end, "what actually happened must for ever remain a secret of the workshop" (HH 1:261).

One thing is clear: the pre-Socratics did not manage to forge a new "spiritual" frontier for their culture. This leads to a further depletion of the organism's strength, and "the decline keeps pace" (WP 864). Nietzsche never tired of trying to find the "secret of the workshop." The more he tried to understand this mystery, the more Socrates' "instinct-disintegrating influence" (BT 13) came to the fore as a decisive factor. The pre-Socratics, he says, were "well on the way toward *assessing correctly* the irrationality and suffering of human existence" (SSW 136; M 6:108). In this, early "Hellenism *revealed its strengths in its succession of philosophers*" (SSW 133; M 6:105). But "thanks to Socrates, *they never reached the goal*" (SSW 136; M 6:108). The movement of Greek culture, he says, "is so accelerated that a single stone thrown into its wheels makes it fly to pieces. Socrates, for example, was such a stone" (HH 1:261).

The tone of Nietzsche's descriptions of the pre-Socratics is, at times, that of hero worship. Granted my use of his youthful references to the pre-Socratics, he still attributes the same heroic status to them in his later writings.[6] In short, there is a certain unqualified, naive reverence for the early Greek cosmologists throughout his philosophical life. Be that as it may, the face of Socrates, on the other hand, even if objectionably ugly (T 3:3), also compelled Nietzsche to recognize, yet again, the face of a hero. Socrates was, Nietzsche says, a decadent; hence, the Apollonian light surrounding this philosophical giant has a dark source.

The pre-Socratics were the products of what may be called the treacherous health of Greek culture. Socrates, like his predecessors, was possible as a pure philosophical type because of things "hidden, reserved, subterranean" (T 3:4). But unlike the pre-Socratics, there is something "defective" in him. The term "defect" has to be put into quotation marks, since I use it for its physiological significance.

The symptoms of sickness Nietzsche identified with Socrates are multiple and provide for him the various avenues he takes in attacking Socrates. A few of these symptoms are Socrates' rationality (T 3:10), his role in destroying tragic art (BT 12), his moralizing (WP 443), and his failure as a physician of culture (T 3:11). But an examination of Nietzsche's relation to Socrates that was too spellbound by these symptoms would fail. I mean, detailed descriptions of them would fail to get at precisely what unifies these symptoms in Socrates. The examination would be limited to symptoms, when the *sickness* is "even more instructive" (G 3:9).

Understanding the illness Nietzsche attributes to Socrates is beneficial to my purposes in several ways. First, it clarifies the seemingly disparate features of Nietzsche's critique of him. Second, Socrates' sickness is exposed as characteristic of Greek culture. And finally, the symptoms of this same illness are made recognizable in philosophy *after* Socrates. But appreciating Nietzsche's diagnosis of sickness in Socrates requires development of a feature of the physiology I only touched upon in Chapter 1: namely, human consciousness.

Consciousness

Origins

Consciousness, Nietzsche says, is "innocent of any of the essential processes of our preservation and our growth" (WP 646). But if consciousness is "in the main *superfluous*" to these processes, why has it

6. See, for example, E BT:3; T 4:2, and especially WP 437.

become integral to the human animal? A proper response to this question is possible, Nietzsche says, "when we begin to comprehend how we could dispense with" consciousness entirely. And the path to this comprehension lies in "physiology and the history of animals" (GS 354). Consciousness is intimately related to the organic as will to power, but it "is the last and latest development of the organic and hence also what is also most unfinished and unstrong." The human race has flourished thanks to powerful instincts, not consciousness. Without "the former," Nietzsche says, "humanity would have long disappeared" (GS 11).

But the question still remains: why any consciousness at all? Even if tentative and weak, consciousness is rooted in the organic, and its growth presupposes the physiological dynamics of will to power. Nietzsche notes these dynamics in pointing out that "the subtlety and strength of consciousness always were proportionate to a man's (or animal's) *capacity for communication.*" Somehow, then, whatever "strength" we attribute to consciousness corresponds to our ability to communicate. But if the conditions of growth and preservation do not require consciousness, is our ability to communicate equally superficial? Nietzsche would answer yes if we were speaking about "man's individual existence," but our ability to communicate and the proportionate development of consciousness is essential to our "social or herd nature" (GS 354).

"[U]nder the pressure of the need for communication . . . particularly between those who commanded and those who obeyed" (GS 354), consciousness emerged. That is, it developed in "unfavorable conditions" wherein life was threatened and there was the "need to reach agreement quickly and easily about what must be done" (B 268). It was "only in proportion to the degree of this utility" that consciousness emerged and the "degree of this utility" was determined by an already familiar instinct, self-preservation. Consciousness matured because the human being, as "the most endangered animal . . . *needed* help and protection." This animal "needed his peers"; and it was precisely this need, as the perspective of the instinct of preservation, that forced us to learn "to communicate and understand each other quickly and subtly." And man, "to express his distress and make himself understood . . . needed 'consciousness' first of all," because "he needed to 'know' . . . what distressed him, he needed to 'know' how he felt, he needed to 'know' what he thought" (GS 354).

What can Nietzsche mean in saying the human animal "needed to 'know' what he thought?" This distinction between "knowing" and "thinking" is pursued when he points out that we think "continually without knowing it" but that "the thinking that rises to *consciousness* is only the smallest part of all this." And "only this conscious thinking *takes the form of words, which is to say signs of communication*, and this fact uncovers the origin of consciousness" (GS 354).

The Deception of Grammar

In Chapter 1, I pointed out that consciousness reflects "the last scenes of reconciliation" after the drives have battled to establish power relations among themselves. For Nietzsche, only "the end of this long process rise[s] to our consciousness" (GS 333). Consciousness simply mirrors the "cumulative perspective" of an order of rank among the drives. It is our drive-perspectives "that interpret the world . . . their For and Against" (WP 481). What we communicate is already determined by the "great intelligence" (Z 1:4) of the body. This is "the essence," Nietzsche says, "of phenomenalism and perspectivism as *I* understand them." Because of "the nature of *animal consciousness*, the world of which we can become conscious is only a surface- and sign-world" (GS 354).

All the fictions and deceptions typical of the "spirit," determined by the law of life in a multiplicity of perspectives toward preservation and growth, would never have become "conscious" without the necessity to articulate these primordial interpretations in "the form of words." It is only insofar as we ever had to communicate that it became necessary for us to "know," that is, level off and stabilize a "thousandfold complexity as a unity" (WP 523). This "unity" is merely an acoustical sign (B 268) "that is a unit only as a word" (B 19). When the unconscious cumulative perspective of a multiplicity of drives is mirrored in "conscious thought," it "*becomes* by the same token shallow, thin, relatively stupid, sign, herd signal." In short, it takes the form of words, a "reduction to superficialities, and generalization" (GS 354).

Knowledge, then, is only what appears in conscious thinking. "Knowledge and becoming," Nietzsche says, "exclude one another" because "knowledge is possible only on the basis of belief in being" (WP 517–18). The deception of stability peculiar to self-preservation has already "impose[d] upon becoming the character of being" (WP 617). With this belief we "have projected the conditions of *our* preservation as predicates of being in general." For Nietzsche, precisely these predicates constitute formal ontology insofar as logic has a "usefulness for life . . . *not* that something is true" (WP 507). Logic and reason function "only after a fundamental *falsification* of all events is assumed" (WP 512). But this "falsification" is essential because "we have to be stable in our beliefs if we are to prosper" (WP 507).

We could have gotten along without consciousness, language, reason, and logic if we had remained solitary animals. But since the deceptions of "spirit" had to be articulated, what was "incomparably personal" was "translated back into the perspective of the herd" (GS 354). The passion of knowledge characteristic of philosophy naturally translates into the herd perspective. Conscious thought is herd thought. For Nietzsche this is neither right nor wrong; in the end, as always, its "value for *life* is ultimately decisive" (WP 493).

This value is life affirming in the case of the pre-Socratics, who revealed the potent instincts of a culture exploding with vitality. As the products of a genuinely healthy culture, they displayed the passion to conquer the cosmos through their "truths." These "truths" were, from Nietzsche's point of view, the new deceptions, the new "spiritual" frontiers, through which the *growth* of Greek culture might be secured within the destruction of the old.

Socrates, on the other hand, was also the product of his culture. His role, like that of his predecessors, was that of destruction. But his emphasis on consciousness, reason, and dialectics, on "conscious thinking" as the path to "Truth," betrayed a sickness in his exhortation to "Know thyself." Socrates, like the pre-Socratics, articulated "Truth" within the perspective of the herd. But unlike his predecessors, his "Truth" exposed the dark role philosophy plays in a culture that is *ill*. Through Socrates, life as will to power provided a deception through which the Greek culture embraced death.

The Case of Socrates

Much has been made of the philosophical relation between Nietzsche and Socrates, and my observations on it here are by no means meant as the "last word" on the matter.[7] Some, deceived by Nietzsche's polemical

---

7. In addition to those mentioned below, there are studies by Ernst Sandvoss, *Sokrates und Nietzsche* (Leiden: E. J. Brill, 1966), and Hermann-Josef Schmidt's *Nietzsche und Sokrates: Philosophische Untersuchungen zu Nietzsches Sokratesbild* (Meisenheim am Glan: Hain, 1969) presents a remarkably detailed account of this relation.

tone, have said that he hated Socrates.⁸ Walter Kaufmann has, however, successfully shown that this assessment is false. But Kaufmann is really *too* successful here.⁹ Nietzsche certainly admired Socrates, but Kaufmann is conspicuously silent about Nietzsche's attack upon him. I think Werner Dannhauser is correct to say that Kaufmann oversimplifies Nietzsche's view of Socrates "by making [Nietzsche] seem at once less ambiguous and less interesting than he really is."¹⁰ But is Nietzsche as ambiguous toward Socrates as Dannhauser and others have suggested?¹¹

No doubt Nietzsche's references to Socrates make the assessment of ambiguity almost irresistible. For example, Nietzsche says he admires "the courage and wisdom of Socrates in everything he did, said—and did not say" (GS 340). On the other hand, he says Socrates is "a dangerous force that undermines life" (E BT:1). There are many other perceptions of Socrates besides Nietzsche's, but since my task here is pursue Nietzsche's portrait of him, I will proceed according to the physiology established thus far. This physiology no more settles "The Problem of Socrates" than it settles the other problems in Nietzsche's thought. However, if nothing else, Nietzsche's "clinical standpoint" helps to dispel the idea of Nietzsche's ambiguity toward Socrates. His observations on Socrates are, in many respects, those of a diagnostician noting the symptoms of a great, though decadent, philosophical type.

Deformities

The reformation Nietzsche identified with pre-Socratic thought never occurred, and the ebbing of the vitality of Greek culture continued

---

8. See, for example, Richard Oehler, *Nietzsche und die Vorsokratiker* (Leipzig: Dürr'schen Buchhandlung, 1904); T. Ziegler, "Nietzsche gegen Socrates," *Suddeutsche Monatshefte* 10 (1913): 277–89; Ernst Bertram, *Nietzsche: Versuch einer Mythologie* (Berlin: Bondi, 1918), 309; Crane Brinton, *Nietzsche* (Cambridge: Harvard University Press, 1941), 83; A.H.J. Knight, *Some Aspects of the Life and Work of Nietzsche, and Particularly of His Connection with Greek Literature and Thought* (New York: Russell & Russell, 1967), 55n.

9. See chapter 13 of Kaufmann's *Nietzsche: Philosopher, Psychologist, Antichrist*, 3d ed. (New York: Vintage, 1968), 391. For a sustained and penetrating critique of Kaufmann's views on Nietzsche's relation to Socrates, see Tracy B. Strong's *Friedrich Nietzsche and the Politics of Transfiguration* (Berkeley and Los Angeles: University of California Press, 1975), 112–23.

10. Dannhauser, *Nietzsche's View of Socrates* (Ithaca: Cornell University Press, 1974), 32.

11. See Karl Jaspers, *Nietzsche: An Introduction to the Understanding of His Philosophical Activity*, trans. Charles F. Wallraff and Frederick J. Schmitz (South Bend, Ind.: Regnery/Gateway, 1979), 35; Marianne Cowan, introduction to *Philosophy in the Tragic Age of the Greeks*, trans. Marianne Cowan (Chicago: Regnery/Gateway, 1962), 13; and Alan D. Schrift, *Nietzsche and the Question of Interpretation: Between Hermeneutics and Deconstruction* (New York: Routledge, 1990), 63.

unabated. No new "spirituality" emerged through which a new aristocracy could do "what needed to be done" (T 10:47), that is, exploit the weaker drives within the social organism toward a transfiguration of the goal of power. By the time Socrates appeared on the scene, the old nobility was only a shadow of its former self, and this is evidenced in the social mobility of those elements formerly repressed and exploited by the aristocracy. The discipline of the old order of rank had broken down, the distance between ruler and ruled was lacking, and "degeneration was everywhere silently preparing itself: the old Athens was coming to an end" (T 3:9).

Symptomatic of this degeneration was the fact that Socrates, who "in his origins" belonged "to the lowest orders" (T 3:3), actually "*got himself taken seriously*" (T 3:5). "Socrates," Nietzsche says, "was rabble" (T 3:3), but his access to "the aristocratic circles of Athens" (T 3:8), indicated that the culture's physiological function of excluding "forms of decline and decay" (WP 339) was seriously debilitated.

To emphasize Socrates' degenerate origins, Nietzsche mentions "how ugly he was." The polemical tone of such a remark is undeniable. But there is more to it than that, since Nietzsche says that the physiological significance of ugliness lies in its frequently being "the sign of . . . a development *retarded* by interbreeding. Otherwise it appears as a development in *decline*." In his elaboration of the idea that ugliness is physiologically suspect, Nietzsche associates it, and therewith Socrates, to the sordid side of any society: "Anthropologists among criminologists tell us the typical criminal is ugly: *monstrum in fronte, monstrum in animo*" (T 3:3).

These remarks are dubious. Clearly, an "ugly" face is not necessarily a criminal face. But the hermeneutic of suspicion characteristic of Nietzsche's clinical standpoint allows him to highlight the idea that among the Greeks ugliness was "almost a refutation." If this is so, then the question how Socrates could fascinate his contemporaries becomes more intense. That Socrates exercised this fascination reveals something about his fellow Athenians as well. Why did they not object to Socrates from the start? In this vein, Nietzsche wonders if the Socrates who was convicted at his trial was "a typical criminal." He then speculates upon the opinion of Zopyrus, a "famous physiognomist" who, "passing through Athens . . . told Socrates to his face that he *was a monstrum*—that he contained within him every kind of foul vice and lust. And Socrates answered merely: 'You know me, sir!' " (T 3:3).[12]

---

12. Nietzsche takes this conversation from Cicero, who tells the story of the "'physiognomist' Zopyrus" (*De Fato*, Loeb ed., trans. H. Rackham [London: William Heinemann,

When Zopyrus revealed to Socrates that he was "a cave of every evil lust," Nietzsche says, "the great ironist uttered a phrase that provides the key to him. 'That is true,' he said, 'but I have become master of them all.'" That Socrates should attain self-mastery is important, especially since, for Nietzsche, his case is "only the most obvious instance of what had at that time begun to be the universal exigency." In this decadent age "no one was any longer master of himself . . . the instincts were becoming mutually *antagonistic* (T 3:9).

At such times all the instincts demand satisfaction and lack the coordination of an order of rank. This state of affairs rendered the age of Socrates one of "physiological weariness" (BT S:4). And in ages of exhaustion, when all the drives "seek satisfaction, a man of profound mediocrity must result" (WP 677). But Socrates was by no means mediocre. Yet in light of "the admitted . . . anarchy of his instincts which indicates *décadence* in Socrates" (T 3:4), the real question for Nietzsche was, "*How* did Socrates become master of *himself*?" (T 3:9).

When Nietzsche looks at Socrates, he first determines "what order of rank the innermost drives of his nature stand in relation to each other."[13] The instincts, as I have shown, are such that "every single one . . . would like only too well to represent just *itself* as the ultimate purpose of existence." Nietzsche goes on to say that "every drive wants to be master—and it attempts to philosophize in *that spirit*" (B 6). In "the case of Socrates" (T 3:7), it is the "spirit," or deception, peculiar to the instinct of preservation that philosophizes.

Symptoms of Decadence

In conditions of exhaustion the instinct of preservation consolidates its power by dominating the weakest drives of the organism. In this way

---

1942], v. 10). Zopyrus, "who claimed to discern every man's nature from his appearance, charged Socrates in company with a number of vices which he enumerated, and when he was ridiculed by the rest who said they failed to recognize such vices in Socrates, Socrates himself came to [Zopyrus's] rescue by saying that he was naturally inclined to the vices named, but had cast them out of him by the help of reason" (*Tusculan Disputations*, Loeb ed., trans. J. E. King [London: William Heinemann, 1927], 4.37.80. Nietzsche does not mention Cicero's other version of this encounter: "Again, do we not read how Socrates was stigmatized by the 'physiognomist' Zopyrus, who professed to discover men's entire characters and natures from their body, eyes, face and brow? He said that Socrates was stupid and thick-witted because he had got hollows in the neck above the collar-bone—he used to say that these portions of his anatomy were blocked and stopped up; he also added that he was addicted to women—at which Alcibiades is said to have given a loud guffaw!" (*De Fato*, v. 10).

13. He does the same thing with Jesus of Nazareth. Nietzsche's critique of any

its perspective gains in influence over the more powerful drives, which, in their fatigued state, are more easily defeated. As preservation gains in strength, the intensity of the most powerful drives is leveled off and devitalized to the extent that the organism gains stability and the constant feuding of the others is suspended. Preservation is the first instinct of "spirit," and its deception of stability is vitally important in rendering a stable and fixed world of "being" for any healthy organism. Upon this deception the more powerful drives manipulate the world according to whatever affirms growth in power. But in the case of decadence, the instinct of preservation reveals its perspective, not toward growth, but in a ruthless antagonism to whatever threatens stability.

In a healthy organism the combined power of its drives is harnessed toward growth. In decadence the situation is reversed: the instinct of preservation becomes dominant, and the strength still evident in the constant feud between drive-perspectives is devitalized and leveled off for the sake of stability. The organism is worn out by the constant battle among its multiple drives. And the instinct of preservation, recognizing the threat of further depletion of strength, emerges as a *reaction* to a state of siege. It will suspend, and indeed undermine, the power of those drives essential to growth. But insofar as preservation must negate the activity of the other instincts, it conforms to "the formula for *décadence*"—the physiological need "to combat one's instincts" (T 3:11).

For Nietzsche, "the case of Socrates" reveals a dominating instinct of preservation, and Socrates "philosophize[s] in *that spirit*" (B 6). Socrates could honestly say to Zopyrus that he suspended the "anarchy of his instincts" (T 3:4). But the cheerful optimism typical of Socrates' self-mastery was possible because the law of life as will to power was denied. Life requires growth in power, not mere self-preservation. Socrates *had* to combat his instincts to attain equilibrium, and here he betrayed "the formula for *décadence*." Thanks to the deceptions peculiar to the "spiritualizing" activity of preservation, all of which are articulated by Socrates, he was instrumental in "the dissolution of Greece" (T 3:2). These deceptions, those of "conscious" thought—"logic," "reason," "being"—are precisely those fictions through which we project "the conditions of *our* preservation" (WP 507).

Nietzsche recognized something defective in Socrates' extraordinary intellect as early as 1872, in *The Birth of Tragedy*, and this is echoed again

---

individual or culture generally hinges on the physiological status of the individual or culture in question. That is, he determines the status of the instincts, and he rarely, if ever, displays a lack of confidence in his ability to make these determinations.

in 1888, in *Twilight of the Idols*. In the former, Nietzsche mentions Socrates' astonishment at his contemporaries, who "were without a proper and sure insight, even with regard to their own professions, and that they practiced them only by instinct." With the phrase " 'Only by instinct' . . . we touch," Nietzsche says, "upon the heart and core of the Socratic tendency." This "tendency" is referred to in *The Birth of Tragedy* as a "hypertrophy [of] the logical nature" (BT 13). Then sixteen years later it is called a "superfetation of the logical" (T 3:4), and this and the "clarity of reason . . . are abnormalities, both belong together" (WP 433).

These are abnormalities insofar as Socrates' rational capacity betrayed a *dominant* perspective of preservation demanding a "rational" fixed world of "being" to combat the instincts essential to the law of life as becoming. He was himself infected with the disease of his age, "the antagonism of the passions; two, three, a multiplicity of 'souls in one breast' " (WP 778). He realized a "cure" for this anarchy by negating within himself the activity of his other drives. Yet the path to health lies in the combined strength of all our drives. His success in attaining self-mastery came at the cost of declaring war "against the preconditions of life, against the value feelings of life, against partisanship in favor of life" (WP 461). This warfare is expressed by Nietzsche when he places into the mouth of Socrates the following words: "The instincts want to play the tyrant; we must devise a *counter-tyrant* who is stronger" (T 3:9). This counter-tyrant is "Reason," and therefore all the deceptions of conscious thought determined by the drive for preservation.

In Socrates, consciousness, the weakest and "latest development of the organic" (GS 11), was hypertrophied. Since consciousness and language go "hand in hand" (GS 354), Socrates' excessively developed capacity for conscious thought rendered him a virtuoso in *articulating* the fictions of a fixed, static world. He was the most exquisite example of an existence lived within the "absolute coldness and neutrality of . . . consciousness," and he consistently embraced consciousness as "the precondition of perfection—whereas the opposite is true—" (WP 434). Socrates was the wise man who, affirming "rationality at any cost" (T 3:11), resorted to "clarity, severity and logicality as weapons against the ferocity of the drives" (WP 433).

The Philosophical Type of Decadence

Socrates entered an abstract world where the "body and its great intelligence" (Z 1:4), manifest in the struggle for power among our drives, is deemed false and irrational. This world of becoming and chaos was instinctively repulsive to him. The world as will to power, a whirligig of death, "change, age, as well as procreation and growth" (T 4:1) was judged "good for nothing" because it was "not the 'real world' " (WP 461). Socrates' survival depended on the negation of this flux by means of acoustical signs (B 268). He was magnificent in his vision of Truth, Reality, Perfection and Virtue as *eternally* accessible to us via conscious thought—the thinking that *"takes the form of words"* (GS 354).

After all, those who cannot justify themselves according to conscious thought are fools. Nietzsche points out that with Socrates "Greek taste undergoes a change in favour of dialectics." Then he asks, "[W]hat is really happening when that happens?" and responds, "It is above all the defeat of a *nobler* taste; with dialectics the rabble gets on top." In the healthier age of Greek culture, "the dialectical manner was repudiated in good society . . . one was compromised by it . . . such presentation of one's reasons was regarded with mistrust" (T 3:5). Dialectics seemed somehow dishonest to the old nobility. It was seen as indicative of weakness. "Why this display of reasons? Why should one demonstrate? Against others one possessed authority. One commanded: that sufficed. . . . One simply had no place for dialectic" (WP 431). Among the old warrior aristocracy "the dialectician is a kind of buffoon: he is laughed at" (T 3:5).

But Socrates, flourishing in a degenerate age, was "the buffoon who *got himself taken seriously*" (T 3:5). He represents a physiological revaluation of the values of Greek antiquity. No longer does Greek culture seek the enhancement of power; no longer is a life of victory and conquest the mark of nobility. On the contrary, the rational man, the dialectician, is the new hero; this "profound *illusion*," Nietzsche says, "first saw the . . . world in the person of Socrates." He is the embodiment of the fictions of conscious thought and of "the unshakable faith that thought, using the thread of logic," is capable not only of penetrating "the deepest abysses of being . . . but even of *correcting* it" (BT 15).

Wherever Socrates fails to see reason, he recognizes falsehood. That is, his instinct of preservation insists on *its* interpretation to the extent that life as the chaos of will to power is judged to be not as it "ought" to be. In this way he "infers the essential perversity and reprehensibility of what exists" (BT 13). This is the genuine Socratic *ignorance* of "all the presuppositions of the 'noble Greek' of the old stamp" (WP 435). The morality of the old nobility affirmed and was founded on life as will to power, but with Socrates the old values "are torn from their conditionality, in which they have grown and alone possess any meaning, from their Greek and Greek-political ground and soil." Now the "great concepts 'good' and 'just' are severed from the presuppositions to which they belong" and degenerate into "objects of dialectic." Simultaneously with this revaluation comes the invention of "the abstractly perfect man as well:—good, just, wise, a dialectician . . . a plant removed from all soil" that cherishes "a humanity without any . . . regulating instincts" and "a virtue that 'proves' itself with reasons." The ultimate result of this "denaturalization of moral values was," Nietzsche says, "the creation of a degenerate type of man—'the good man,' 'the happy man,' 'the wise man' " (WP 430). And insofar as Socrates promoted "the greatest seduction to make oneself abstract" (WP 428), he "represents a moment of the profoundest perversity in the history of values" (WP 430).

A "Detestable Pretension to Happiness"

The Greeks of the old nobility, unified with the law of life, demanded "victory, opponents overcome, the overflow of the feeling of power across wider domains than hitherto" (WP 703). The drive to power was their virtue, and victory was their happiness. With Socrates the virtuous man always sees the advantage of "Reason," that is, preservation. In other words, the "good" does not demand that one *"live dangerously"* (GS 283). After all, living dangerously puts one's life in jeopardy. "Good" people do not seek the greatest resistance; they deny the necessity of life as *"essentially* appropriation, injury, overpowering of what is alien and weaker" (B 259). Lured by the deception of stability, they judge the law of life "unreasonable" and therefore "bad." These individuals hold that nobody "wants to do harm to himself, therefore all that is bad is done involuntarily." For nobody would *consciously* choose to be bad, that is, risk self-destruction. "Hence the bad are bad only because of an error; if one removes the error, one necessarily makes them—good" (B 190).

This kind of thinking is the mark, Nietzsche says, of a "profoundly average creature" who (WP 873), from the standpoint of the old warrior elite, is a coward. But in "the age of Socrates, among men of fatigued instincts" (B 212), nobody "had the courage to conceive virtue as a consequence of immorality (of a will to power)." The old virtues stood "in the service of the species (or of the race or *polis*)." But in this degenerate age, the virtues through which Greek culture became possible were "considered immorality" (WP 428). And "[b]eginning with Socrates, the individual all at once began to take himself too seriously" (SSW 132; M 6:103). A certain "anxiety concerning oneself [became] the soul of philosophy" (SSW 135: M 6:107), culminating in morbid concerns over "the 'salvation of the soul' or the question 'what is happiness?' "

(SSW 144; M 6:117). This self-centered tendency negated any future philosophical vision of the Greeks as intimately unified with all life and therewith any possibility of a *telos* greater than the mere preservation of the individual.

The once passionate joy of victory deteriorated into an obsession with "being happy." Nietzsche says that "as long as life is *ascending*, happiness and instinct are one" (T 3:11). In healthy cultures and individuals, only success in overpowering the greatest resistance "*brings happiness*" (WP 1022), that "triumphant consciousness of power and victory" (WP 1023). This consciousness reflects the affects characteristic of individuals who overcome the obstacles through which life as will to power realizes its highest types. In the age of Socrates, the main obstacle to both culture and individuals was the "*monstrum in animo*" (T 3:9). The chaos within and without was the enemy, and the only expression of strength suitable to such an age was the negation of the exhausting demands of multiple drive-perspectives. Happiness was no longer a consequence of the victorious unity of these drive-perspectives over a resistance; rather, it resided in extirpating the most powerful instincts of life. What better way to negate them than through a flight into a "Real" world, where there is no resistance, where one "knows" that anarchy, whether within or without, is proof of "immorality"? True "happiness" is attained when the fixed, eternal "Realities" of conscious thought subdue the "illusions" of the body.

The voice of reason "corrects" the "error" of conflict essential to life and affirms stability as good. In seeing the good, the rational person is necessarily virtuous because "it is supremely rational and because rationality" as the source for all the fictions of preservation "makes it impossible to err in the choice of means: it is as *reason* that virtue is the way to happiness" (WP 434). Reason always corrects the world with a fiction of "Being," the appreciation of which makes us good and allows us the "happiness" of an abstract world devoid of struggle and the battle for power.

This is how Nietzsche understands the "Socratic equation reason = virtue = happiness . . . that bizarrest of equations . . . which has in particular all the instincts of the older Hellenes against it" (T 3:4). The "older Hellenes," guided by the most powerful drives, lived in unity with life as power; their virtue, their justice, their right and wrong, expressed the values of a natural order of rank. They were "a sovereignly developed type . . . in which everything has become instinct," and possessed a "real morality, i.e., instinctive certainty in actions" (WP 423). They did "not reflect on their rights, on the principles on which they act[ed]" (WP 423); they "commanded: that sufficed" (WP

431). But with Socrates "the *instincts of decadence* [are] translated into the formulas of morality" (WP 423).

Paralysis

The exhausted, decadent organism is ever on the verge of a physiological implosion. In a state of tension and "constant irritability in the face of all natural stirrings and inclinations . . . [he feels] as if his self-control were endangered." He cannot, Nietzsche says, "entrust himself to any instinct or free wingbeat; he stands in a fixed position . . . armed against himself" (GS 305). Anything that manifests spontaneous, healthy life only threatens this type, which resents those who, feeling no need to justify themselves, reveal a "proof of strength" in their love of "bravado . . . fearlessness, indifference to life or death" (WP 800).[14] In short, this type despises the strength of the healthy type, who has an instinctive and therefore unconscious conviction of self-worth.

Confronted with this healthy, noble individual, the "rational" person reveals a symptom of decadence in a *reactionary* attempt to negate the value of the former. In this way the decadent lashes out at life itself. In this sense, Nietzsche sees dialectics as "a form of *revenge* in the case of Socrates" (T 3:7). Socrates laughed at the "noble Athenians who, like all noble men, were men of instinct and never could give sufficient information about the reasons for their actions" (B 191). Here we find the irony that concealed "the malicious Socrates" (G 3:7). He was an actor playing the humble, ignorant man seeking knowledge of justice, goodness, and beauty, but he "made mock when morality did not know how to justify itself logically" (WP 430). In this vein, Nietzsche says Socrates "leaves it to his opponent to demonstrate he is not an idiot: he enrages, he at the same time makes helpless. The dialectician *devitalizes* his opponent's intellect" (T 3:7).

The "intellect" Nietzsche refers to is that unconscious "primeval mechanism" of the body (GS 111). With Socrates, one must prove one's worth according to conscious thought, that is, dialectically. Noble individuals only fail in this enterprise, and when they do, they become confused and lose the instinctive certitude of themselves and their value. This is the devitalizing, paralyzing effect of Socratic revenge, on the basis of which Nietzsche considers Socrates "as an instrument of Greek disintegration, as a typical decadent" (E BT:1). After instilling the doubt of one's value because one fails to justify oneself dialectically, Socrates poses as one's benefactor. The noble cannot win against this

---

14. I look in greater detail at the physiology of *ressentiment* in the next chapter.

"superior dialectician" (B 191), who "makes others furious and helpless, while . . . [remaining] the embodiment of cool, triumphant reasonableness" (WP 431). Dialectics is "a merciless weapon in one's hands" (WP 431), and with it Socrates renders the noble individual impotent. Here the instinct of preservation reveals *its* will to power.

Decadence is that condition wherein the lowest instincts in the individual or cultural organism are exploited by that of preservation to devitalize the most powerful drives. Socrates is the physiological representative of his culture's lowest drives; hence, Nietzsche's references to Socrates as "the *roturier*" (WP 431), "*canaille au fond*" (WP 432), and "rabble" (T 3:3) can be seen in this physiological context. He is a sublime manifestation of the instinct of preservation and the advocate of all the weakest instincts in the cultural organism: "the weak and underprivileged . . . of the *abortus* in what is lofty and what is petty" and those "who need a noble interpretation of their condition (WP 423).

For Nietzsche, dialectics is the most exquisite product of this state of affairs. Socrates, as the dialectician par excellence, can always "prove" that following reason is the path to virtue and happiness. The old nobility, on the other hand, could "prove" neither its superiority nor, therefore, its right to lead and determine the values of its culture. Through the example of Socrates the dialectician becomes "popular." It is, after all, fascinating to see the noble actually lose in combat to Socrates, "the wisest chatterer of all time" (GS 340). The dialectician becomes the new hero; he is more "conscious" of himself, the one who "knows himself" *and can prove it*. Now everyone—even the aristocrat—can be happy. With Socrates, the rabble, long enslaved, makes its play for power. Dialectics is a means to undermining the authority of the old nobility, its customs and traditions. It is the perfect vehicle for the values of the herd because it reveals its essential instinct, self-preservation. The values of the herd, unlike those of their old masters, can be "demonstrated."

An Infected Physician

Unable to "prove" its right to rule through reason, the old nobility continued to lose its authority, and "the mob achieved victory with dialectics," that "form of mob revenge" through which "the ferocity of the oppressed finds an outlet in the cold knife-thrust of the syllogism" (WP 431). For Nietzsche, thanks to Socrates "the rabble gets on top" (T 3:5); positing "proofs as the presupposition for personal excellence in virtue signified nothing less than the disintegration of Greek instincts" (WP 430).

The foregoing may give the impression that the demise of the old aristocracy was accelerated only when the market rabble took up dialectics and simply outtalked those in power. This, of course, is absurd. For Nietzsche, it is more accurate to say the aristocracy talked itself out of its right to rule. After all, this was an age of decay. It may be that with Socrates "Greek taste undergoes a change in favour of dialectics" (T 3:5), but this "taste" was determined by "the aristocratic circles of Athens" (T 3:8), not the dregs of society. The general state of exhaustion characteristic of the culture pointed to that of the aristocrats themselves. The "conservatives of ancient Athens," whose ancestors originally coined Greek values, "let themselves go—'toward happiness,' as they said; toward pleasure, as they acted—and . . . all the while still mouthed the ancient pompous words to which their lives no longer gave them any right" (B 212).

Socrates was a decadent, but his "case was . . . only the extreme case, only the most obvious instance of what had at that time begun to be the universal exigency: that no one was any longer master of himself" (T 3:9). In degenerate ages "the refuse, the waste, gain importance," and the "sick and weak have fascination on their side" (WP 864). Socrates was an "abnormality" (WP 433) from "the lowest orders. . . . One knows, one sees for oneself, how ugly he was" (T 3:3). His ugliness intimated "the way in which Socrates could repel"; consequently, "it is . . . necessary to explain the fact *that* he exercised fascination" (T 3:8).

In degenerate types there is always a morbid fascination with the repulsive and deformed. Socrates "exercised fascination as this extreme case—his fear-inspiring ugliness expressed it for every eye to see." But unlike the "aristocratic Athenians," he had "become master of *himself.*" For this very reason, "he fascinated even more, it goes without saying as the answer, as the solution, as the apparent *cure* for this case." With this *"cure"* Socrates enchanted the aristocrats of Athens. He was the embodiment of "self-discipline" at a time when "everywhere people were but five steps from excess" (T 3:9). He seemed unmarked by the fevers of his age and, proclaiming "Reason" as the path to virtue, "Socrates exercised fascination: he seemed to be a physician, a saviour" (T 3:11).

It is in this role as physician that Nietzsche identifies Socrates as a philosopher. Just as the pre-Socratics "tended toward the healing and purification" of the Greek culture, so did Socrates. But in Socrates the philosophical type was infected with the disease of his epoch. He recognized the degeneration of his age and "grasped that *his* case, the idiosyncrasy of his case, was no longer exceptional. The same kind of degeneration was everywhere silently preparing itself." This insight inflamed the pride typical of the philosophical type, and "Socrates understood that all the world had need of him—his expedient, his cure, his personal art of self-preservation" (T 3:9).

The formula for this cure was "reason = virtue = happiness. It was with this absurdity of a doctrine of identity that he fascinated" (WP 432). But given the physiological circumstances of the Greek culture at this time, the "fanaticism with which the whole of Greek thought throws itself at rationality betrays a state of emergency." "Rationality," Nietzsche says, "was at that time divined as *saviour* . . . one was in peril, one had only *one* choice: either to perish or—be *absurdly rational*." In the end, "neither Socrates nor his 'invalids' were free to be rational or not . . . it was *de rigueur*, it was their *last* expedient" (T 3:10).

In Socrates, Nietzsche again sees a pure philosophical type convinced of his "truth," sees the "Socratic sarcastic assurance of the old physician and plebian who cut ruthlessly into his own flesh, as he did into the flesh and heart of the 'noble.' " And throughout his dialectical incisions, Socrates could look into the face of any aristocrat "with a look that said clearly enough: 'Don't dissemble in front of me! Here—we are equal' " (B 212). Now the aristocracy through which the health of Greek culture was forged was the "patient" of Socrates. This was a dangerous revaluation of the values of Greek antiquity. The old nobility would have *instinctively* despised Socrates as "rabble." But their degenerate offspring *"prefer[red]* what is harmful" (A 6) and saw him as a physician. Here was the "equality" and camaraderie of sickness.

Socrates had to deny the most powerful instincts of life as the means to physiological equilibrium. But in combating the drives with his "reason = virtue = happiness," he fought the sources of vitality fundamental to that form of will to power that is human. When he prescribed this cure to his culture, he was actually promoting a "physiological self-contradiction" (T 10:41). But here the philosophical type revealed the sinister role of philosophy in decadent cultures. His "cure" was actually a deception through which his culture would desire death. The philosopher as a physician of culture thus stood in accord yet again with the law of life that "requires that the ill-constituted, weak, degenerate, perish" (WP 246). The Greek culture had spiraled into sickness and decay, and Socrates' "cure" was actually a potent drought of poison.

The Death Wish

To the extent that Socrates' "reason = virtue = happiness" was irresistible to his age, his culture meets the criterion of sickness for cultures or individuals. When any organism actually *"prefers* what is harmful to it" (A 6), we find the unmistakable symptom of illness. "[T]he good severe will of the older Greeks" (BT SC:4) craved everything destructive, and they also had a preference for what was "harmful"; but they had other "regulating instincts" that (WP 430), *unified* with preservation, affirmed the growth required by life. In the case of illness, the preference for what is harmful lacks the affects of the more powerful instincts of life. Indeed, the denial of these for the purpose of preservation constitutes "a physiological defect . . . tak[ing] step upon step as practice and procedure, as innovation in principles" (C 7).

Through this defect the weakness of the organism is actually enhanced as it sinks to lower levels of vitality. "Not that it grasps this," Nietzsche says; on the contrary, it dreams "that it is getting back to wholeness, to unity, to strength of life," and "thinks it will be in a state of redemption when the inner anarchy, the unrest between those opposing value drives, is at last put an end to" (WP 351). But in striving for mere preservation, unthinkable to the older Hellenes, the organism stands opposed to the law of life and is thereby bent on its own destruction.

Socrates was essential to preparing an exhausted and decadent culture for death. His "reason = virtue = happiness" is "no more than a form of sickness" (T 3:11). Life requires that the "weak and ill-constituted shall perish" (A 2), and in Socrates, life provides the philosophical type in whom wisdom appears "as a raven . . . inspired by the smell of carrion" (T 3:1).

Philosophy is always to be regarded from the standpoint of its "value for *life*" (WP 493); hence, its value is a "biological question" (WP 41). As "the most spiritual will to power" (B 9), it is the source of new deceptions, new "spiritual" frontiers for culture. The philosopher, Nietzsche says, "simply *cannot* keep from transposing his states . . . into the most spiritual form and distance: this art of transfiguration *is* philosophy" (GS pref.:3). The pre-Socratics were guided by the *ascending* instincts of life. But Socrates, guided by preservation and a ruthless desire for stability, had to combat the instincts through which cultural growth is possible. And in this he represents the "wisdom" of life—which is devoid of pity for what is ill.

Like the pre-Socratics, Socrates exhibits a profound pride in passing judgment "on the whole fate of man . . . on the highest fate that can befall individual men or entire nations" (U 3:3). But he also betrays a symptom of decadence: that is, he knows "as little as possible about physiology" (WP 423). Socrates is naive to think he is restoring or curing his culture through "Reason." He is led by the utility of preservation, the fictions of which are brilliant in the light of conscious thought. But "his cure, his personal art of self-preservation" (T 3:9), is a "physiological self-contradiction" (T 10:41). In recognizing the body to be "infected with every error of logic there is" (T 4:1), he makes a dangerous error *"in physiologicis"* (WP 454).

Threatened by the most powerful instincts of life, Socrates sees "rationality at all costs" as a "counter-tyrant" to fight them. In the midst of his combat, "this shrewdest of all self-deceivers" (T 3:12) decides that the degeneration of his own culture is due to the body and its implacable drives. Through him, "everything genuinely Hellenic is made responsible for the state of decay. . . . The decline of Greece is understood as an objection to the foundations of Hellenic culture. . . . Conclusion: the Greek world perishes. Cause: Homer, myth, the ancient morality, etc." (WP 427).

After Socrates, "the philosophers are the *décadents* of Hellenism, the countermovement against the old, noble taste" (T 11:3). The "quarrelsome and loquacious hordes of the Socratic schools" (HH 1:261) preached the Socratic virtues *"because* the Greeks had lost them. . . . Not that it would have done any good" (T 11:3). The old virtues were now misunderstood as attainable if bled of the vitality inherent to the ascending instincts of life. Socrates was only the first "to spill this magic potion into the dust" (BT 13). Thus Nietzsche, quoting Goethe's *Faust*, laments:

> What demigod is this to whom the chorus of the noblest spirits of mankind must call out:
>
> > *Alas!*
> > *You have shattered*
> > *The beautiful world*
> > *With brazen fist;*
> > *It falls, it is scattered.*
> >   (BT 13)

Perhaps a healthier epoch would have been "lucky enough to find the cup of hemlock with which one could simply dispose of such a character" (BT 15). But at this time "of impending old age, and of physiological weariness" (BT SC:4), all "the poison that envy, calumny, and rancour created did not suffice to destroy that self-sufficient splendour" (BT 15).

This splendor shone in the dazzling light of the dialectics through which Socrates introduced "the disease of moralizing" (WP 443). Those who could justify themselves with "reason" thereby proved their "virtue." In this way "he touched on the agonal instinct of the Hellenes—he introduced a variation into the wrestling-matches among the youths and young men" (T 3:8). The love of combat, which the older Greeks "evaluated and determined as good" (D 38), was now revealed in the decline "of good taste in spiritual matters" (WP 427). That is, the agonal instinct had degenerated into petty bickering over justice, virtue, and the good, thanks to the "measly fact that the agonal instinct in all these born dialecticians compelled them" to posit their "personal ability as the highest quality and to represent all other good things as conditioned by it" (WP 442). With dialectics Socrates "discovered a new kind of *agon* . . . he was the first fencing-master in it for the aristocratic circles of Athens" (T 3:8). Consequently, this "mocking and enamored monster and pied piper of Athens, who made the most overweening youths tremble and sob" (GS 340), was really "the corrupter of youth after all" (B pref.).

But dialectics is only "a *last-ditch weapon* in the hands of those who have no other weapon left" (T 3:6). In the end, the Socratic "cure," reason = virtue = happiness, and the dialectics through which it was administered meant "merely: one must imitate Socrates and counter the dark desires by producing a permanent *daylight*—the daylight of reason" (T 3:10). But since this "cure" is *itself* symptomatic of the illness Socrates tried to combat, is "it necessary," Nietzsche asks, "to go on to point out the error which lay in his faith in 'rationality at any cost'?" Philosophers and moralists delude themselves, Nietzsche says, when they embrace "Rationality" as the means to "making war on *décadence*." They do not "therewith elude *décadence* themselves." Insofar as "Reason" is understood here as the means to fighting the instincts of life, "what they select as an expedient . . . is itself only another expression of *décadence*—they *alter* its expression, they do not abolish the thing itself" (T 3:11).

Socrates revealed the genuine task of the philosopher to be that of a cultural physician. But this great model of the philosopher for succeeding millennia necessarily promoted the sickness he understood himself to be fighting. With his "reason = virtue = happiness . . . he fascinated: the philosophers of antiquity never again freed themselves from this fascination" (WP 432). Socrates was the gateway through which all the instinct-disintegrating symptoms of decadence and sickness found philosophical expression. Hence, "Socrates was a misunderstanding: *the entire morality of improvement . . . has been a misunderstanding. . . .*"[15]

---

15. The latter ellipsis points are Nietzsche's.

He improved nothing, his "cure" was "another form of sickness—and by no means a way back to 'virtue,' to 'health,' to happiness" (T 3:11).

The Order of Rank

The Greek culture gave birth to the philosophical type out of the abundance of a vitality revealed both in the pre-Socratics at the zenith of its philosophical health and in the destructive forces unleashed in its philosophical decay. Nietzsche contends that every level of health in an organism requires an equivalent one of sickness. This built-in level of sickness is the threat essential to life as overcoming. The pre-Socratics represent the vitality through which sickness might have been kept at bay. "I conceive of them," Nietzsche says, "as the *forerunners of a reformation of the Greeks*, but not as the forerunners of Socrates." Socrates does not represent an advance in the growth of the philosophical type. When the reformation Nietzsche identified with the pre-Socratics fizzled out, "all that remained was Socrates" (SSW 134; M 6:106). Through him, the great forces of sickness and destruction, the repression of which was essential to the growth of Greek culture, were sanctioned as "Good" and "True." Thus, Socrates also reveals the "steely necessity which binds a philosopher to a genuine culture" (PTA 1:33–34; M 4:159). He was there to kill off a failed culture, a failed experiment of life as will to power.

The pre-Socratics, Nietzsche says, "tended toward the healing and the purification" of their culture (PTA 2:35; M 4:160). That is, through their "truths" they were to destroy whatever threatens culture, and preserve whatever was useful for the future. Socrates was quite *conscious* of himself as a physician for his culture, but was as naive as his predecessors in his function. What he "selected" according to the "spiritualizing" activity of his instincts "as an expedient, as a deliverance, [was] itself only another expression of *décadence*" (T 3:11).

It should come as no surprise that Socrates' decadence is the basis of Nietzsche's attack on him. But strange as it may sound, it is also the basis of Nietzsche's admiration of him. Here is an admiration, not for sickness per se, but for the Socrates who stood in accord with the law of life by revealing the task of the philosopher in a decadent age. Only the Greek culture, Nietzsche says, "can answer our question as to the task of the philosopher" (PTA 1:33; M 4:159). Socrates was by no means an accident, like his predecessors; he also "possessed that virtuous energy of the ancients, herein excelling all men since" (PTA 1:31; M 4:156). But his is the energy of philosophical *décadence*; he demonstrates that there are times when, confronted with illness, the physician's only "cure" is a lethal injection.

Aware of himself as a physician for his culture, Socrates confirmed the dictum "Know Thyself" through conscious thought, thinking that can only be "translated back into the perspective of the herd" (GS 354). In this he concealed what was most unique to himself, the silent destiny of his philosophical task. And in this Nietzsche admired Socrates not only in what he did and said but also in what he "did not say" (GS 340). Socrates seduced his culture into the din of dialectics as the path to improving it, yet all the while he was unconsciously luring it to its death. He was astonished at the "ignorance" of his contemporaries, their lack of a "proper and sure insight, even with regard to their own professions, and that they practiced them only by instinct" (BT 13). Yet Socrates himself also lacked insight into the task of philosophy, which he practiced "only by instinct." This was not a question of choice; neither he "nor his 'invalids' were free to be rational or not—it was *de rigueur*" (T 3:10). He was the pure philosophical type through which life as will to power is affirmed by providing an irresistible death wish for a culture worthy of destruction. Hence, Nietzsche's rhetorical questions: "O Socrates, Socrates, was that perhaps *your* secret? O enigmatic ironist, was that perhaps your—irony?" (BT SC:1).

When the Greek culture slipped irredeemably into exhaustion and illness, the decadent philosophical type emerged to euthanize it. Nietzsche certainly attacks Socrates as the one in whom wisdom took the form of a scavenger "inspired by the smell of carrion" (T 3:1). But this wisdom Nietzsche refused to deny, and in this he also recognized greatness in Socrates. "All other cultures are put to shame," Nietzsche said, by the "philosophical company represented by the ancient Greek masters Thales, Anaximander, Heraclitus, Parmenides, Anaxagoras, Empedocles, Democritus, and Socrates." Socrates is among the giants of Western philosophy because he is among those who invented *"the archetypes of philosophical thought"* (PTA 1:31; M 4:156–57). Like his predecessors, he wanted to heal and purify his culture, "protect and defend his native land" (PTA 2:35; M 4:160), and bring about a reformation. But as a "a monstrosity *per defectum*" (BT 13), his only "cure" was the destruction of his culture.

This "mischief . . . reached its climax in Plato" (WP 430), who, "more innocent . . . and lacking the craftiness of the plebeian" (B 191), was "seduced by the *roturier* Socrates" (WP 435). Plato embraced "reason = virtue = happiness" and dedicated himself to reading "something refined and noble into the proposition of his teacher" (B 190). Plato's success in this "provided the example of the most complete severance of the instincts from the past." Socrates was the dark power of death, and his "seduction" of Plato is the evidence of his having corrupted youth. Under the spell of Socrates' instinct-disintegrating influence, Plato became "profound, passionate in everything *anti*-Hellenic" (WP 435).

Plato, however, is not simply Nietzsche's whipping boy. Nietzsche refers to Plato as "Europe's greatest misfortune,"[16] and this must be seen in two ways. First, Plato enables Christianity to "make itself possible philosophically." Through him Christianity takes on "Greek refinement in word and form" (WP 195). The transcendent world of the "Good" affirmed by Plato becomes the "other worldly" God of Christianity, and in this he is a "great viaduct of corruption" (WP 202). Second, Plato is "the most beautiful growth of antiquity" (B pref.), having "the greatest strength any philosopher so far has had at his disposal" (B 191). Nietzsche laments that such a profound "spiritual" power (evidenced in Plato's influence on Western philosophy) was squandered on the Socratic program. He also wonders "whether, if he had not come under the spell of Socrates, Plato might not have discovered an even higher type of the philosophical man who is now lost to us for ever" (HH 1:261). In considering the decadence in Plato's philosophy, Nietzsche says that "as a physician one might ask: How could . . . [he] contract such a disease?" Nietzsche answers with the rhetorical questions, "Did the wicked Socrates corrupt him after all? Could Socrates have been a corrupter of youth after all? And did he deserve his hemlock?" (B pref.).

Nietzsche recognized "the pre-Platonic philosophers as . . . one homogeneous company" (PTA 2:34; M 4:159); hence, Socrates remained one of the great "ancient Greek masters" (PTA 1:31; M 4:156). But "with him the line of original and typical '*sophoi*' is exhausted."[17] Socrates was the last shadow of the strength that gave rise to Greek culture. The wisdom in the necessity of death is revealed in him, the final and most impoverished of the great sages of Greece. Socrates was a product of the organic life of his culture, and the strength of his siren song of death "spread over posterity like a shadow that keeps growing in the evening sun" (BT 15). In this Nietzsche saw the wisdom of life as will to power in a culture whose philosophers were great both in life and death. But as a cultural physician himself, Nietzsche attacked Socrates as "a dangerous force that undermines life" (E BT:1).

16. Nietzsche to Franz Overbeck, January 1887, SPL 94 (BKG III[5]:9).
17. This reference is taken from an unpublished lecture probably written in 1876. The translation is from Walter Kaufmann's *Nietzsche: Philosopher, Psychologist, Antichrist*, 397 (M 4:364).

His high estimation of the pre-Socratics is that of a physician who stands on the side of life and health. Socrates is among the original *sophoi* of Greek culture, but "as an instrument of Greek disintegration," he is, compared to his predecessors, lowest in the order of rank. The attempts to grasp whether Nietzsche admired, rejected, or hated Socrates are understandable, though it is vexing to reconcile his attack on one of the most revered figures of Western philosophy with his simultaneous admiration for him. Nietzsche's relation to Socrates is full of twists. I have shown a few here and show others in the chapters to come.

The virtues of the ancient cosmologists were unified with and affirmed the law of life. But what was once a tyrannical drive to rule the universe had, in the age of Socrates, degenerated into justifications of existence according to the moral dictates of reason, that is, conscious thought. The days of the great cosmologists were over, and thanks to Socrates, the most poisonous form of philosophizing—metaphysics—saw the light of day. In metaphysics the drive to preservation dominating Socratic dialectics became the new "spiritual" paradigm, and the cosmologist gave way to the metaphysician, "the scarecrow of the ancient philosopher: a plant removed from all soil" (WP 430).

The Physician Heals Himself

As Nietzsche emphasizes, self-preservation is not the goal of life. But if this instinct dominates, it devitalizes the most powerful drives; this is the "physiological self-contradiction" (T 10:41) promoted by Socrates. As the cultural organism continually fights to keep the anarchy of its drives in check, it is simultaneously promoting its own destruction. A weariness sets in whose cumulative affect is a longing for a condition where there is no resistance to it, where it no longer has to cope with the potential anarchy of its drives. In short, it wants the perfect stability of "Being"—it wants to die. And as the decadent philosophical type and an instrument of the law of life, Socrates reveals that the "right of altruism cannot be derived from physiology; nor can the right to help and to an equality of lots" (WP 52). Since the organism has not developed under the *threat* of illness but has succumbed to it, the philosopher here is "the hand that considerately—kills" (B 69).

Nietzsche sees the death wish at work in Socrates, who, "before his subtle conscience," saw that there was no rational-moral justification for existence. "This was the real *falseness* of that great ironic, so rich in secrets . . . at bottom, he had seen through the irrational element in moral judgments" (B 191). Socrates saw that "reason" was an expedient means to protect himself from the "anarchy of his instincts" (T 3:4). However, he "privately and secretly . . . laughed at himself" (B 191). He saw that his rationality and its inherent "good" justified neither this world nor his own existence. And so he "who had lived cheerfully and like a soldier in the sight of everyone" was only putting on an act "while concealing all his life long his ultimate judgement, his inmost feeling. Socrates, Socrates *suffered life*!" (GS 340).

In the end, even "Socrates had had enough of it" (T 3:1). Nietzsche says he wanted death, not exile, and when he got his wish, he lacked the "natural awe of death." Predictably, in this decadent age, the *"dying Socrates* became the new ideal . . . of noble Greek youths," and "above all . . . Plato, prostrated himself before this image with all the ardent devotion of his enthusiastic soul" (BT 13).

Nietzsche finds Socrates' death wish revealed in his last words; he "said as he died: 'To live—that means to be a long time sick: I owe a cock to the saviour Asclepius' " (T 3:1). In *The Gay Science* Nietzsche offers what, coming from him, is a more detailed explanation for Socrates' reference to the god of healing. Nietzsche speculates whether "it was death or the poison or piety or malice—something loosened his tongue at that moment and he said: 'O Crito, I owe Asclepius a rooster.' " This "terrible 'last word' means for those who have ears: 'O Crito, *life is a disease.*' " With his reference to Asclepius, Socrates betrayed himself and, says Nietzsche, "revenged himself—with this veiled, gruesome, pious, and, blasphemous saying" (GS 340). Socrates opted for suicide and in so doing betrayed his "ultimate judgement" on life: death is preferable to life; *it* is the cure.

"Socrates *wanted* to die—it was not Athens, it was *he* who handed himself the poison cup" (T 3:12). Nietzsche says that when Socrates took a good look at his condition, " 'Socrates is no physician,' he said softly to himself: 'death alone is a physician here. . . . Socrates himself has only been a long time sick . . .' " (T 3:12).[18] In committing suicide, Socrates betrayed that his "reason = virtue − happiness" not only was antagonistic to "the preconditions of life" (WP 461) in himself but was a negation of life *in toto*. This is why Nietzsche says his philosophizing was only an apparent cure (T 3:9) for the sick and decadent. Whatever they chose as a cure was symptomatic of their condition. Inevitably they chose their own destruction and, cleaving to Socrates as their physician, were mesmerized by "that famous old serpent" (B 202) who said,

---

18. The ellipses points are Nietzsche's.

"[T]hose who tackle philosophy aright are simply and solely practicing dying, practicing death, all the time, but nobody sees it."[19]

Nietzsche holds that in Socrates' suicide he reveals his genuine wisdom in disposing of himself. This, Nietzsche says, is "the *wisdom* of his courage for death" (T 3:12). Zarathustra says, "The man consummating his life dies his death triumphantly, surrounded by men filled with hope and making solemn vows." This would be an apt description of the death of Socrates, but Zarathustra goes on to request that one's death "not be a blasphemy against man and the earth" (Z 1:21). When Socrates blasphemed in saying *"life is a disease"* (GS 340), he betrayed "a poison-worm eat[ing] at his heart" (Z 1:21).

The "poison-worm" he carried was the "physiological self-contradiction" lying at the core of the new "spiritual" paradigm; and this error *"in physiologicis"* infected all philosophy after him. Here, as I said earlier, is the beginning of metaphysics, a brand of philosophy that from its inception "is a secret raging against the preconditions of life, against the value feelings of life, against partisanship in favor of life" (WP 461). Thus, the instinct-disintegrating influence of Socrates has continued "down to the present moment and even into all future time" (BT 15).

Concluding Remarks

My look at Socrates shows how Nietzsche applies the dynamics of will to power in terms of the physiology of humans and culture. Many might dismiss Nietzsche's "Socrates" for having no resemblance to the man whose heroic status still shines today. Nor does Nietzsche seem even remotely inclined to conform to a correct, or "historically accurate," picture of Socrates. With regard to the historical Socrates, I think Nietzsche's attack on him owes a lot to Plato. Without Plato, this attack would have little force, since it is directed at the man Plato gave us. On the other hand, Nietzsche sees physiology at work not only in Plato's Socrates but in the whole enterprise of history as a discipline.

Indeed, history, as an interpretation, is determined by the physiology of the cultures and individuals who create it. History, like philosophy or any other interpretative enterprise, is a text of *symptoms* the health or sickness of which Nietzsche determines from his clinical standpoint. He is not, therefore, indifferent to history; on the contrary, it provides a reservoir of data through which he comes to terms with the illness of modernity he calls nihilism. For Nietzsche, the demand for an objec-

---

19. *Phaedo* 63A. This reference is taken from *Great Dialogues of Plato*, trans. W.H.D. Rouse (New York: Mentor, 1956), 466–67.

tively "True History" of Socrates is itself symptomatic of "the more recent and decadent Hellenism" (SSW 131; M 6: 102–3) promoted by Socrates' pathos for a "True World," a "True Reality." Such a demand reflects a desire for a "history" that bleeds and mummifies cultures and individuals, that places "events" into the mausoleum of its "discipline," where, petrified into artifacts, they are *preserved* from the inscrutable face of becoming. Nietzsche does not conform to objectively "True History," because he wants to avoid its sickness—a sickness he believed Socrates promoted.

The Socrates found in Nietzsche's texts is one whose heroic status is diminished but by no means shattered. The Socrates of the dialogues bravely defended himself against the very charges Nietzsche dredges up yet again. Plato's Socrates is a man of courage, willing to die for his convictions. Nietzsche portrays a man whose death is not particularly courageous, since he wanted to die anyway. Indeed, Nietzsche implies that Socrates would have been disappointed with anything less than a death sentence. However, Nietzsche does not see Socrates as a coward. The question of cowardice did not interest him. In his eyes Socrates is a philosophical hero because he had the most tragic of philosophical fates. He was dragged along by the forces of life as will to power. As a pure philosophical type, he stood in accord with his predecessors, who also came to heal their culture. But necessary to the organic life of his culture, Socrates the "physician says 'incurable' " (A 47).

Nietzsche says he admired "the courage and wisdom of Socrates in everything he did, said—and did not say" (GS 340). This is the courage and wisdom of a philosopher whose task provided one of *"the archetypes of philosophical thought"* (PTA 1:31; M 4:156). But it is a courage and wisdom that, determined by the law of life, is as effortless as any force of nature. This is the source of Nietzsche's admiration for the Socrates who, while engaged in dialectics, fulfilled the role of the philosopher in a decadent age. This was a role determined by the activity of his instincts, an activity equally admirable, since, as unconscious, it remained unspoken.

Nietzsche recognized the symptoms of decadence and its attendant masks of sickness in Socrates. But he also recognized that his own situation was painfully similar to that of Socrates. After all, did not Nietzsche recognize his own epoch as sick? And did not this same Nietzsche consider himself infected with the same disease, the same nihilism symptomatic of modernity? Is it any surprise that Nietzsche wanted "to acknowledge the fact: *Socrates* is so close to me that I am almost continually fighting with him?" (SSW 127; M 6:118). The *agon* between these two philosophers certainly has a hint of what one commentator has called Nietzsche's envy "of the accomplishments of Socrates."[20] Socrates has had the most profound impact of any Western philosopher, and there is no doubt that Nietzsche wanted at least to equal this accomplishment. But more than jealousy, there is also Nietzsche's combat with the most influential cultural physician to date. Socrates was correct in his diagnosis of his culture as decadent, but the "cure," so potent, so deadly, infected all philosophy after him in the guise of metaphysics. Yes, Nietzsche was very close to Socrates; he identified with him as the most commanding "physician" hitherto. But as a cultural physician himself, Nietzsche's task was a revaluation of the values inherent to the Socratic "cure." In short, Nietzsche admired the power of his dark philosophical adversary but had to fight him tooth and nail. And in the midst of this battle, Nietzsche, though unambiguous concerning the identity of this great enemy, was, I think, haunted by him. He was afraid that he might *unconsciously* commit the same mistake as Socrates: that is, promote the illness of the age that infected himself. No wonder Nietzsche says he "required a special self-discipline: to take sides against everything sick in me" (C pref.). In this he had to walk a very thin line; he had to take sides against the Socratic task he himself attempted as a physician of culture.

---

20. Tracy B. Strong, *Friedrich Nietzsche and the Politics of Transfiguration*, 113.

4 Jesus Christ and the Origins of Christianity

> I tell you solemnly, unless you change and become like little children you will never enter the kingdom of heaven.
> —Matt. 18:3–4.

Within Nietzsche's furious attack on Christianity there is a portrait of Jesus Christ that has remained fairly obscure. At times, Christ is seen to possess the characteristics of nobility (Z 1:21) and is called, "with some freedom of expression . . . a 'free spirit' " (A 32). At other times, to "speak with the precision of the physiologist a quite different word would rather be in place here: the word idiot" (A 29). Referring to Jesus of Nazareth as an idiot certainly has a polemical value. But to the extent that Nietzsche wanted to speak here with physiological precision, "the word idiot" must be taken as seriously as "free spirit." There are obviously views of Christ radically opposed to Nietzsche's. My concern in this chapter is not to "defend" Nietzsche but to demonstrate that his portrait of Christ can be understood in terms of a "precision" founded upon his clinical standpoint.

Toward this end, I do not give a lot of attention to his critique of Christianity. This does not mean it is unimportant for the purposes of this investigation—quite the contrary. But I want to remain within the nexus of the physiology that constitutes Christianity as an *illness*. In doing this, I get to the dynamics underlying Nietzsche's well-known critique of Christianity and avoid repeating the well-known *symptoms* of this sickness that he constantly points to throughout his critique. My approach to Nietzsche's perception of Christianity is similar to that of the last chapter; just as Nietzsche's views on Socrates presuppose those on the physiology of Greek culture, so his views on Christ presuppose those on the physiology of Hebrew culture. An examination of ancient Hebrew culture reveals: (a) why "Jesus Christ was possible only in a Jewish landscape" (GS 137) and (b) why "Christianity can be understood only by referring to the soil out of which it grew" (A 24). At the same time, this examination yields the concomitant elucidation of the distinction Nietzsche makes between Jesus of Nazareth and the religion of Christianity.

The Ancient Jewish Culture

Preliminary Considerations: Ressentiment

Understanding Nietzsche's views on Christianity is impossible without a good grasp of his perception of the ancient Jewish culture. An examination of Christianity devoid of its organic origins in the soil of this culture would fail to disclose (a) the physiological dynamics through which a profound sickness saw the light of day and (b) the strength of the Jewish culture in having excluded this illness from itself. The "significance of the Jewish people," Nietzsche tells us, is that "they mark the beginning of the slave rebellion in morals" (B 195). This "significance" hinges on the physiological dynamics that allow Nietzsche to distinguish between master and slave moralities.

The genesis of master morality was concurrent with that of the old Greek nobility. Among the ancient Hellenes the healthiest, strongest, most dangerous individuals represent the dominating instincts of their culture—the instincts of ascending life. Those dominated by lesser drives constitute the lower echelons of the society. As always, the order of rank among the drives of individuals constitutes them as healthy, sick, exhausted, or decadent. And for Nietzsche, each of us "transports the order of which he is the physiological representative into his relations with other human beings and with things" (T 7:2).

The healthy individual is the blueprint for that of any healthy culture. The aristocracy, representing a culture's most powerful instincts, extorts the strength of those who represent lesser, weaker instincts. Thus, slavery and "many degrees of bondage" are "the precondition of every higher culture" (WP 464). The values of the nobility, that is, the perspective of a healthy culture's dominating instincts, subdue those of the lesser classes—or, to say the same thing, subdues the perspectives of the culture's weaker instincts. The process of enslaving and exploiting weaker individuals is by no means gentle. But just as the lesser, weaker drives of a healthy individual are brought under control, so are the lower classes of a healthy culture. Those *"born* to command" (GS 40)—that "species of severe, warlike, prudently taciturn men, close-mouthed and closely linked" (B 262)—harness the strength of the weak. And the fictions, that is, values, through which this aristocracy glorifies itself, eventually serve as the dominating "spirituality" of a healthy culture. This provides that "unity of style" Nietzsche saw in architecture, painting, poetry, sculpture, religion, etiquette, domestic rituals, political leadership, mode of combat, and so forth. Of course, it is the healthy epoch of Greek culture that provides him the standard of excellence in this arena.

Master morality, as the expression of the ascending instincts of life, "is self-glorification." Here "the exalted, proud states of the soul are experienced as conferring distinction and determining the order of rank." Hence, the "noble human being separates from himself those in whom the opposite of such exalted, proud states finds expression: he despises them." The noble is *instinctively* contemptuous of people who are bent "on narrow utility . . . those who humble themselves . . . the begging flatterers, above all the liars." In this vein, Nietzsche says "it is part of the fundamental faith of all aristocrats that the common people lie. 'We truthful ones'—thus the nobility of ancient Greece referred to itself." Generally, in master morality "the opposition of 'good' and 'bad' means approximately the same as 'noble' and 'contemptible' " (B 260). It is "the sign language of what has turned out well, of *ascending* life, of the will to power as the principle of life" (C epilogue).

Slave morality, on the other hand, is the sign language of the weakest instincts of life and, hence, the lowest echelons of any culture. Because they are enslaved, the weakest instincts of an individual or culture "cannot assert [their] degree of independence—here there is no mercy, no forbearance" (WP 630). They want "freedom"; hence, "solidarity is felt as tyranny: they want no authority, no solidarity, no lining up with the rank and file" (WP 442). These qualities are typical of the rancorous individual, possessed of a combination of "pessimistic gloom . . . fatalism, disappointment, and fear of new disappointments," along with an "ostentatious wrath, a bad mood, the anarchism of indignation, and whatever other symptoms and masquerades of the feeling of weakness there may be" (GS 347).

The nobility, dominated by the most powerful instincts of life, have their accumulated strength harnessed toward "precision and clarity of the direction." The weak betray a "disgregation of impulses and the lack of any systematic order among them," resulting in "oscillation and the lack of gravity" (WP 46). Pulled hither and yon by their instincts, the weak are at the beck and call of an "abundance of disparate impressions" that constantly "erase each other: one instinctively resists taking in anything, taking anything deeply." These people "unlearn spontaneous action, they merely react to stimuli from outside" (WP 71).

For Nietzsche, these individuals are not weak because they are slaves; rather, they are slaves because they are weak. And slave morality determines as good whatever enables the weak to tolerate their condition. Predictably, Nietzsche points out that in slave morality "those qualities are brought out and flooded with light which serve to ease existence for those who suffer." "Slave morality," he says, "is essentially a morality of utility." Honored here are "pity, the complaisant and obliging hand, the warm heart, patience, industry, humility, and friendliness" because "these are the most useful qualities and almost the only means for enduring existence" (B 260).

The word "utility" again invokes the domain of the instinct of preservation. As the first instinct of the "spirit" (T 9:2), it enables the weak to create the fictions essential to sustaining their condition. And strange as it may seem, the famous Nietzschean idea of *ressentiment* has to be understood as a fiction fundamental to the survival of those who want "rest, relaxation, peace, calm—the happiness of nihilistic religions and philosophies" (WP 703).

Ressentiment is not only integral to slave morality but indeed serves as its basis; while "every noble morality develops from a triumphant affirmation of itself, slave morality from the outset says No to what is 'outside,' what is 'different,' what is 'not itself.' " This negation of "what is 'not itself' " is a truly "creative deed" and constitutes "the essence of *ressentiment*" (G 1:10). *Ressentiment* is "[b]orn of weakness" (E 1:6) and, as an effective means for the survival of the weak, does not allow the weak to look too closely at their own weakness or their lack of discipline and direction. Here preservation channels the *"need* to direct one's view outward instead of back to oneself." And this "inversion of the value-positing eye" (G 1:10) is displayed when the weak seek "someone whom . . . [they] can make responsible" for their condition.

The "instinct of revenge and *ressentiment* appears here in both cases as a means of enduring, as the instinct of self-preservation" (WP 373).

The Pleasure of Weakness

"Spirit" provides a shield and spear for the human animal. In the case of the strong, it protects them from the hideous aspects of existence and from too lucid a perception of the dangers surrounding them. It also gives them a spear, the fictions through which they can grow in strength, whether as an individual or a caste. In the case of the weak, "spirit" shields them from too lucid a perception of their cowardice and worthlessness compared to the strong. The spear here is in the revenge they take by denigrating the strong as "unfriendly," "self-centered," "unsympathetic." *Ressentiment*, then, is what in the present day goes by the name of a victim mentality.

What would happen if the weak were not protected from too lucid a perception of themselves? It *"would be unbearable"* (WP 765), Nietzsche says, and lead to a self-hatred that "takes the form of self-destruction" (WP 55). But the necessary fiction that "someone or other must be to blame" (G 3:15) emerges, and the "underprivileged . . . revolt on account of themselves and need victims so as not to quench their thirst for destruction by destroying themselves" (WP 765). Here is "the hatred of the ill-constituted . . . which destroys, *has* to destroy, because what exists, indeed existence itself, all being itself, enrages and provokes it" (WP 846). Thus, their own desire for self-destruction is channeled outward and into "relations with other human beings and with things" (T 7:2).

Ressentiment lies like a constantly festering wound within slave morality and reveals itself as "the profoundest hatred there is" (T 10:20). It is a hatred that seeks scapegoats and revenge for the fact "that I am wretched!" (WP 765). In "order to exist," Nietzsche says, "slave morality always first needs a hostile external world" (G 1:10). And the weak invariably "make the ruling classes responsible" (WP 765) for their misery. The "slave's eye," Nietzsche says, "is not favorable to the virtues of the powerful." On the contrary, and quite predictably, "he is skeptical and suspicious, *subtly* suspicious, of all the 'good' that is honored there—he would like to persuade himself that even their happiness is not genuine" (B 260).

Being in no position to vanquish the masters, the slaves, consumed by *ressentiment*, "are denied the true reaction, that of deeds, and compensate themselves with an imaginary revenge" (G 1:10). In "the man of *ressentiment"* the desire for self-destruction is kept in check through the self-preservative fiction not only that the powerful are to blame for his condition but that he is "better" than the powerful. By means of this fantasy, he indulges in an imaginary negation of the "cause" of his misery. Through the utility of this illusion, he realizes a vicarious revenge on all that "enrages and provokes" him: that being life itself. Here once again the "creative deed" of the "spirit" is the instinct of preservation providing a deception "as a condition of life" (B 4). It is a fantasy essential to the life of one who "is neither upright nor naive nor honest and straightforward with himself." This is an individual whose "soul *squints"* and whose "spirit loves hiding places . . . everything covert entices him as *his* world, *his* security, *his* refreshment." And this furtive little weasel "understands how to keep silent, how not to forget, how to wait, how to be provisionally self-deprecating and humble" (G 1:10).

This individual suffers from the very fact of existence and for this reason will *"lie himself out* of actuality." With "its roots in *hatred* of the natural," *ressentiment* is a taking of revenge on all that affirms life. It is, however, a revenge that, nurtured by hatred, remains perhaps the finest pleasure for the weak because, as imaginary, it is a fiction essential to the unmitigated shame of cowardice. To "suffer from actuality means," Nietzsche says, "to be an abortive actuality." And within such miscarriages, *ressentiment* as a function of "spirit" betrays the symptoms of decadence and sickness. Indeed, in the case of Socrates the physiological necessity to fight the most powerful drives "provides the *formula* for *décadence"* (A 15). And there can be no doubt that these drives are the would-be victims of *ressentiment*.

The Warrior God: Jewish Master Morality

We can readily imagine slave morality to have existed "against the aristocratic values of the *ancient* world" (WP 134) and flourishing among the physiologically "underprivileged" (WP 55). But why would Nietzsche attribute this "morality of utility" (B 260) to the entire Jewish race? He did not think the Jews were always "a people 'born for slavery,' as Tacitus and the whole ancient world say" (B 195); there was a time when master morality did flourish among the ancient Hebrews. This means that the most powerful drives in the cultural organism were manifest in a strong warrior aristocracy. Hence, originally, "above all in the period of the Kingdom, Israel too stood in a *correct*, that is to say natural relationship to all things" (A 25).

The best evidence of master morality in the ancient Jewish culture lies in its particular "spiritualization" of the world. Its instinct of preservation provided the fiction of "stability," of "being," of that which abides. This fiction was that of the one God of Israel, which, when exploited by the most powerful drives in the culture, that is, the ruling class, was adorned with the values of a warrior elite. Yaweh embodied the identity of this culture—determined by its most powerful instincts for war, conquest, and "justice." This deity was "the expression of their consciousness of power, of their delight in themselves, their hopes of themselves: in him they anticipated victory and salvation." Within them flourished the conviction of those born to rule: since this God was *their* God, it was unthinkable that Yaweh could be anything but a "God of justice." This, Nietzsche says, is "the logic of every nation that is in power and has a good conscience about it" (A 25).

This "good conscience" is peculiar to "the older parts of the Old Testament" (WP 145), wherein there are "human beings, things, and speeches in so grand a style that Greek and Indian literature have nothing to compare with it" (B 52). The Old Testament presents a God "both useful and harmful, both friend and foe—he is admired in good and bad alike." For Nietzsche, Yaweh is a marvelous expression of a genuine "people, the strength of a people, everything aggressive and thirsting for power in the soul of a people" (A 16). This, he says, is what "an *affirmative* Semitic religion, the product of a *ruling* class, looks like" (WP 145). Such a religion reveals a whole culture holding in awe "the conditions through which it has prospered" and projecting "its feeling of power on to a being whom one can thank." This warrior God demands nothing less than adoration, and those who fail in this are subjected to a terrifying justice. His every gesture of gratitude and destruction is emblazoned with infinite power; and since the ancient Hebrews attributed the very fact of existence to Yaweh, then to them a God "who knew nothing of anger" and "acts of violence" would have been of no consequence. "One would not understand such a God: why should one have him?" (A 16). Nietzsche is famous for his proclamation of the death of God. But when master morality flourished in the ancient Jewish culture, the Holy was "fundamentally a word for every happy inspiration of courage and self-reliance" (A 25). In short, this God was very much alive.

So, what happened? Why does Nietzsche attribute slave morality to the same culture wherein, like the Greeks, master morality was at one time quite apparent. From his clinical standpoint, he saw a physiological deterioration setting into both these cultural organisms when the order of rank among the drives was radically altered. One might expect the "spiritual" decay of the Hebrew culture would be similar to that of the

Greek—at least to the extent that the symptoms of ascending life could be traced into those of decline via morality. But the physiological circumstances of the ancient Jews were quite different, and in this respect, we really must keep in mind Nietzsche's claim that corruption "is something totally different depending on the organism in which it appears" (B 258).

The Greek culture collapsed into decadence when the stored-up strength of the organism could no longer be contained and it exploded with its finest fruit. These were the "times of corruption," when those who carried the "seeds of the future" fell from the tree of a genuine culture (GS 23). A few of these seeds sprouted in the guise of pre-Socratic thought, and the transformation of the Greek culture seemed at least possible. But nothing came of it, and the reformation, that re-creation of a new order of rank among the drives of the organism, failed. No new "spiritual" deception emerged to provide the stability through which the power of Greek culture could be harnessed. This led to further depletion of its strength, old age set in, and the inevitable revenge of the weakest instincts of life led to decadence.

When Nietzsche looks at the ancient Jewish culture, he notes a remarkable lack of the feeble and decrepit characteristics of decadent Greek culture. The Greeks had become fed up with "the old, used-up 'fatherland,' which had been touted to death" (GS 23). Yet among the Jews the virtues of its warrior caste "long remained the ideal, even after it had been tragically done away with." This culture "retained as its supreme desideratum that vision of a king who is a good soldier and an upright judge." Nietzsche is vague on how the old Jewish nobility was destroyed, calling it a "misfortune" that took the shape of "anarchy within, [and] the Assyrian from without" (A 25). His brevity regarding this "calamity" (WP 173) is perhaps explicable in light of the importance events *after* the demise of the warrior elite had for him.[1] Be this as it may, events after the destruction of the aristocracy among both the Greeks and the Jews provide an occasion for distinguishing between the physiological makeups of both cultures.

A "Spiritual" Weapon and Revaluation

The disintegration of the old order of rank in the Greek culture brought no other dominating drive to the fore, and this resulted in dissipation

---

1. Nietzsche refers to the strange demise of pre-Socratic philosophy as "a secret of the workshop" (HH 1:261) and at least speculates upon this mystery (see the subsection entitled "The Failure of Greek Cosmology," in Chapter 3). On the Jewish warrior elite, he is remarkably quiet.

of the strength of the organism. But with the fall of the Jewish aristocracy, one drive did emerge strong enough to seize power and establish a chain of command to prevent cultural decline: the instinct of preservation.

This drive, honed during "the Exile, the long years of misfortune" (A 26) stored up "their capital in will and spirit accumulated from generation to generation in a long school of suffering." Thanks to "the most grief-laden history of any people" (HH 1:475), the Jewish culture acquired "the toughest national will to life which has ever existed on earth" (A 27). Thus, Nietzsche says that the Jews are "a people firmly attached to life," and attached to it even "*more* than the Greeks" (D 72; emphasis added). The instinct of preservation is the physiological clue to how the Jewish culture avoided the fate of the Greeks. This may seem strange in light of the Greek experience: when the most powerful Greek drives waned in strength, the weakest ones rallied around preservation to form an alliance deadly to the health of the organism as a whole.

Greek culture was already in a state of exhaustion when preservation co-opted the weakest instincts in the organism. And insofar as this alliance was necessary, the instinct of preservation was *itself* debilitated and in no position to usurp power on its own. But the situation was quite different with the Jewish culture. Though its warrior caste had been vanquished, this drive was by no means exhausted, and it stepped into the place of the old nobility quite *independently* of the weakest drives in the culture. Thus, Jewish culture did not sink into decline when the drive to preservation came to power.

Naturally, when preservation took power, it harnessed the power of the remaining drives toward its own ends. Nietzsche sees the Jewish instinct of preservation embodied in "the priestly caste" (G 1:7), which seized power upon the demolition of the old nobility. With the destruction of the latter, the culture was "placed in impossible circumstances." However, the priests representing "the profoundest shrewdness in self-preservation" emerged to exploit the lowest orders of the Jewish culture as a means to cultural survival. Like the Greek culture, an alliance formed between preservation and the weakest instincts. But, for Nietzsche, the essential difference between the Greek and Jewish cultures is how the Jews were *never* dominated by the weakest instincts within their culture (A 24). Insofar as the Jewish instinct of preservation could exploit the weakest instincts and simultaneously keep them at a *distance*, the culture realized precisely what is essential to any genuine culture—an order of rank. Hence, "they [had] the priests—and then immediately the chandala" (WP 184). As simple as its order of rank was, it was enough to avoid decadence even "after they had fallen into slavery" (WP 427).

But such a power lay in the weakest instincts that the Jewish culture not only remained intact but actually "tried to prevail" (WP 184) after the destruction of its warrior class—such a power within "the chandala" that not only enabled the priests to remain dominant but also provided a weapon to use against their enemies. This power, which in the hands of the priests was "only a *means*" (A 24), was the hatred typical of *ressentiment*. As a manifestation of the instinct of preservation, the priest fights, Nietzsche says, "against anarchy and ever-threatening disintegration within the herd, in which the most dangerous of all explosives, *ressentiment*, is constantly accumulating." This arsenal of hatred, forever seeking some object, has to be given a direction, so "that it does not blow up herd and herdsmen." And here Nietzsche states the "essential art" and "value of the priestly existence in the briefest formula . . . the priest *alters the direction of ressentiment*" (G 3:15).

Since slave morality resides in "the very seat of *ressentiment*" (WP 167), it naturally existed among the decadent, that is, the weakest, instincts of the Jewish culture. But in the hands of the priests it came in very handy upon the destruction of the warrior elite. Here was a nation forced into servitude, but "the Jews held firm as a 'people' after they had fallen into slavery" (WP 427). This was possible, Nietzsche says, because the priestly caste manipulated the *ressentiment* typical of "the underprivileged" (WP 55). When its warrior caste was vanquished, the Jewish culture confronted great hostility because it was "faced with the question of being or not being" (A 24). But the fiction of "imaginary revenge" (G 1:10) essential to slave morality was now used in a completely original manner. Through the *ressentiment* of slave morality this culture survived by rejecting "all that represents the *ascending* movement of life." Now "the instinct of *ressentiment* here become genius had to invent *another* world from which . . . life-affirmation would appear evil, reprehensible as such" (A 24).

In harnessing the *ressentiment* inherent to slave morality, the priests channeled it as a weapon against the virtues by which strong cultures, *including their own*, had originally been established. At that time, says Nietzsche, the Jews "were ultimately satisfied with nothing less than a radical revaluation of their enemies' values, that is to say, an act of the *most spiritual revenge*" (G 1:7). The ancient Jewish culture lacked its former ability to meet its enemies on the battlefield. Nevertheless, by maintaining the discipline of an order of rank, it was never assimilated by its enemies. The *ressentiment* of slave morality, governed by the first instinct of "spirit," namely preservation, provided yet again the "shield and spear" (T 10:38) characteristic of strong cultures.

The shield was the very hatred of authority typical of slave morality, and the spear was the imaginary *revenge* "of outranking those who actually possess power." Here we find "the invention of new tables of value" and therefore a new "order of rank that permits judgement even of the more powerful" (WP 774). It was precisely this "invention" that constituted *"the slave revolt in morality."* And this revolt was founded on a conviction physiologically determined by the instinct of preservation embodied in the priestly caste. That conviction consisted of the necessary *fiction* that "the wretched alone are the good; the poor, impotent, lowly alone are the good; the suffering, deprived, sick, ugly alone are . . . blessed by God"—while of course "the powerful and noble, are on the contrary the evil" and "shall be in all eternity the unblessed, accursed, and damned!" (G 1:7).

The Mask of Decadence

In attributing slave morality to the Jewish race, Nietzsche does not thereby consider them physiologically degenerate. This morality served as a means to cultural survival and as a weapon against its enemies. This is why he says the "Jews are the counterparts of *décadents*: they have been compelled to *act* as *décadents*." Theirs was a culture that, "placed in impossible circumstances," learned to simulate decadence out of "the profoundest shrewdness in self-preservation." It therefore took sides with "all *décadence* instincts—*not* as being dominated by them but because it divined in them a power by means of which one can prevail *against* 'the world' " (A 24).

This, for Nietzsche, is one of the most remarkable features of the Jewish culture. Through its very negation of "the world," it managed to remain there. This was possible because essential features of life as will to power were affirmed. First, by maintaining an order of rank among the drives of the cultural organism, it displayed a "tremendously tough will to exist and to power" (WP 180). Through this order, it attained, no matter how "imaginary," the privilege of rank over its enemies (G 1:7). Second, "the continual fight against ever constant *unfavorable* conditions" (B 262) cultivated this culture's great "spiritual" strengths, its "power of invention and simulation" (B 44). This is typical of "all strong races" (WP 352) that affirm "the primordial law of things" (B 265). Will to power "can manifest itself only against resistances" (WP 656): the Jewish culture was faced with annihilation upon the destruction of its most warlike drives, but it still possessed its remaining powerful instinct of preservation, which stepped into the breach to resist total destruction. Consequently, the Jews "preferred, with a perfectly uncanny conviction, being *at any price*" (A 24).

Ironically, they affirmed life as will to power through a negation of it as such. This culture said yes to life by harnessing "the most dangerous of all explosives, *ressentiment*" (G 3:15), and thereby overcame life in a manner unheard of before. Here we find "Jewish 'holiness' and its natural basis," that is, a "moral law made sovereign . . . to the point of becoming the antithesis of nature" (WP 299). And in this Nietzsche recognized the Jews as "the most remarkable nation of world history" (A 24).

But having used the power of *ressentiment*, "the price they had to pay was the radical *falsification* of all nature, all naturalness, all reality." In order to survive and to affirm their superiority over the masters of the earth, they had to see themselves in opposition to everything through which their culture saw the light of day. In this vein, Nietzsche says they had to define "themselves *counter* to all those conditions under which a nation was previously able to live, was *permitted* to live; they made of themselves . . . the *contradiction of their natural values* (A 24). This *"denaturalizing* of natural values" (A 25) took place in the hands of a "priestly aristocracy" (G 1:6) that began coining the values of the culture. The priests, as the manifestation of the instinct of preservation, did what any dominating caste does: strive to retain its power by keeping itself in the first rank. But a basic difference between this caste and the old nobility is that the latter embodied the culture's warrior drives, its willingness to risk destruction for the sake of growth in power. And, as I have shown throughout, preservation cannot do this; its perspective is wholly absorbed with the stability of the organism. Clearly, the priestly caste, which was essential to the stability of Jewish culture, was also "disadvantageous for it when it comes to war" (G 1:7) .

It comes as no surprise, then, that in spite of the Jewish culture's desire for "a king who is a good soldier and an upright judge . . . every hope remained unfulfilled." Thus, with the dissolving of the warrior class, it became clear that the "old God *could* no longer do what he formerly could." Nietzsche suggests that in this situation "[o]ne should have let him go." But no, "the conception of him" was altered, and "at this price one retained him." Yaweh was kept as their God but, "in the hands of priestly agitators," was predictably stripped of all the virtues he possessed as a warrior. He became, says Nietzsche, "the God of 'justice'—*no longer* at one with Israel, an expression of national self-confidence: now only a God bound by conditions." Thanks to the priests, Yaweh was used "henceforth [to] interpret all good fortune as reward, all misfortune as punishment for disobedience of God, for 'sin.' " This was a God "who *demands*—in place of a God who helps . . . who is fundamentally a word for . . . courage and self-reliance." This emasculation of God brought with it a morality that no longer expressed "a nation's deepest instinct of life"; morality had "become abstract, become the antithesis of life—morality as a fundamental . . . 'evil eye' for all things" (A 25).

This process of denaturalization took place in the Jewish culture through that "parasitic kind of human being which prospers only at the expense of every healthy form of life, the *priest*" (A 26). Through the priestly caste God and his law became "thoroughly realistic formalization[s] of certain conditions for the self-preservation of a community" (WP 204). "From now on all things of life [were] so ordered that the priest [was] *everywhere indispensable*; at all the natural events of life . . . there [appeared] the holy parasite to denaturalize them" (A 26).

Thus, from Nietzsche's ironical standpoint, what remained was the "concept of God falsified; the concept of morality falsified," by priests undermining the law of life in both morality and religion. Of course, "the Jewish priesthood did not stop there. The entire *history* of Israel was useless: away with it!" (A 26). When the instinct of preservation emerged among the Greeks, cultural decline was "understood as an objection to the foundations of Hellenic culture" (WP 427). Similarly, when this drive gained power in the Jewish culture via the priests, they made "the *great* epoch in the history of Israel . . . an epoch of decay, the Exile, the long years of misfortune, was transformed into an eternal *punishment* for the great epoch—an epoch in which the priest was as yet nothing." They turned the mighty "figures of Israel's history into . . . pathetic cringing bigots or 'godless men' " (A 26).

With the priestly simplification of "every great event into the idiotic formula 'obedience to *or* disobedience of God' " (A 26), "all the remaining unnaturalness follows forthwith" (A 25). "Disobedience of God, that is to say of the priest, of 'the Law,' now acquires," Nietzsche says, "the name 'sin.' " The only ways "of 'becoming reconciled again with God' are, as is only to be expected, means by which subjection to the priest is only more thoroughly guaranteed: the priest alone 'redeems.' " By means of the fictions of sin and guilt for every natural inclination, the priestly caste consolidated its power: " 'sins' are indispensable in any society organized by priests: they are the actual levers of power." The "priest *lives* on sins," and his "Supreme law" is, Nietzsche says, " 'God forgives him who repents'—in plain language: *who subjects himself to the priest*" (A 26).

Nevertheless, it was precisely through this subjection that the Jewish culture maintained an order of rank and not only survived but, more important, held firm to the possibility of looking down on their enemies and keeping them at a profound distance. The price was embracing values antithetical to life and the constant, dismal conviction of sin. Here punishment and reward were scaled according to various degrees of guilt, interpreted by an oppressive caste of priests that through *ressentiment* compelled this culture to deny all that affirmed life.

The Case of Christ

Though Nietzsche believed Jesus Christ and Christianity derived their physiological origins from the Jewish culture, Nietzsche's vision of Christianity as a perversion of Jesus' "glad tidings" constitutes his consistent distinction between Christianity and Jesus of Nazareth.

I have shown that the Jewish instinct of preservation was embodied in the priestly caste "at the head of the chandala—against the noble orders" (WP 184). Fundamental to the power of this caste, and therewith to the preservation of the Jewish culture, was the "*denaturalizing* of natural values" (A 25) through which this culture realized its "*last* possibility of remaining in being, the residuum of its separate political existence" (A 27). This capacity for "denaturalizing" the values of ascending life eventually developed into an efficient physiological mechanism perfect for "communal self-preservation under foreign rule" (WP 175). Nietzsche referred to this wonderfully adapted drive as "the Jewish instinct" (A 27).

Christ must be seen as both diametrically opposed to precisely this Jewish instinct *and its natural consequence*. He is, therefore, a negation of everything essential to his culture's survival, as well as its physiological result. "I confess," says Nietzsche, "there are few books which present me with so many difficulties as the Gospels do" (A 28). "What *I* am concerned with," he says, "is the psychological type of the redeemer. For it could be contained in the Gospels in spite of the Gospels" (A 29). By "the type of the redeemer" Nietzsche means that which is as "physiological[ly] representative" (T 7:2) of the ancient Jewish culture as the philosophical type is of the Greek. In either case, genuine cultures "constitute the 'body' for the production of isolated valuable individuals, who carry on the great process" (WP 679) of life as will to power. The type of the redeemer is, like that of the philosopher, yet another promise of the future, but as always, this "promise" physiologically represents the level of sickness or health of the culture wherein is arises.

Physio-Psychoanalyses

Nietzsche's investigation into "the psychological type of the redeemer" determines his portrait of Christ, and, of course, this psychoanalysis is done by ascertaining "what order of rank the innermost drives of his nature stand in relation to each other" (B 6). "A Jesus Christ," Nietzsche says, "was possible only in a Jewish landscape—I mean one over which the gloomy and sublime thunder cloud of the wrathful Jehovah was brooding continually" (GS 137). It sounds strange, but for Nietzsche, "Jesus of Nazareth, the incarnate gospel of love," was the product of "the profoundest and sublimest kind of hatred" (G 1:8). The instinct of preservation in the Jewish culture had for generations exploited the hatred inherent to *ressentiment*, and it finally cultivated its most subtle expression in Jesus Christ.

Nietzsche demonstrates this by coming to terms with what he calls "two *physiological realities*" in the case of Christ. The first of these is, he says, an *"[i]nstinctive hatred of reality"* that is the "consequence of an extreme capacity for suffering and irritation" inherited from his culture. But Christ is an organism in which the instinct of preservation is so finely tuned that it "no longer wants to be 'touched' at all because it feels every contact too deeply" (A 30). As always, the activity of the drives is the basis of Nietzsche's psychology. Their subterranean dynamics, "a host of partly contradictory, partly congruous stimuli" (A 14), affect consciousness as the "will" of the organism. The profound suffering that marks the very fact of existence for Christ is psychological. In saying, for example, that Christ reveals a "morbid susceptibility of the *sense of touch*" (A 29), Nietzsche does not mean that Christ felt physical pain when holding an object. Rather, he is translating an abnormally developed instinct of self-preservation's affect on the consciousness of Christ, rendering the world a constant source of pain—something to be avoided.

The second "physiological reality" Nietzsche finds in Christ is an *"[i]nstinctive exclusion of all aversion, all enmity, all feeling for limitation and distancing."* This is, again, the consequence of his culture's "extreme capacity for suffering and irritation," but in his case "all resisting, all need for resistance, [is] an unbearable *displeasure* (that is to say [is] *harmful*, [is] *deprecated* by the instinct of self-preservation)." Christ, unlike his culture, "knows blessedness (pleasure) only in no longer resisting anyone or anything" (A 30). Here Nietzsche finds an instinct of preservation so hypersensitive that all capacity for struggle, resistance, anger, and revenge is nonexistent. "*Denial* is precisely what is totally impossible for him" (A 32). He preserves himself through nonresistance, through "love . . . as the *last* possibility of life" (A 30).

In saying that Christ is the physiological consequence of the Jewish instinct, Nietzsche means that the hatred essential to denaturalizing everything remotely akin to ascending life finally expresses itself in a perfectly emasculated individual. Christ's instinctive hatred of reality is not to be characterized as the *ressentiment* through which his culture managed to survive. It is more accurate to say that, from Nietzsche's point of view, this hatred is transformed in Christ, who lives it as an unmitigated torment and suffering from life itself. Feeling "every contact too deeply," he has a sensitivity to pain terrifying to imagine; and worst, he is virtually defenseless. That is, he lacks any capacity for anger, antagonism, and revenge. Christ inherited the profound drive to preservation typical of the Jewish instinct, but as a very "specific culture plant" (WP 864) he is entirely purged of any of the instincts of command, warfare, and revenge. In short, he utterly lacks the instincts of ascending life. Generations of hatred for these very instincts finally made possible the birth of an individual who is devoid of them. He is the physiological result of the process of denaturalization so essential to the existence of his culture. Indeed, he is denaturalization made flesh.

This is why Nietzsche says that from the tree of Jewish culture "there grew something equally incomparable, a *new love*, the profoundest and sublimest kind of love—and from what other trunk could it have grown?" It is naive to think this love "grew up as the denial of that thirst for revenge, as the opposite of Jewish hatred!" On the contrary, it grew out of this hatred "as its triumphant crown spreading itself farther and farther into the purest brightness and sunlight" (G 1:8).

A Most Interesting Decadent

So Christ is a physiological consequence of the Jewish instinct, and he is also its negation. In spite of the suffering that marks his existence, he completely lacks any capacity to blame or to want revenge because of this suffering. In this, he is in direct opposition to the Jewish instinct. He is the antithesis of his culture because, as Nietzsche says, he reveals "the freedom from, the superiority *over* every feeling of *ressentiment*" (A 40). Christ is a perfectly refined manifestation of the instinct of preservation, but the *ressentiment* characteristic of this drive in the Jewish culture has been bred out of him to such an extent that "the opposite of all contending, of all feeling oneself in struggle has here become instinct." Thanks to the fictions of an imperious drive to preservation, "the incapacity for resistance here becomes morality." And it is in precisely his *"inability* for enmity" (A 29) that Christ is the negation of the Jewish instinct. In his inability for resistance a fundamental feature of life as will to power is denied, and therewith the possibility for the future existence of the Jewish culture.

The Jewish instinct forged not only an order of rank through which its culture realized the "possibility of remaining in being" (A 27) but, more important, a process of denaturalizing natural values that allowed it to strike back with "nothing less than a radical revaluation of [its] enemies' values." This "act of the *most spiritual revenge*" (G 1:7) may have compelled the Jews to *"act* as *décadents"* (A 24), but all this dissembling proves that they never abandoned life itself. As a uniquely specialized expression of the Jewish instinct, the hatred of reality in Christ was magnified and transformed into a hatred of *"every* reality" (A 29). He was the embodiment of the physiological revaluation of all values that the Jewish culture exploited but did not in reality embrace. In strong cultures "it is one of life's processes to exclude the forms of decline and decay" (WP 339). For this reason the Jewish culture had to "exclude" Christ. He inherited the Jewish *"hatred* of the natural" (A 15), but in him this hatred had *advanced* to an "instinctive hatred of *every* reality" (A 29), including life itself. This profound sickness had to be rejected because it threatened "the pile-work upon which the Jewish nation continued to exist at all" (A 27).

If fighting the instincts of ascending life "is the formula for *décadence"* (T 3:11), Christ fits the formula. But his fight is not, as was Socrates', through a "conscious" battle to tyrannize them. On the contrary, he is a living example of their annihilation: there is no "battle" here, or rancor, or *ressentiment*—only the quintessential expression of an instinct of preservation negating all reality insofar as reality is suffered. Christ cannot help expressing, in everything he does and says, a negation of all the instincts of ascending life, because he is living proof of their absence. What he requires as a possibility to endure is a state of peace, one wherein the flux of life as becoming is completely negated. And this is the negation Nietzsche sees in the love of Christ—a love physiologically determined by an inherent incapacity for resistance of any kind. Christ's yes to all things is rooted in a no to the law of all life. This betrays a condition wherein the organism desires precisely what the instinct of preservation in all exhausted organisms requires: perfect stasis, an end to all suffering. As Nietzsche puts it, the love of Christ ultimately *"seeks* death" (B 269).

The death wish is symptomatic of decadence. Unlike Socrates, however, Christ is not a typical decadent. In Socrates the anarchy of the drives pulled him in a multiplicity of directions, and it was precisely this multiplicity that he set out to destroy until he "had enough of it" (T 1:1). But Christ, "as a *decadence* type, *could* in fact have been of a peculiar multiplicity and contradictoriness: such a possibility cannot be entirely excluded. But everything speaks against it" (A 31). What particularly speaks against it is not only the lack of powerful, warlike drives in Christ but also, and even more interesting, his "superiority *over* every feeling of *ressentiment*" (A 40). The chaos and multiplicity of drive-perspectives found in Socrates is *lacking* in Christ. That the latter suffered life indicates his possession of very weak instincts, but precisely the *ressentiment* typical of these has been vetoed by self-preservation.

Like everything in Nietzsche's philosophy, we must look at revenge "from the perspective of the sick toward *healthier* concepts . . . and, conversely, looking again from the fullness and self-assurance of a *rich* life down into the secret work of the instinct of decadence" (E 1:1). From the standpoint of health, revenge is quite typical of powerful, life-affirming warlike drives. On the other hand, it can be rooted in the *ressentiment* characteristic of the weakest instincts. What is remarkable about Christ "as a *décadence* type" is his lack of both forms of revenge. Hence, compared to Socrates, Jesus is the "most interesting *décadent*" (A 31). His instinct of preservation permeates him to the extent that the revenge characteristic of the weakest instincts of life is wholly nullified. His weakest drives rally round that of preservation; their cumulative affect is that of a weariness and suffering in the face of existence. Unlike Socrates, Christ is *not* pulled in a multiplicity of directions; on the contrary, he is a unified organism to the extent that he is wholly directed toward preserving himself from suffering, as "the *last* possibility of life" (A 30).

Ultimately, Socrates went to war against the multiplicity within himself. This battle against the most powerful drives naturally led to a negation of his strength until a weariness with life emerged with its attendant desire for death. Christ, on the other hand, does not war against a multiplicity within himself, since there is no anarchy among his drives. He is so constituted that he is *already* a weariness with life and utterly incapable of going against anything. In this Nietzsche certainly sees Christ as an individual *born* to suffer and die.

The Idiot

As a unique form of decadence, Christ "spiritualized"—that is, created—fictions essential to an individual devoid of the ascending instincts of life. Preservation is the first instinct of "spirit," but in the case of Christ, preservation is the undisputed master drive. Unlike Socrates', Christ's drive to preservation is unfettered by combat with the instincts of ascending life, since he possesses none of these. The weakest instincts of life, on the other hand, are in a state of perpetual exhaustion, and the *ressentiment* typical of them, in the normally weak person, has been vetoed, as it were, by preservation. Here preservation "is on the right track insofar as doing nothing is more expedient than doing something" (WP 45). Christ's incapacity for resistance is the affect of the perspective of preservation, which "understands" that the organism simply cannot afford *ressentiment*. In short, passivity becomes, not a conscious choice, but a technique, a means through which Christ can endure existence.

Naturally, the fictions that sustain an individual like Christ are quite different from those of a Socrates. Indeed, it is precisely in the "errors" through which Christ preserves himself that Nietzsche recognizes "a combination of the sublime, the sick and the childish" (A 31). In Christ, Nietzsche says, the "concept, the *experience* 'life' in the only form he knows it is opposed to any kind of word, formula, law, faith, dogma." He inhabits a world wherein "the whole of reality, the whole of nature, language itself, possesses for him merely the value of a sign, a metaphor" (A 32). Here is an individual so insulated from the world that the fictions already determined by preservation and articulated in conscious thought reflect the physiological hieroglyphs of "a symbolist *par excellence*."

He articulates *his* experience of life, an experience that flies in the face of the religion through which his culture survived. Hence, Christ "never had reason to deny 'the world,' he had no notion of the ecclesiastical concept 'world'" (A 32). Christ does not argue over "Truth," he inhabits an impregnable psychological bubble wherein all contact with reality is "*deprecated* by the instinct of preservation" (A 30). Since the world and life are only an "occasion for metaphors," then predictably "[d]ialectics are likewise lacking, the idea is lacking that a faith, a 'truth' could be proved by reasons." Christ's proofs, Nietzsche says, "are inner 'lights,' inner feelings of pleasure and self-affirmations, nothing but 'proofs' by potency." This is the potency of preservation and the pleasure *felt* in affirming a "world" disconnected from "all experience of the world." And since "[d]enial is precisely what is totally impossible for him," such a "doctrine" does not "argue: it simply does not know how to imagine an opinion contrary to its own" (A 32).

Being incapable of any form of resistance and suffering the very fact of existence, Christ naturally reveals the fictions essential to his own preservation. Socrates' "form of ferocity" (T 3:7), even if degenerately expressed in dialectic, betrays an agonal instinct nonexistent in Christ.[2] The latter possesses an instinct of preservation that "spiritualizes" existence according to *"inner* realities" (A 34) that confine him to a world devoid of "all experience of the world, all acquirements, all politics, all psychology, all books, all art" (A 32). In this sense Christ embodies a technique through which life as will to power creates its own contradiction. That is, he "redeems" insofar as he represents the perfect means—nonresistance—for the preservation of the weak and physiologically depraved. The fictions essential to Christ affirm strictly protective measures, those that insulate him from a world of becoming; there is no affirmation of attack or vengeance. Hence, it is "on condition that nothing he says is taken literally that this antirealist can speak at all" (A 32).

Not surprisingly, Nietzsche thinks that with "everything pertaining to nature, time, space, history" (A 34), Christ's " 'knowledge' is precisely the *pure folly* of the fact *that* anything of this kind exists" (A 32). The "physiological *habitus*" of preserving the negation of all ascending instincts determines a "spirituality" at "home in a world undisturbed by reality of any kind" (A 29). And it is exactly this *habitus*, as "the inmost thing" (A 32), that determines Christ's "relations with other human beings and with things" (T 7:2). Such a condition renders Christ's "faith" effortless, that is, "not a faith which has been won by struggle—it is there, from the beginning, it is as it were a return to the childish in the spiritual domain" (A 32). In this "domain" "[b]eing a soldier, being a judge, being a patriot; defending oneself; preserving one's honour; desiring to seek one's advantage; being *proud*" (A 38) are simply impossible. On the contrary, such a faith "is not angry, does not censure, does not defend itself." There is no need here, Nietzsche says, to prove itself "by miracles or by rewards and promises . . . it is every moment its own miracle . . . its own proof, its own 'kingdom of God' . . . this faith . . . *lives*, it resists formulas" (A 32).

This resistance to all formulas does not mean a conscious refusal on the part of Christ to put forth a doctrine; it means simply an inability to "imagine an opinion contrary to its own." As Nietzsche says, this is a *living* faith. Christ has no need to prove or dispute anything; he is the proof of his "glad tidings" and "kingdom of Heaven" in the way a child is convinced he is the center of the universe, while knowing nothing of what "the universe" or "having convictions" means. It is in this connection "to *children*" that Nietzsche recognizes in Christ an "occurrence of

---

2. On agonal instinct, see the subsection entitled "The Death Wish," in Chapter 3.

retarded puberty undeveloped in the organism as a consequence of degeneration . . . familiar at any rate to physiologists" (A 32). Indeed, Christ is, for Nietzsche, like a child, or to "speak with the precision of the physiologist a quite different word would rather be in place here: the word idiot" (A 29). Here is "a being immersed entirely in symbols and incomprehensibilities" and very much a child in the manner of one who is emotionally and psychologically underdeveloped. Everything Christ does and says is indicative of that helpless and self-absorbed world of " 'childlike' idiocy" (A 31).

Much has been made of Nietzsche's use of the term "idiot" to describe Jesus, specifically in reference to the influence of Dostoevsky. Walter Kaufmann, for example, says Nietzsche's regret that "no Dostoevsky lived in the neighbourhood of this most interesting *décadent*" (A 31) is "one of many indications that Nietzsche's image of Jesus was decisively influenced by Dostoevsky's portrait of Prince Myshkin in *The Idiot*."[3] This is, I think, certainly true, but Kaufmann concentrates on the "psychology of the redeemer" only to indicate Dostoevsky's influence on this "psychology." Kaufmann's reticence to acknowledge the importance of physiology in Nietzsche's philosophy leads him to ignore the "two *physiological realities* upon which, out of which the doctrine of redemption has grown" (A 30). Kaufmann says that in Nietzsche's later period he "repudiated 'physiologism.' "[4] Why, then, does Nietzsche want to "speak with the precision of the physiologist" in the last year of his creative life—particularly where "the word idiot" (A 29) applies to Jesus? Indeed, in the notes of this same year (1888–89), Nietzsche refers to Saint Francis as "neurotic, epileptic, a visionary, like Jesus" (WP 221). I suspect that Nietzsche saw Myshkin's epilepsy to be an important physio-psychological factor in Dostoevsky's *Idiot*, and in this Nietzsche took the physiology of Prince Myshkin far more seriously than Kaufmann believed.

Of course, the "milieu in which this strange figure moved," says Nietzsche, "must have left its mark upon him" (A 31). The "mark" of his milieu was ultimately rather arbitrary in that chance, "to be sure, determines the environment, the language, the preparatory schooling of a particular configuration of concepts." Hence, Christ employed "*only* Judeo-Semitic concepts." But "one must be careful not to see in this anything but a sign-language, a semeiotic, an occasion for metaphors." If Christ had lived among Indians, "he would have made use of

---

3. Kaufmann, *Nietzsche: Philosopher, Psychologist, Antichrist* (New York: Vintage, 1968), 340–41.
4. Ibid., 294.

Sankhyam concepts, among Chinese those of Lao-tse—and would not have felt the difference" (A 32). Thus, it was "only in a Jewish landscape" that Jesus could "dream of his rainbow and ladder to heaven" (GS 137) and find God "walking before him and coming alive within him" (WP 176). But as the negation of the Jewish instinct—that is, being devoid of *ressentiment*—Christ was the antithesis of the Jewish conception of Yaweh, of sin and, of course, of the messiah.

Nevertheless, Nietzsche points out that it "is quite another question whether he was conscious of any such antithesis—whether he was not merely *felt* to be this antithesis" (A 28). In the end, it was precisely the feeling of *ressentiment* among his "followers" that "*misunderstood* [Jesus] to be . . . a *No* uttered towards everything that was priest and theologian" (A 27). Due to "*inner* realities" (A 34) that fortified him from a world already "*deprecated* by the instinct of self-preservation" (A 30), Christ lived with a childlike conviction that he was "the son of God" (A 34). He had, says Nietzsche, no real conception of reality and certainly "no notion of the ecclesiastical concept 'world' " (A 32). This was an individual submerged in a world of childish fictions whose language was that of a culture steeped in the concepts God, sin, and messiah. He copied this language in the same way a child does, and was equally ignorant of its significance. Christ could no more be responsible for a revolution "against the Jewish Church" (A 27) than could a child be responsible for mimicking his or her parents.

The Gift of Preservation

Jesus possessed, says Nietzsche, "the most innocent and desirous heart" (B 269), and he was murdered for reasons that, to this holy simpleton, were incomprehensible, since cruelty, vengeance, punishment, hate, and *ressentiment* did not exist in his " 'real' world" (A 29). He had no doctrines to defend, or "any formulas, any rites for communicating with God." He knew that it was "through the *practice* of one's life" that one is "at all times a 'child of God.' " It is precisely this practice, "*not* 'penance,' *not* 'prayer for forgiveness' which leads to God: *evangelic practice alone* leads to God, it *is* God." But in this practice "the whole of Jewish *ecclesiastical* teaching was denied" (A 33).

What Jesus teaches, Nietzsche says, is a "new way of living, *not* a new belief." In him "[b]lessedness is not promised, it is not tied to any conditions: it is the *only* reality—the rest is signs for speaking of it." He is the living example of a "new *practice*, the true evangelic practice." The genuine Christian "is distinguished by a *different* mode of acting," embodied in Christ, who made "no distinction between foreigner and native, between Jew and non-Jew. . . . He is not angry with anyone, does not disdain anyone. . . . The life of the redeemer," says Nietzsche, is "nothing else than *this* practice," which points back to "fundamentally *one* law, all consequences of *one* instinct" (A 33). The instinct of preservation in Christ provided the fictions necessary to living with pain and suffering. And total passivity, as the key to negating the affects of *ressentiment*, was the means to his survival. The "physiological *habitus*" that sustained him constitutes the "glad tidings."[5]

Christ, therefore, "bequeathed to mankind . . . his *practice*" (A 35), that is, a technique for enduring suffering. Consequently, even "today such a life is possible, for *certain* men even necessary: genuine, primitive Christianity will be possible at all times" (A 39).

With Christ the abyss between God and humanity was bridged insofar as he felt no contradiction between himself and God. In him existence is "to feel oneself 'in Heaven,' to feel oneself 'eternal,' while in every other condition one by *no* means feels oneself 'in Heaven': this alone is the psychological reality of 'redemption' " (A 33). For Nietzsche, the significance of Christ's teaching does not lie in eternal rewards and punishment but in living according to his example. Hence, Christ's "words to the *thief* on the cross contain the whole Evangel. 'That was verily a *divine* man, a child of God!'—says the thief. 'If thou feelest this'—answers the redeemer—'*thou art in paradise*, thou art a child of God' " (A 35).

Christ redeemed by providing a means to "happiness" in the midst of suffering. In his compassion for human suffering, Nietzsche says, lay "*Christ's error.*" As he puts it, Jesus "thought that there was nothing of which men suffered more than their sins" (GS 138). This was understandable in a world over which "Jehovah was brooding continually." Only here was the "sudden piercing of the gruesome and perpetual general day-night by a single ray of the sun experienced as if it were a miracle of 'love' and the ray of unmerited 'grace' " (GS 137). Christ's error was in thinking men suffered from sin; hence, "his soul grew full of that wonderful and fantastic compassion for a misery that even among his people, who had invented sin, was rarely a very great

---

5. In this light, Nietzsche makes the interesting observation that what died with Christ was "an absolutely primary beginning to a Buddhistic peace movement, to an actual and *not* merely promised *happiness on earth*" (A 42). A comparison between "the *two* physiological facts upon which . . . [Buddhism] rests" (A 20) and "the two *physiological realities*" (A 30) inherent to the psychology of the redeemer reveals means for the endurance of suffering. Insofar as the above physiological concerns are *primarily* related to this endurance, Buddhism and "genuine, primitive Christianity" (A 39) are both "*décadence* religions" (A 42).

misery" (GS 138). His error was that of "one who felt that he was without sin and who lacked firsthand experience" (GS 138). Wherever Christ saw suffering, he would not think it was due to the *ressentiment* of thwarted will to power; he would think that it was "sin" in the failure to love unconditionally.

Socrates provided "his expedient, his cure, his personal art of self-preservation" (T 3:9). Christ has his self-preservative technique as well, in "love as the sole, as the *last* possibility of life" (A 30). Like Socrates, Christ's perception of the world "is a symptom of certain physiological conditions, likewise of a particular spiritual level of prevalent judgments" (WP 254). In both cases, preservation seeks the avoidance of suffering as a means to "happiness." Hence, both fictionalize the world in terms of what is essential to their own survival. With the former, it is reason; with the latter, it is love.

A Physiological Redemption

The compassion Christ has for humans points not only to an error regarding the source of suffering but also to the root of *all* suffering. For Christ, love is the means to a negation of suffering and the way of bringing "happiness" to men. But actually to want to undermine all suffering and make men "happy" leads, as with Socrates, to "errors *in physiologicis*" (WP 454). These errors are determined by the physiology of Christ, for whom it is constitutionally impossible to see that all life strives for power, "*not* an increase in 'happiness' " (WP 704). Suffering is by no means to be eliminated, since it is inherent to "the primordial law of things" (B 265), according to which any drive "seeks that which resists it" (WP 656). Christ provides "the formula for *décadence*" (T 3:11) to the extent that his lack of ascending instincts allows him to estimate human suffering only as pathetic, something to be negated through a "love" that, as nonresistance, is opposed to the struggle, strife, and suffering essential to life as will to power. In short, here one preserves oneself via avoidance of the conditions essential to growth. And this physiological evasion is precisely the technique through which Christ "redeems" the weak and degenerate: he embodies a means to their preservation.

Naturally, the Jewish culture had to exclude Christ and his love from itself insofar as it was decadent; strong races will find Christ's love a threat to their existence, but the weak will find him irresistible. Christ's pity, then, is directed at the suffering of the physiologically depraved, since this is *his* suffering. His love is a means to his own preservation as well as to that of the weak in general. By representing a means to preserving the ill-constituted, Christ, like Socrates, provides "as a deliverance . . . only another expression of *décadence*—[Christ and Socrates] *alter* its expression, they do not abolish the thing itself" (T 3:11).

The weak are constitutionally incapable of realizing an order of rank among their instincts. Pulled hither and yon by competing drive-perspectives, they lack the "economy" through which their strength can be both saved and spent. Trying to satisfy all their drives, they are constantly reacting to stimuli, and this is the path to physiological exhaustion.[6] In Christ, however, abides a profound resistance to stimuli insofar as his instinct of preservation dissuades as *"harmful"* (A 30) all contact with reality. Here, says Nietzsche, the "instinct is on the right track insofar as doing nothing is more expedient than doing something" (WP 45). What is required, then, is the realization of a state wherein the organism's inability to avoid reaction is brought under control. That is to say, it requires a state of total passivity. Christ's nonresistance to stimuli is fundamentally the affect of an instinct of preservation basically leaving him numb to all contact with reality. His incapacity for resistance of any kind is therefore not the discipline inherent to an order of rank among the drives but the affect of the instinct of preservation conserving energy that would be dissipated if the organism was actually "touched" (A 30) by reality.

This state of affairs is manifest in various monastic "orders, the solitary philosophers, the fakirs," who "are inspired by the right value standard that a certain kind of man cannot benefit himself more than by preventing himself as much as possible from acting" (WP 45).[7] This is the physiological basis of asceticism, and it should not be confused with a "doctrine" that insists on one's mortifying the flesh to attain proximity to God. Such mortification would presuppose *ressentiment* and taking revenge on one's body. Christ taught an asceticism that is not a "formula for holiness" but is, rather, more in line with Nietzsche's idea of the asceticism of Buddhism: that is, an attempt on the part of the individual to realize a state, not of antagonism toward oneself or the world, but of such complete passivity that no matter what happens, one is indifferent.

The love of Christ is precisely a nonresistance to anything, a not fighting for or against anything. It is precisely this practice that enables the exhausted to realize "happiness" in a sublime indifference to every-

---

6. See the subsections "Weakness" and "Exhaustion" in Chapter 1.
7. Once again, the parallels to Buddhism here are interesting. See, for instance, A 20–22 and WP 155 and 159. See also note 5 above.

thing. This happiness is the release from the burdensome affects of *ressentiment*. It is a state of physiological hibernation wherein all possible sources of strength are channeled toward the preservation of the individual. It is a technique of relaxation and rest from the world, a world that, from the standpoint of *ressentiment*, is despised. This is the "Kingdom of Heaven," this is living as a "child of God," and this is why Nietzsche says "Christianity is possible as the most *private* form of existence" (WP 211). It has nothing to do with the necessity to deny the body or the world as a means to salvation in the hereafter.

In organisms pulled in multiple directions by the anarchy of their drives, energy is dissipated in multiple directions, leading to its fragmentation. The prevention of this dissipation is the object of Christ's saying, "[R]esist not evil!" which, says Nietzsche, is "the profoundest saying of the Gospel, its key in a certain sense" (A 29). Ultimately, Christ is the "redeemer" of the physiologically "underprivileged" (WP 55) because his love, like Socrates' "rationality at any cost" (T 3:11), is the "*last* possibility of life" (A 30).

The Little Prince

Nevertheless, like the Socratic cure, Christ's love is symptomatic of the death wish typical of all exhausted organisms. In organisms dominated by the instinct of preservation, Nietzsche translates their need for peace and repose into a longing for a fixed and static world wherein the flux of becoming is entirely negated. Socrates wanted to inhabit a world entirely devoid of the chaos of becoming and strove to inhabit a "good" world, one entirely "fixed" through dialectic. But Socrates' "subtle conscience and self-examination" (B 191) showed him that "rationality" and its inherent "good" justified neither this world nor his own existence, and finally he "handed himself the poison cup" (T 3:12). Unlike Socrates, Christ was fundamentally incapable of becoming transparent to himself; thus, the former "possessed the finer intellect" (PN 69).[8]

Nietzsche takes the idea of Christ as a harmless idiot quite seriously and recognizes a death wish in Christ's conviction that he was "at all times a 'child of God' " (A 33), actually feeling himself "in heaven" and "eternal." For Nietzsche, since Christ "is purely inward" (WP 160) and steeped in fictions essential to avoiding contact with reality, the " 'hour of death' . . . time, physical life and its crises, simply do not exist for the teacher of the 'glad tidings' " (A 34). In this sense Christ was a living death and genuinely occupied that perfectly static state characteristic of

---

8. This is from "The Wanderer and His Shadow," HH 2:86.

the perspective of the instinct of preservation. He was "dead" to this world in all but the physical reality of death. Socrates may have "possessed the finer intellect," but "this shrewdest of all self-deceivers" (T 3:12) could not attain, as Christ did, a state of equilibrium. The latter never had to "strive" to convince himself of anything. In Christ, the "'kingdom of heaven' is a condition of the heart" (A 34) betraying a condition "of retarded puberty" (A 32). In this sense, he was perhaps not unlike Dostoevsky's "idiot" who "was utterly a child . . . he was like an adult only in stature and face, but in development, soul, character, and perhaps even in mind—he was not an adult and so he would remain."[9]

C. S. Lewis said that we have three ways to explain Christ: he was either the Devil or a lunatic, or he was telling the truth.[10] Nietzsche takes the second option, lamenting that "no Dostoevsky lived in the neighbourhood of this most interesting *décadent.*" Only someone like Dostoevsky could have approached Jesus of Nazareth and articulated "the thrilling fascination of such a combination of the sublime, the sick and the childish" (A 31).

In a letter, Dostoevsky described his *Idiot* as an attempt *"to portray the perfectly good man."* In another letter, he said there "is only one positively good figure in the world—Christ—so that the phenomenon of that boundlessly, infinitely good figure is already in itself an infinite miracle."[11] Dostoevsky attempted to portray the good man so that such a one must be seen by others as an idiot. In this vein, Dostoevsky would have seen Nietzsche as one of those others. The difficulty of attempting such a portrait was clear to Dostoevsky. He pointed out that success in this endeavor had been attained in such figures as Cervantes' Don Quixote, Dickens's Pickwick, and Hugo's Jean Valjean. The "success" of the first two hinged on the reader's compassion for people who were ridiculed for their goodness, whereas Valjean elicited compassion not in being ridiculed but as a victim of social injustice. But in *The Idiot* "there is nothing of this sort . . . that is why I am afraid it will be a positive failure."[12] Nietzsche's portrait of Christ as a combination of the sick, sublime, and childish is a psychological one based on certain *"physiological realities"* (A 30). And Dostoevsky's portrait of the good man, based

---

9. This quote is from part 1, chapter 6, of Dostoevsky's *Idiot*. The translation is found in Konstantin Mochulsky, *Dostoevsky: His Life and Work*, trans. M. A. Minihan (Princeton: Princeton University Press, 1967), 375.
10. C. S. Lewis, *Mere Christianity* (London: Fontana, 1975), 52.
11. *Selected Letters of Fyodor Dostoevsky*, ed. Joseph Frank and David I. Goldstein, trans. A. R. MacAndrew (New Brunswick, N.J.: Rutgers University Press, 1987), 262, 269–70.
12. Ibid., 270.

on the illness of epilepsy, shares similar physiological concerns. But Dostoevsky believed Christ was God, hence incomprehensible to humanity.

Nietzsche sees Christ, not as God, but as a gentle, harmless man whose *example* is equally incomprehensible because it is blurred by the *ressentiment* of his contemporaries. Christ is sublime insofar as he embodies an effortless affirmation of the perfection of every moment. He is a perfectly innocent child who, devoid of arrogance or anger, is beyond even beginning to doubt that gods and men should love him. Moving through a world of inner fictions that insulate him from all reality, he may appear a kind of redeemer, but this redemption, at least from Nietzsche's point of view, is only that wherein the resistance essential to life as will to power is neutralized by the perspective of self-preservation.

Socrates fascinated his contemporaries as the supreme example of the rational man with his passions under control. His dialectical wizardry was an enchanting display of the formula for decadence, a path to war against the instincts of life. What is peculiar to Christ, on the other hand, is the total *lack* of competing drive-perspectives typical of mutually antagonistic instincts. He spoke with gentleness and compassion of loving one's enemy, giving up all one's possessions, and being in a state of blessedness here and now. And being without *ressentiment*, he was also a fascinating creature to his contemporaries, the perfect example of a certain "control" through which the physiologically "ill-constituted" (WP 846) could *endure*. The longing for stasis, peace, and the negation of struggle typical of the weak and exhausted was perfectly realized in Christ. In him there was no desire for worldly power or to become "the master." He was, from Nietzsche's standpoint, a child, among individuals whose lives had been so dominated by interpretations of guilt and sin that "the rare and sudden piercing of the . . . general day-night by a single ray of the sun [was] experienced as if it were a miracle of 'love' and the ray of unmerited 'grace' " (GS 137).

Seeing Christ as the most exquisite example of an utter lack of ascending instincts and thereby physiologically exhausted from the outset, Nietzsche does not have to look very far for symptoms of decadence and sickness. The "two *physiological realities*" (A 30) constituting Nietzsche's "psychology of the redeemer" show that, like Socrates, Christ suffered life to the extent that he was an "abortive actuality" (A 15). In this vein, as in the case of Socrates, it is pointless to debate here whether Nietzsche "admired or repudiated" Christ. One respects, admires, and combats one's enemies, and in this sense, Socrates was a worthy opponent. Christ was not. Nietzsche admires Socrates but is consistently antagonistic toward him. Christ, on the other hand, is in Nietzsche's eyes not unlike a retarded child. Though fascinated by this "combination of the sublime, the sick and the childish," Nietzsche is not particularly inclined to admire or repudiate a "retarded puberty . . . familiar at any rate to physiologists" (A 32). One does not admire illness, and where Christ is concerned, Nietzsche is not interested in picking on a child who was murdered in particularly ugly circumstances. To Nietzsche, Christ is at best only of secondary importance and in his time served merely as an occasion for the hatred through which he was deified.

Christianity

The "physiological realities" Nietzsche recognizes at work in Jesus of Nazareth constitute the great divide between his portrait of Christ and that of the Christian tradition. Clearly, Nietzsche sees Christ, not as divine, but rather as a harmless, childish man who moved in a world wholly fabricated by the fictions essential to his preservation. The contrast between the Nietzschean and Christian portraits of Christ does not rest on whether Christ is divine. I have shown the physiology through which Christ becomes an inoffensive, gentle simpleton, but Nietzsche sees this hypervulnerable and pathetic creature elevated to the status of a god through the machinations and hatred characteristic of *ressentiment*. What I explore here are the physiological dynamics through which Nietzsche recognizes murder and cowardice as the source of Christ's "divinity."

Distortions

When he looks at the New Testament and the portraits of Christ characteristic of the historicism of his day, Nietzsche is ill at ease to say the least. Fascinated by the redeemer type, the one who would go "over man," Nietzsche is always in search of the physio-psychological configuration of such an individual. Hence, when it comes to Christ he is concerned with, "[n]ot the truth about what he did, what he said, how he really died: but the question *whether* his type is still conceivable at all, whether it has been 'handed down' by tradition." In this regard, Nietzsche's rejection of the "scientific procedures" fashionable in the historicism of his day makes an interesting comparison to Søren Kierkegaard's inquiry in *Philosophical Fragments*. Kierkegaard thought the task of Christian *faith* was by no means enhanced through "knowledge" of historical facts about the life of Christ. Nietzsche disparages the historical facts because the attempt to get "to the facts" only deals with "the contradictions of 'tradition.' " This "tradition" consists of the Gospels and legends, and Nietzsche is deeply suspicious of both. Consequently, "to apply . . . scientific procedures *when no other records are extant* seems to [Nietzsche] wrong in principle—mere learned idling" (A 28). In the end, Kierkegaard thought historical facts about Christ meant nothing in regard to the task of *faith*; for Nietzsche, they meant little in regard to the problem of "the psychological type of the redeemer." He says that the attempts he knows of "to extract even the *history* of a 'soul' from the Gospels" seem "proofs of an execrable psychological frivolity." For example, Ernest Renan "appropriated for his explication of the type Jesus the two *most inapplicable* concepts possible in this case: the concept of the *genius* and the concept of the *hero*" (A 29).[13] Nietzsche is predictably appalled at the concept of genius in this case. The idea of the hero is equally untenable, since it is foolhardy to see Jesus as one who brings "the sword" (A 32).

This echoes something I have already touched upon. Generally speaking, Nietzsche identifies decadence in terms of the "multiplicity and contradictoriness" (A 31) of competing drive-perspectives that lack an overall dominating instinct. Now, as "a *decadence* type," Christ, *lacking* mutually antagonistic instincts, was particularly interesting. Indeed, in Nietzsche's portrait of Christ, "everything speaks against it" (A 31), since any kind of "antagonism" is "*deprecated* by the instinct of self-preservation" (A 30). He is bereft of the ascending instincts of life, and preservation as the dominating instinct negates the possibility of the harmful affects of *ressentiment*, which the organism simply cannot afford.[14] To this extent, then, his is a *unified* physiology, an organism that, lacking conflicting drive-perspectives, reveals a perfect synchronicity. He lacks that multiplicity of unharnessed drive-perspectives that usually exhaust the typical decadent—Socrates, for example. Christ is physiologically integrated by a dominant instinct of preservation keeping him in a state of physiological suspended animation and creating the fictions

---

13. Ernest Renan (1823–92) wrote a popular text entitled *The Life of Christ*, published in 1863, and it is to this text that Nietzsche refers.

14. Interestingly enough, this is also the order of rank within the Jewish culture. The caste of priests embody the culture's instinct of preservation and "negate" *ressentiment* to the extent that they direct this "explosive" at the enemies of the Jewish culture. The essential difference here is that although Christ has inherited the profoundly powerful instinct of preservation characteristic of his culture, he is utterly lacking in the *ressentiment* through which his culture managed to survive.

essential to the least amount of contact with the greatest source of pain—that being the world.

Nietzsche also denies a multiplicity of drive-perspectives in Jesus because for the contrary to be true "the tradition would have to have been remarkably faithful and objective: and we have reasons for assuming the opposite" (A 31). Nietzsche maintains that it is tradition that provided a "Christ" who possesses opposing and conflicting drive-perspectives. In the "actual" Christ, Nietzsche himself recognizes none of the "disgregation of impulses" he sees in Socrates (WP 46); on the contrary, he sees Christ as a unified physiological phenomenon. But when Nietzsche looks at the "Christ" of the Gospels, he notes a "contradiction between the mountain, lake and field preacher . . . and the aggressive fanatic, the mortal enemy of theologian and priest which Renan has wickedly glorified as *'le grand maitre en ironie'* " (A 31). For Nietzsche, Jesus is a simpleton incapable of attacking anything and has no conception of the extent to which he "could one day cause dissention" (A 32). In short, Nietzsche concludes that within the Christian tradition "the type of the redeemer has been preserved to us only in a very distorted form" (A 31).

Revolution

How is it that the Christian tradition portrays Christ as one who brings "the sword" (A 32), as a semiwarrior type? This, says Nietzsche, is "comprehensible only with reference to warfare and the aims of propaganda" (A 31).

At the top of the order of rank within the ancient Jewish culture were "the priests—and then immediately the chandala"—the Jewish priesthood retaining a sense of "caste, the privileged, the noble" (WP 184). The authority of the priestly caste rested on the power of *ressentiment*. Yet for Nietzsche, the hatred of authority and rank characteristic of the lowest orders existed in the Jewish culture just as it does within any culture. In the Jewish culture this hatred was directed at the authority embodied in the ruling caste of priests. When this hatred could no longer be repressed, there came "a revolt of the chandala: the origin of Christianity" (WP 184).

The Gospels, says Nietzsche, introduce us to a "strange and sick world" wherein the "refuse of society, neurosis and 'childlike' idiocy seem to make a rendezvous" (A 31). Out of the sewers of the Jewish culture, the *ressentiment* of the weakest drives, so long held in check by the priestly caste, could not be entirely contained. That profound hatred of all reality, so essential to the life of the Jewish culture, exploded into a negation of reality in toto. Hence, Nietzsche points out that "one understands nothing of the psychology of Christianity if one takes it to be the expression of a newly arisen national youthfulness and racial invigoration." Indeed, the case is quite the opposite; "it is a typical form of decadence, the moral hypersensitivity and hysteria of a sick mishmash populace grown weary and aimless." It is a swamp, full of "neurosis . . . the absence of duties, the instinct that everything is really coming to an end, that nothing is worth while anymore" (WP 180).

Christianity is a sect the religiosity of which can only appeal to "the lower masses, the women, the slaves, the non-noble classes" (WP 196)—a religion in which "the instincts of the subjugated and oppressed come into the foreground: it is the lowest classes which seek their salvation in it" (A 21). At the beginning of Christianity this "salvation" was guided by the instincts of *ressentiment* that flourished among the "outcasts and the condemned" (WP 207) of the Jewish culture. The background of Christianity was a vengeful mob, "insurrection, the explosion of stored-up antipathy towards the 'masters,' the instinct for how much happiness could lie, after such long oppression, simply in feeling oneself free" (WP 209). To the extent that this was a revolt against the priestly caste, it was also a threat to the order of rank through which the Jewish culture retained its very existence. Therefore, the "salvation" sought by the Christians stood opposed to the last reality never abandoned by the Jewish culture—that of life itself. And insofar as Christianity fought this "laboriously-achieved *last* possibility of remaining in being" (A 27), it was not only deadly to this culture but a profound expression of the death wish typical of the exhausted.

For Nietzsche, Christ has nothing to do with any of this. Of course, there are physiological similarities between Christ and these "lepers of all kinds" (WP 207), such as exhaustion, sickness, and decadence. In Christ, however, these similarities are only apparent because he lacks one important factor: *ressentiment*. Christ provides an example of a *"way of life"* (WP 212), a means for the weak and decadent to preserve themselves from the fragmentation inherent to exhaustion. The indifference to external stimuli, the passivity of asceticism, is the essential physiological technique "he bequeathed to mankind" (A 35).[15]

However, "[t]he founder of Christianity had to pay for having directed himself to the lowest class of Jewish society and intelligence. They conceived him in the spirit they understood" (WP 198). That is to say, they saw him in the "spirit" of *ressentiment*, and he became the center of

---

15. See note 5 above and related text, and the subsection "A Physiological Redemption," in this chapter.

"a popular uprising within a priestly people—a pietistic movement from below" (WP 182). And since the "symbolism of Christianity is based on the Jewish, which had already resolved all reality . . . into a holy . . . unreality" (WP 183), the "followers" of Christ required "nothing less than 'the Son of God' to create a faith for themselves" (WP 182).

For Nietzsche, this "faith" presupposes the interpretation of the death of Jesus. Jesus was crucified because he was fundamentally "a political criminal, insofar as political criminals were possible in an *absurdly unpolitical* society." Christ was perceived to be in revolt "against the Jewish Church . . . against 'the good and just,' against 'the saints of Israel,' . . . against caste, privilege, the order, the social form." This revolt "is what brought him to the Cross: the proof is the inscription on the Cross. He died for *his* guilt—all ground is lacking for the assertion, however often it is made, that he died for the guilt of others" (A 27).

A "Spiritual" Parricide

As I noted above, it is, says Nietzsche, "quite another question" (A 28) whether Christ was conscious of the motives behind his crucifixion. And indeed, given Nietzsche's portrait of Christ, it is clear that taking him to the Cross was equivalent to torturing a child to death.[16] Nevertheless, "this unexpected shameful death" led his disciples to confront "the real enigma: *'Who was that? What was that?'* " But no sooner had the riddle been posed than two questions struck like lightning: *"Who killed him? who* was his natural enemy?" And the answer, "*ruling* Judaism, its upper class," marked the point where Jesus of Nazareth was put on the road to divinity. As Nietzsche put it, "The affair could not possibly be at an end with this death: one required 'retribution.' " If the caste of priests caused his death, then naturally "one felt oneself in mutiny *against* the social order." And here Jesus is brought into focus in a novel way, "as having been *in mutiny against the social order*. Up till then this warlike trait . . . was *lacking* in his image; more, he was the contradiction of it" (A 40).

From Nietzsche's point of view, this reaction to the death of Christ is the origin of the traditional view of him as the hero bringing "the sword" (A 32). His "disciples were far from *forgiving* his death. . . . *revengefulness* . . . again came uppermost" (A 40). Thanks to *ressentiment*,

---

16. In this connection it is interesting to recall Dostoevsky's *Brothers Karamazov*, in which Ivan states his refusal to put humankind into the state of paradise if what is required is the torturing to death of one innocent child. This refusal is essential to Ivan's argument for "atheism." God had an innocent child, his own son, tortured to death for the sake of the human race. This is a "love" both Ivan and Nietzsche reject.

Christ was painted and promoted as a warrior type strictly "with reference to warfare and the aims of propaganda" (A 31). This was the war of the lowest social orders within the Jewish culture against *"ruling Judaism."* The image of Christ as a righteous soldier was the product of *ressentiment* and betrayed "a sign of how little they understood" him, since his followers *"failed* to understand" his "freedom from . . . [and] superiority *over* every feeling of *ressentiment"* (A 40).

Now, out of *ressentiment,* all the religious symbols that constituted "the pile-work upon which the Jewish nation continued to exist" (A 27) were dredged up, and predictably the "popular expectation of a Messiah came . . . into the foreground; an historic moment appeared in view: the 'kingdom of God' is coming to sit in judgement on its enemies" (A 40).

The contempt and bitterness toward everything that was "theologian and priest" was adjusted to Christ "according to their requirements" (A 31). At this point "everything [was] misunderstood," since Christ had been "precisely the existence . . . the *actuality"* of the "kingdom of God." But his followers could not endure the "evangelic equal right of everyone to be a child of God" and, "just as the Jews, in revenge on their enemies, had previously separated their God from themselves and raised him on high"; so Jesus' disciples took their revenge by *"exalting* Jesus in an extravagant fashion, in severing him from themselves." The result, Nietzsche says, was the *"one* God and the *one* Son of God: both products of *ressentiment"* (A 40).

Having missed the point of Christ's teaching, Christ's followers were faced with "an absurd problem . . . : 'How *could* God have permitted that?" And they "found a downright terrifyingly absurd answer: God gave his Son for the forgiveness of sins, as a *sacrifice.* All at once," Nietzsche says, "it was all over with the Gospel!" Now came the *"guilt sacrifice,* and that in its most repulsive, barbaric form, the sacrifice of the *innocent man* for the sins of the guilty!" But this had nothing to do with Jesus, because he "had done away with the concept 'guilt' itself—he had denied any chasm between God and man, he *lived* this unity of God and man as *his* 'glad tidings.' . . . And *not* as a special prerogative!" (A 41).[17] Yet from the standpoint of *ressentiment* Christ is a "mere 'motif' " (WP 177) for "this *indecency* of an interpretation" (A 41). With this interpretation of Christ's death, "the whole and sole reality of the Evangel . . . is juggled away" for "the doctrine of a Judgement and a Second Coming, the doctrine of his death as a sacrificial death, the doctrine of the Resurrection . . . for the benefit of a state *after* death!" (A

---

17. The ellipsis points are Nietzsche's.

41). It is in this that Christianity is "something fundamentally different from what its founder did and desired" (WP 195).

Christ's love was a means through which the exhausted and weak could at least *survive* and at least ward off the death wish typical of decadence. To this extent, then, he stood on the side of life. His practice was "above all a *not*-doing of many things" (A 39), because within the perspective of preservation, the weak can be preserved by avoiding action, not to mention the affects of *ressentiment*: hatred, rancor, and the fatiguing experience of a thwarted passion for revenge. The "glad tidings" are "*[n]ot* to defend oneself, *not* to grow angry, *not* to make responsible. . . . But not to resist even the evil man—to *love* him . . ." (A 35).[18]

But from Nietzsche's point of view, Christianity completely misunderstood the "bringer of glad tidings." This "faith" has always been "only a cloak, a pretext, a *screen*, behind which the instincts played their game—a shrewd *blindness* to the dominance of *certain* instincts" (A 39). In Christianity the dominant instincts of decadence, and the *ressentiment* typical of them, "spiritualized" a profound hatred of life into God's love for the weak and sick, and the most degenerate individuals were esteemed by God more than anyone else. Not surprisingly, from Nietzsche's point of view, everything antagonistic to life rallied around such a doctrine. Christianity is, he says, "the great antipagan movement of antiquity," which exploited "the life, teaching and 'words' of the founder of Christianity . . . in an absolutely arbitrary way after the pattern of fundamentally different needs" (WP 195).

Christ taught "*a way of life*, not a system of beliefs" (WP 212). He "wanted to bring peace and the happiness of lambs" (WP 195), not a life swollen with rancor and seen "through the eye of contempt" (WP 193). Yet it is precisely among "the weak, the inferior, the suffering, the oppressed" (WP 195) that the hatred of life flourishes and seeks "freedom." And this desire for liberty is actually the old death wish characteristic of exhaustion and decadence. "Christian faith" is opposed to Christ because it shifts "the centre of gravity of life *out* of life into the 'Beyond'—into *nothingness*" (A 43). Its appeal throughout the ancient world lay in being "a degeneracy movement composed of reject and refuse elements of every kind" (WP 154).

The Harvest

The hate Nietzsche identifies with Christianity is "not racially conditioned." After all, *ressentiment* is characteristic of the physiologically

---

18. The ellipsis points are Nietzsche's.

weak and degenerate in any culture. But the *power of ressentiment* peculiar to Christianity, Nietzsche says, requires race. Only a strong culture, one that clings to life at all costs via generating and exploiting *ressentiment*, can provide the soil wherein the most poisonous of flowers can take root. The profound hatred for everything healthy that Nietzsche sees in Christianity is, he says, the product of "a schooling and technique pursued with the utmost seriousness for hundreds of years." The process, the technique, of denaturalization through which the Jewish culture had managed to survive "attains its ultimate perfection" in Christianity. This unparalleled life-negating power is an offshoot from the tree of the Jewish culture. "[I]t is *inheritance*" Nietzsche says; "only as inheritance does it have the effect of a natural quality" (A 44).

But Christianity is by no means symptomatic of decline in the Jewish culture (WP 154). No doubt the language, symbols, concepts, and so forth, are "Judeo-Semitic" (A 32), and like any strong culture, it required threats to its health. But its potent instinct of preservation, embodied in the caste of priests, fought off this illness, an illness that proved irresistible to the degenerate elements of all cultures in the ancient world. Yes, *ressentiment* may characterize the most decadent drives of any culture, but here was a *ressentiment* that, having served as a means to the survival of the Jewish culture, was a draught of poison too potent for other cultures to withstand. Hence, from the beginning Christianity was "an agglomeration of forms of morbidity crowding together and seeking one another out—It is therefore not national, not racially conditioned; it appeals to the disinherited everywhere." It is "founded on a rancour against everything well-constituted and dominant: it needs a symbol that represents a curse on the well-constituted and dominant" (WP 154). Unfortunately, "Jesus of Nazareth was the sign by which they recognized themselves" (WP 182), and hence there was "only one Christian, and he died on the Cross" (A 39).

For Nietzsche, Christianity emerged from the gutter of Jewish society, and its hatred of authority was typical of the "already existing . . . religions of the lower masses" (WP 196) throughout the ancient world. This is what Nietzsche means in saying that Christianity does not require race, though the force behind its animosity did. It was "forged out of the *ressentiment* of the masses," and this was the *"chief weapon"* (A 43) of "every other already existing subterranean religion" (WP 195) at the time. In saying Christianity does not require race, Nietzsche means that it lacks a fundamental feature of any strong culture—order of rank. Indeed, this order was the perfect stimulant for its hatred. It simply borrowed the symbols of power that reflected the "spirituality" of the Jewish ruling class it repudiated. Nevertheless, it was a sect within which Nietzsche sees a rendezvous of all life-negating drives. All those things indicative of "strong races" (WP 352) are here denied. With Christianity, the total lack of *"meaning* in living . . . now becomes the 'meaning' of life." All the things essential to preserving the Jewish culture—"public spirit . . . gratitude for one's descent and one's forefathers . . . co-operation, trust, of furthering and keeping in view the general welfare"—collapse into so "many 'temptations,' so many diversions from the 'right road' " (A 43).

Unlike the culture from which it was spawned, Christianity is not racially conditioned, because it does not discriminate against decadence and hence appeals to the decadent instincts of *all* cultures at *all* times. It flourishes in "thoroughly morbid soil" everywhere (A 51). All that is required is that "one must be sufficiently sick for it" (A 51). The Jewish culture may have taken "the side of all *decadence* instincts," but it was not "dominated by them." Decadence and *ressentiment* were "a power by means of which . . . [it] could prevail *against* 'the world' " (A 24), and with Christianity, it quite inadvertently came up with its most exquisite weapon.

The God of the sick is invested with all the characteristics valued by them, because when the "prerequisites of *ascending* life, when everything strong, brave, masterful, proud is eliminated from the concept of God," then "he declines step by step to the symbol of a staff for the weary, a sheet-anchor for all who are drowning . . . the poor people's God, the sinner's God, the God of the sick" (A 17). In such a deity "all *décadence* instincts, all cowardliness and weariness of soul have their sanction" (A 19). This, for Nietzsche, is the "low-water mark in the descending development of the God type . . . the *contradiction of life* . . . nothingness deified, the will to nothingness sanctified!" (A 18).

Nietzsche claims that the Jews mark "the *beginning* of the slave rebellion in morals" (B 195; emphasis added). With Christianity the slave rebellion in morals gained real momentum. Under its banner the instincts of decadence everywhere could find a home, and Nietzsche sees it taking root and spreading throughout "the *underworld* of the ancient world" (A 22).

The influence of Christianity went hand in hand with that of decadent Greek philosophy. Indeed, the brand of philosophy that emerged from Socrates onward is seen by Nietzsche to be a "preparation of the soil for Christianity" (WP 427). As far as he is concerned, the two decadence movements of post-Socratic philosophy and Christianity spread throughout Western culture like a cancer.

5 Visions of Innocence

> To love a man, it's necessary that he should be hidden, for as soon as he shows his face, love is gone.
> —Fyodor Dostoevsky, *The Brothers Karamazov*

In the preceding chapters, I have explored Nietzsche's conception of physiology not only to establish his "clinical standpoint" but also to show that this standpoint functions within his diagnosis of cultural health and sickness. It would be ridiculous, however, to suggest that Nietzsche, no matter how much he delighted in it, was primarily concerned with finding a physiological interpretation for all possible phenomena. Possessed of a passion that, standing on its own, would not be thwarted by love or danger, he did not care about intellectual glass-bead games like "physiology" or "the clinical standpoint." In short, though his understanding of physiology permeates his critique of ancient Greek and Hebrew culture, Nietzsche, no less than Socrates, was a *physician* of culture; that is, he did not stop at mere critique, diagnosis of a disease, he also proposed a *cure* based on this physiology.

He recognized Greek metaphysics and Christianity as two modes of physiological decadence that, having fed off each other, realized the ultimate disease he called nihilism. His diagnosis of this sickness is famous, but the cure, if not notorious, is often regarded as incomprehensible. I speak here of the interdependent themes of the eternal recurrence and the overman. Nietzsche's name is virtually synonymous with these conceptions and with the rubric under which they stand: the revaluation of all values. The road to this revaluation constitutes the first part of this chapter; there I look at both the origins of nihilism and how it became a disease peculiar to modernity. In the second part I look at the revaluation of all values: the battle plan Nietzsche devised to fight nihilism, a plant with its roots in antiquity. In the third part I want to look at the eternal recurrence and the overman as strategies essential to the cure Nietzsche devised for nothing less than the *possibility* of a future for the human race.

Nietzsche's task as a philosopher underlies all the concerns of this chapter. My look at his clinical standpoint has revealed the ruthless violence inherent to his perception of the philosopher's task—judging what deserves to live and die. Nietzsche once said that every great philosophy is "the personal confession of its author and a kind of involuntary and unconscious memoir" (B 6). In this chapter violence, destruction, and cruelty by no means disappear. On the contrary, strange and terrifying highways still lie ahead. But if Nietzsche's philosophy is his "personal confession," then I seek to confirm his observation: "I speak only of what I have lived through, not merely of what I have thought through; the opposition of thinking and life is lacking in my case."[1]

I think Nietzsche experienced a terror that makes his legendary illness and loneliness secondary. There are many who have suffered remarkable illness and loneliness; in this Nietzsche is not unique. But what if this suffering is devoid of meaning or purpose? This, he says, is the greatest pain—one that lies, he says, in the "meaninglessness of suffering, *not* suffering itself." Unless humans are "shown a *meaning* for it, a *purpose* of suffering," they self-destruct. When Nietzsche raised the "crying question" (G 3:28) of meaningless suffering, silence was the only answer, and he sought "deterrence from the *deed of nihilism*, which is suicide" (WP 247).

Again, in this Nietzsche was not extraordinary; there are many who fight the death wish when their suffering appears pointless. His uniqueness consists in recognizing his own pain, in the midst of

---

1. This is from a discarded draft for section 3 of "Why I Write Such Good Books," in *Ecce Homo*. The translation, by Kaufmann, is found in section 2 of the appendix to EH. For the German text, see *Friedrich Nietzsches Werke des Zusammenbruchs*, ed. Erich F. Podach (Heidelberg: Wolfgang Rothe, 1961), 215–16.

meaningless suffering, to be symptomatic of the "spiritual" disease of his age and a specter that would haunt "the history of the next two centuries." He witnessed within himself the collapse of everything that formerly sustained those within the most profound suffering. He called it the *"advent of nihilism"* (WP pref.:2); with nihilism the incapacity to affirm anything worth living or dying for becomes a world-historical event.

Nietzsche despised this debility both within himself and his epoch. Nevertheless, he saw it as unavoidable—something that, like any illness, had to be endured and defeated. He claimed success in this by becoming "the first perfect nihilist of Europe," the first to have "lived through the whole of nihilism, to the end, leaving it behind, outside himself" (WP pref.:3). For Nietzsche, this success provided precisely what nihilism had undermined: the ability to stand on the side of life and the bravery to make the sacrifices necessary to creating new mores, new values, perhaps even new gods.

Nietzsche saw within himself the disease of his age, and by overcoming nihilism in himself, he, like Socrates, believed he had found a cure. But wary of the Socrates who, as a cultural physician, only promoted the illness he set out to fight, Nietzsche looked again at the philosophical giants "of the two centuries *before* Socrates" (E BT:3) and would settle for nothing less than the high philosophical rank he identified with the pre-Socratics. From them he derived his vision of the genuine philosophical type, who heals through new deceptions and is, of course, "most useful when there is *a lot to be destroyed*, in times of chaos or degeneration" (PAC 72; M 6:68).

Nietzsche believed much had to be destroyed within himself, and within the philosophers of his own age, he saw nothing but "spiritual" infection—and this to such an extent that he decided "nothing comes of this situation. Why indeed? *They are not philosophers for themselves.* 'Physician heal thyself!' is what we must shout to them" (PH 115; M 7:26). Nietzsche shouted this at himself loudest of all and was precisely the physician who attempted to heal himself. His prescription for curing nihilism reflects an experiment he made with himself. I do not intend to reduce Nietzsche's philosophy to his biography, but it is clear that in saying "people shall say after I am dead that I was a *good* physician—and not only in my behalf,"[2] he described his own philosophical passion.

---

2. Nietzsche to his mother, around July 9, 1881, *Nietzsche: Unpublished Letters*, ed. and trans. Karl F. Leidecker (London: Peter Owen, 1960), 83 (BKG III¹:103).

Nihilism

Physiological Genealogy

For Nietzsche, Greek metaphysics and Christianity are two forms of cultural sickness with much in common: both (*a*) emerge in times of cultural dissolution, (*b*) constitute a revaluation of the values essential to the foundation of their respective cultures, and (*c*) originate from the lowest ranks of the social hierarchy and represent, therefore, the weakest instincts. For Nietzsche, Christianity and metaphysics synthesized into a poison spreading throughout Western culture. These two decadence movements ran side by side (WP 427) and inevitably united through the "symbiosis of centuries" (WP 50).

The origins of this symbiosis can be traced back to Plato: "since Plato, all theologians and philosophers are on the same track" (B 191). Plato, having been "seduced by the *roturier* Socrates" (WP 435), took up the proposition "reason = virtue = happiness," and "with all the ardent devotion of his enthusiastic soul" (BT 13) became one of the most powerful promoters of decadence. He became the potent philosophical voice of the Greek "world grown senile and sick" (WP 438), seeking solace in the transcendent, eternal world of dialectics wherein suffering, death, change, procreation, and growth were reduced to "conceptual mummies" (T 4:1).

The desire for a world transcending this one was precisely the means through which Greek metaphysics was a "preparation of the soil for Christianity" (WP 427). In affirming a transcendent reality that "contradicted this world" (WP 461), Plato provided the "decayed soil" where Christianity "could only take root" (WP 438). Greek metaphysics opted for "denaturalized" (WP 430) and hence abstract virtues the origin of which was a world antithetical to this one. Christianity behaved similarly. Its *ressentiment* shifted "the center of gravity of life *out* of life into the 'Beyond' " (A 43) as the source of virtues that, from the clinical standpoint, were "life-poisoning and heart-poisoning errors" (A 39). In both cultures, the dominant instincts of decadence created a "spiritualization" of the world in *"contradiction of life"* (A 18). What Christianity had in common with Greek metaphysics was "the denaturalization of moral values" (WP 430). Nietzsche says these two "decadence movements and extremes run side by side" (WP 427), but this does not mean metaphysics was a necessary condition for the existence of Christianity. Strictly speaking, these two modes of decadence saw the light of day quite independent of each other. Nietzsche's physiological analyses of decadence in each culture are essentially the same, but he would not say the historical manifestations of decadence in both the Greek and Hebrew cultures are interchangeable.

Decadence "belongs to every age and every people" (WP 41) and is held in check by any healthy culture. Clearly, by the time metaphysics emerged in the figures of Socrates and Plato, the Greek culture had lapsed into decadence and was in no condition to fight "the contagion of the healthy parts of the organism" (WP 41). Indeed, the illness only spread in the guise of metaphysics, which "refused to see nature in morality." The process of denaturalization initiated by Socrates was enhanced among the Greeks by Plato, who, says Nietzsche, "debased the Greek gods with his concept 'good' " (WP 202). On the other hand, Christianity appealed "to the disinherited everywhere" (WP 154) and easily adapted "to the needs and the level of understanding of the religious masses of that time"—that is, the religions of "the non-noble classes" (WP 196), the "subterranean cults, those of Osiris, of the Great Mother, of Mithras for example" (A 58). The "latent Christianity" (A 58) of the "non-noble classes" allowed Christianity to insinuate itself into their religious attitudes and rituals: their "hope of a beyond" (WP 196), "blood-drinking" (WP 167), "the bloody phantasmagoria of the sacrificial animal" (WP 196), "the *unio mystica* with the 'sacrifice' " (WP 167), "asceticism, world-denial" (WP 196) and "above all the slowly stirred up fire of revengefulness, of Chandala revengefulness" (A 58).

Christianity also coalesced very nicely with Greek metaphysics insofar as the latter was just ill enough to allow Christianity "to found and make itself possible philosophically." Christianity, Nietzsche says, revealed a "predilection for the ambiguous figures of the old culture, above all for Plato" (WP 195). When Plato placed absolute "Good" in a world transcending this one, he contributed a most noteworthy symptom of Socratic decadence—the moral condemnation of this world. In this, Plato not only deviated "from all the fundamental instincts of the Hellenes," he was also "morally infected . . . an antecedent Christian." He was a "coward in the face of reality—consequently he [fled] into the ideal" (T 11:2). And this flight "was the greatest of rebaptisms" (WP 572), that is, revaluations of the values of his culture. But since this revaluation was "adopted by Christianity, we do not recognize how astonishing it is" (WP 572). In "the great fatality of Christianity," Nietzsche says, Plato was "that ambiguity and fascination called the 'ideal' which made it possible for the nobler natures of antiquity to . . . step on to the *bridge* which led to the 'Cross' " (T 11:2).

In opting for the "Good" and "Truth" of a transcendent world, Plato "reversed the concept 'reality' and said: 'What you take for real is an error, and the nearer we approach the 'Idea,' the nearer we approach 'truth.' " Here was the Greek decadence "adopted by Christianity" (WP 572). Plato was Christianity's most profound, albeit inadvertent, philosophical advocate. He provided the means through which *ressentiment* acquired a philosophical voice. Christianity, Nietzsche says, "is Platonism for the people" (B pref.), that is, an "appalling mishmash of Greek philosophy and Judaism" (WP 169). It proved irresistible to "the scum of previous society of all classes" (WP 50) and "was forcibly disseminated among uncivilized peoples: this is the history of Occidental culture" (SSW 133; M 6:104).

Nietzsche's attack on this history speaks from the standpoint of neither Christianity nor "metaphysics but from animal physiology" (WP 275). Within his clinical standpoint, he thinks that thanks to two thousand years of Christianity, something "sickly, and mediocre has been bred, the European of today" (B 62). Insofar as Christian *morality* has come to dominate the "spirituality" of the West, it has been the "history of the struggle of morality with the basic instincts of life" (WP 274). This antagonism has itself become an instinct with us; it is "in our blood" (WP 765). Everything promising sickness and decay is preserved and honored by Christianity, and to the extent that humanity has embraced it for two thousand years, "they have taken up sickness, old age, contradiction into all their instincts" (A 19).

The ultimate and indeed *natural* consequence of this physiological state of affairs is death. The death wish of Socrates was masked by a metaphysical longing for the "virtue" of a world devoid of "error." The death wish of Christ was exploited and deified by a mob, of whose *ressentiment* he had no grasp. For Nietzsche, the death wish inherent to all decadence and cultivated for two millennia finally comes to fruition in modernity. Nietzsche calls it nihilism: "the ultimate logical conclusion of our great values and ideals" (WP pref.:4).

Nihilism is the historical phenomenon wherein *"the highest values devaluate themselves"* (WP 2). This devaluation is, on the one hand, the lucid perception of "God" and "Truth" as *deceptions*. On the other hand, this perception renders a vision of life so terrifying that degenerate modernity stands paralyzed. Since "all of us have, unconsciously, involuntarily in our bodies values" of decadent "descent—we are, physiologically considered, *false*" (C epilogue). With the collapse of the highest values hitherto, our instinctive preference for what is ill renders us almost incapable of overcoming our demise.

This extreme situation leads the physician to take extreme measures regarding both himself and his epoch. Nietzsche's philosophy is a prodigious attack upon everything the human race ever held dear. But this philosophy is not dedicated simply to attack and destruction. It is also committed to creating a new footing for Western culture. "Nothing," he says, "has preoccupied me more profoundly than the problem of decadence." However, Nietzsche says he resisted decadence: "The philosopher in me resisted" (C pref.). The cultural physician must fight decadence within both himself and his epoch. This is the path through which the philosopher sets out to "protect and defend his native land" (PTA 2:35; M 4:160). Socrates tried to save his culture, but being infected himself, his "cure" was only symptomatic of the sickness of his age. Nietzsche also saw himself as "a child of this time; that is, a decadent" (C pref.); and like Socrates, he "grasped that *his* case . . . was already no longer exceptional," since the "same kind of degeneration was everywhere silently preparing itself" (T 3:9). "Physician, heal yourself: thus you will heal your patient too" (Z 1:22): this was Nietzsche's conviction, and when he looked at the "relation between what's called 'improvement' of mankind . . . and the elevation of the species Man,"[3] he experimented with himself "first and last" (C pref.).

Haunted by the fact of his decadence and fearing he might commit the Socratic error of promoting the very sickness one seeks to cure, Nietzsche said he "required a special self-discipline: to take sides against everything sick in me" (C pref.). He was convinced of the necessity for a revaluation of all values, but the means to this revaluation—eternal recurrence, the overman, and the symbol of Dionysus—were by no means hard and fast truths. They were the experiments of a physician who confronted his own death and that of his culture.

The Political Infection

There is always a hiss of contempt in Nietzsche's references to modernity. Compared to the ancients, who lived in accord with life, the "hopelessly mediocre and insipid man" (G 1:11) of today is the price we "pay for having been Christians for two thousand years" (WP 30). We have made ourselves ill, Nietzsche thinks, by having embraced this infection, which, from "the standpoint of general breeding" (WP 246), can only *"worsen the European race"* (B 62). Of course, such a race is destined to "have descendants even more degenerate than they are themselves" (WP 52). Ultimately, the malaise beginning with metaphysics and absorbed by Christianity has brought us to the point where "modern society is no 'society,' no 'body,' but a sick conglomerate of chandalas—a society that no longer has the strength to *excrete*" (WP 50).

---

3. Nietzsche to Jakob Burckhardt, September 22, 1886, SPL 91 (BKG III³:254).

"What does nihilism mean? *That the highest values devaluate themselves.* The aim is lacking; 'why' finds no answer" (WP 2). Our values are only the palest image of what at one time were expressions of a profound health. The pre-Socratic Greek and pre-Christian Hebrew cultures developed a "spirituality" that affirmed the law of life. In both cases, however, decadence movements marked a revaluation of the values through which both modes of decadence retained the values of their respective cultures *in name only*.

Ultimately, Nietzsche puts his finger on Christian morality as the path through which all forms of exhaustion, decadence, and sickness were preserved and promoted up to the present. Consequently, Western culture is so ill that the physiological capacity of "spirit" to create the fictions essential to cultural preservation and growth has atrophied. For Nietzsche, a firmly maintained order of rank is the essence of any healthy "spirituality." On the other hand, he sees Christianity is a profound threat to the necessity of an order of rank determined by life as will to power.

In its hatred of an order of rank, Christianity has always stood "against every feeling of reverence and distance between man and man, against, that is, the *precondition* of every elevation, every increase in culture." There can be no doubt, therefore, that the "aristocratic outlook has been undermined most deeply by the lie of equality of souls" (A 43). In its capacity to absorb sickness from any corner, the God of Christianity "has sat still nowhere . . . he is at home everywhere, the great cosmopolitan," the "God of the 'great majority,' the democrat among gods" (A 17). Christianity has "waged a war to the death" (A 43) with the necessity for the "many degrees of bondage" (WP 464) essential to cultivating the strongest, most "spiritual" human beings; and as soon as "the degenerate and sick [are] . . . accorded the same value as the healthy . . . or even more value . . . then unnaturalness becomes law" (WP 246).

As I have shown, an order of rank provides "an arrangement, whether voluntary or involuntary, for *breeding*" (B 262) human beings who will "carry the seeds of the future" (GS 23). Within this natural greenhouse, it is essential that "the ill-constituted, weak, degenerate, perish" (WP 246). But, says Nietzsche, from Christian *ressentiment*, which has determined the values of our culture, has come the "poison of the doctrine '*equal* rights for all' " (A 43) through which particularly the sick individual was made "so important, so absolute, that he could no longer be sacrificed." Hence, the idea of the individual's "infinite value" and the principle of equality have "from the standpoint of general breeding, no meaning at all" (WP 246). Since the doctrine of equality "has been more thoroughly sowed by Christianity than by anything else" (A 43), it stands as "the counterprinciple to the principle of *selection*" (WP 246). And its dominant physiological effect has been "for eighteen centuries—to turn man into a *sublime miscarriage*" (B 62).

Insofar as Nietzsche thinks the idea that everyone "is equal to everyone else" only breeds a populace of "self-seeking cattle and mob" (WP 752), he is quick to condemn both democracy and socialism. Of the latter, he says, "[T]he human beings or races that think up such a doctrine must be bungled" (WP 125). And democracy, as "the heir of the Christian movement" (B 202), reveals "a tremendous *physiological* process" through which "Europeans are becoming more similar to each other . . . more detached from the conditions under which races originate" (B 242).

Since Nietzsche sees a strong, natural order of rank as "the *precondition* of every elevation, every increase in culture" (A 43), his hatred for "equality" should come as no surprise. He sees our adherence to egalitarian principles as the "real *historical* effect" (WP 246) of the decadence inherent to Christianity. And precisely this diagnosis leads him to articulate his philosophical task thus: "In the age of *suffrage universal*, i.e., when everyone may sit in judgment on everyone and everything, I feel impelled to reestablish *order of rank*" (WP 854).

This task is essential since, without a new order, our "highest values" will be our doom. The conceptions of justice, courage, and the good did not originate in conditions wherein "everyone may sit in judgment on everyone and everything" (WP 854). On the contrary, they presuppose the "spiritual" strength typical of a firmly established order of rank and are, therefore, intimately connected to an affirmation of life on earth. Without this order, the sick and weak have flourished to the point where our culture is equal to "the *sum of zeroes*—where every zero has 'equal rights,' where it is virtuous to be zero" (WP 53).

Our inherited sick "spirituality" that promises cultural destruction is, generally speaking, what is meant by nihilism. Yet how does it happen that the very affirmation of everything "holy" and "good" for the last two millennia has actually compelled us to deny the "holy" and "good"?

The Absurd

From Nietzsche's clinical standpoint, we are the debilitated offspring of decadent antiquity. Our physiological inheritance from Greek metaphysics and Christianity is a "spiritualization" of the world that, as "morality," has poisoned us to the point where we are repulsed at the very idea of order of rank, where we have fallen prey to the death wish Nietzsche perceived both in decadent Greek culture and in Christianity. He saw this death wish as an essential part of our ancient inheritance, an inheritance that, planted within our morality, he saw bear fruit in the age of nihilism.

In decadent organisms, again, the weakest instincts cleave to the instinct of preservation and undermine the vitality of the organism as a whole. And preservation, as the "first instinct of spirituality" (T 9:2), only renders a fiction determined by *its* perspective. That is, it provides the deception of stability essential to the organism. However, since life requires growth in power, not mere preservation, the organism is further devitalized to the point where it seeks the ultimate stability of death.

The paradox of decadence lies in how the very intensity of the organism's search for preservation only enhances the prospect of exhaustion and the death wish. The more it seeks to preserve itself, the more it rushes headlong into the devitalization it is trying to ameliorate. Thomas Mann provides an illustration of this devitalizing spiral into exhaustion and sickness through Hans Castorp, the protagonist of *The Magic Mountain*.[4] In reference to Hans, Mann speaks of how the "unfavourable influence exerted upon a man's personal life by the times in which he lives may even extend to his physical organism." The age Mann has in mind is the dawn of the twentieth century, "an age that affords no satisfying answer to the eternal question of 'Why?' 'To what end?' " As the product of such an age, Castorp "must be considered mediocre," in both the physical and spiritual senses.

Physically, Hans was neither healthy nor ill, but somewhere in between. He was "a little anaemic," but "notwithstanding his thin-bloodedness . . . [he] clung to the grosser pleasures of life as a greedy suckling to its mother's breast." His was that state of hiatus typical of the self-preservative type. Physical exertion "was something to which he was quite definitely disinclined." He preferred the somnambulance and stupor of a medically prescribed "glass of porter," which he found "soothing to his spirits" and which encouraged "a propensity of his . . . sitting staring into space, with his jaw dropped and his thoughts fixed on just nothing at all." Within the spiritual dimension, Mann's protagonist "prolonged a situation he was used to, in which no definite decisions had to be taken, and in which he had further time to think

---

4. All the quotations that follow in this and the next two paragraphs are from Thomas Mann, *The Magic Mountain*, trans. H. T. Lowe-Porter, (New York: Knopf, 1968), 29–34.

matters over and decide what he really wanted to do, which he was far from knowing."

Eventually Hans goes to a health spa, where he rapidly "settles in" to the routine of the "cure." Throughout the novel, Mann weaves together Hans's physical inferiority and his spiritual inferiority. The more Hans devotes himself to regaining his health, the more it remains the same or deteriorates, along with his spiritual torpor and incapacity to make a commitment to anything at all. Indeed, his only commitment is to "getting better," but Mann portrays this as a self-deception insofar as his "resolve" is a means to "further time to think matters over and decide what he really want[s] to do." In the end, this decision is forced upon Hans by the declaration of World War I, and it is only when he *risks* his life, rather than try to preserve it, that he is "saved."

As seen in Chapter 1, decadence is will to power striving for dominance of the whole organism. And its victory is the destruction of its life. The more the perspective of self-preservation is affirmed via the debilitation of the most powerful drives, the more the law of life is affirmed in the necessity for the destruction of the weak. Here life, as will to power, is *affirmed* in the necessity of self-destruction for organisms gone awry. And, for Nietzsche, this physiological necessity is embodied in the "spiritual" illness of nihilism. It is simply nature's way of weeding out degenerate organisms.

Nihilism is attained when *"the highest values devaluate themselves,"* and this results, Nietzsche says, in undermining any sense of purpose; " 'why?' finds no answer" (WP 2). Here the law of life reveals the necessity of self-destruction in an organism gone awry. Our morality, our "highest values," have their origins in a "spirituality" that provided a fiction meant to shield the weak and degenerate elements in both the Greek and Hebrew cultures. These fictions, be they the "virtues" of the dialecticians or the Christians, presuppose an attack on the source of cultural vitality, that is, an order of rank dominated by the most powerful drives. And this "is the formula for *décadence"* (T 3:11).

In cultivating the idea "Everyone is equal to everyone else" (WP 752), we have systematically negated "the *precondition*" (A 43) through which any healthy culture has ever existed. Whether we speak "of an individual or a people" (WP 852), this precondition is an order of rank among the drives. This order is fundamental to "that economy in the law of life" (T 6:6) making possible the "feeling of plenitude, of *dammed-up strength*" (WP 852) essential to the most potent, life-affirming "spiritualization" of the world and ourselves. This is the function of a healthy instinct of preservation rendering an intoxicating vision of beauty "even to things and conditions that the instinct of impotence could only find *hateful* and 'ugly' " (WP 852).

This healthy "spirituality" prevailed in the early Hellenic culture, which, with its instinct of preservation properly ranked *below* the more powerful drives, created tragedy as the means of blunting and falsifying everything "hateful and 'ugly.' " Compared to healthy antiquity, modernity lacks precisely "the *large-scale economy* which justifies the *terrifying*, the *evil*, the *questionable*" (WP 852).

As I showed in Chapter 2, the "spiritualization of *cruelty*" (B 229) was the physiological means through which the Hellenic culture overcame the dark face of life. It assimilated whatever resisted it through fictions that painted life's cruelty and promise of destruction as sources of beauty. "Spirit" provides the means to so "many subtleties of ultimate self-deception, so many seductions to life, so much faith in life!" It is the artistic instinct in us, revealing our "will to appearance, to illusion," and "counts as more profound, primeval" (WP 853). This is why "tragedy is a *tonic*" (WP 851) to early Greek antiquity, it is "the great means of making life possible, the great seduction to life, the great stimulant to life" (WP 853). And in this art is a physiological phenomenon, and we possess it "lest we *perish of the truth*" (WP 822).

This truth is the vision that is capable of stopping us cold in our tracks and that leads us to whisper, "I am better off dead." For Nietzsche, such a truth is the brutal certitude that "there is only *one* world, and this is false, cruel, contradictory, seductive, without meaning—A world thus constituted is the real world" (WP 853). The early Hellenes confronted this phenomenon through the question, "What is a life of struggle and victory for?" Suddenly the meaninglessness of the values for which they suffered and risked death stepped before them. But the "Hellenic genius," their "spiritual" ability, always sustained them "with yet another answer to the question . . . and it gave that answer through the whole breadth of Greek history" (HC 34–35; WKG 3:279).

For Nietzsche, we moderns are a different story; our "spiritual" ability to fictionalize the most terrifying faces of life has degenerated into *preserving* everything sick and weak. Egalitarian principles are the predictable consequence of the perspective of a dominating instinct of preservation inherited from Greek metaphysics and Christian *ressentiment*. Western culture has "spiritualized," that is, "valued" the individual as "so absolute, that he could no longer be sacrificed" (WP 246). From the standpoint of life as will to power, individuals do not, by the fact that they are human, possess infinite value. Nietzsche thinks that after two millennia of "values" wholly dedicated to self-preservation, we are incapable of withstanding, and are destined to be overwhelmed by, the most dangerous truth of life as will to power, the truth that life itself is "an ebb and a flood of its forms; out of the simplest forms . . . toward the most complex, out of the stillest, most rigid, coldest forms toward the hottest, most turbulent, most self-contradictory" (WP 1067). This is the law of madness—the helter-skelter play of power spinning, collapsing, and exploding—wherein that form of power we call human is as significant as the shadow of a flower.

The fictions of "spirit" are meant to conceal the law of madness, to falsify the brutal truth that human suffering is, at bottom, a *danse macabre* without rhyme or reason. Through life-preserving fictions we have possessed the means to conceal the meaninglessness of existence. By these means we have grown in power. Thus, our "truths" have always been the illusions that conceal the absurd, and in this we "are all *afraid* of truth" (E 2:4). In the end, Nietzsche's vision of the will to power is one wherein "unreason crawls out . . . into the light like a worm" (GS 307). This is a truth he never denied. His denial of "Truth" (WP 616) hinges on how it has always been a fiction that has allowed us to believe *we* are the heart of some transcendental *telos* and "the measure of all things." Yes, we are the measure of all things to the extent that our "measures" conceal the madness upon which they rest. For Nietzsche, the deceptions of "spirit" show that "the character of existence is to be misunderstood." This, he says, is the "profoundest and supreme secret motive behind all that is virtue, science, piety, artistry" (WP 853). But where is the "concealed will to death" (GS 344) in our morality?

Moralities, says Nietzsche, are "merely a *sign language of the affects*" (B 187). The master morality of the ancient, warlike Hellenes and Hebrews was the product of a physiological order of rank among powerful, life-affirming drives generating the illusions essential to revering themselves and this world. Their taste for everything "frightful, evil, a riddle, destructive, fatal" (BT S:4) indicates a certain delight in a world that promised destruction. They could *respect* only that which lived dangerously and flirted with inevitable death. What they deemed good and bad was determined by courage, that is, one's ability to confront the darkest faces of existence and still find it deserving of reverence.[5]

---

5. This casts some light on Nietzsche's antagonism to pity. Life as will to power has no pity on the weak and helpless. Consequently, a warrior class that revered and identified as good the violence inherent to life would find the idea of pity alien. To have pity on the weak and helpless would indicate a lack of strength before a brutal fact of life: that one must be strong or be destroyed. This, again, is the code of a warrior elite, a code that echoes a natural order of rank determined by life as will to power. It is in this sense that Nietzsche sees pity as a life-denying concept appropriate only to slave morality.

This was the ultimate test of strength. To feel oneself hurt, insulted, embittered, or angered by the "injustice" of one's inevitable destruction was cowardice. Of course, only the most potent "spiritual" capacity was the path to reverence for life. And only the healthiest races of antiquity had that *"genius in lying"* (WP 853) essential to creating the illusions through which the absurd became a lie. Therefore they could never hate life for its horror, random violence, and suffering. In short, they never fully affirmed the idea that existence is devoid of meaning or value. At the very abyss of the truth of life as will to power, the Greeks and Hebrews displayed the "will of the spirit to let itself be deceived . . . that such and such is *not* the case" (B 230).

"Spirit," as mentioned earlier, embellishes the world according to the dominant perspective of the organism; of course, this may include a "decision in favor of ignorance . . . an internal No to this or that thing." Such constitutes a "state of defense against much that is knowable, a satisfaction with . . . a Yea and Amen to ignorance—all of which," Nietzsche says, "is necessary in proportion to a spirit's power to appropriate, its 'digestive capacity' to speak metaphorically" (B 230). But if " 'the spirit' is relatively most similar to a stomach" (B 230), the Greeks and the Hebrews could not fully digest the absurd. They had their limits determined by a healthy instinct of preservation, "which senses that one might get a hold of the truth *too soon*, before man has become strong enough, hard enough, artist enough" (B 59).[6]

Modern Western morality, on the other hand, led to the cultivation of the "hybrid European" (B 223). Rooted in decadence and hence antagonistic to any semblance of a natural order of rank, it found "a political formula, [in] Europe's *democratic* movement" (B 242). This movement represented "a tremendous *physiological* process" (B 242) of "a radical mixture of classes, and hence *races*" (B 208), leading "to the production of a type . . . prepared for *slavery*" (B 242). How would this type, "all in all, a tolerably ugly plebian" (B 223), cope with the truth that even healthy cultures had to have "thinned down?" (B 59). Doubtless, Nietzsche feared this culture of slaves would proceed to the logical consequence of all decadence: self-destruction.

Self-deception, error, and falsehood in the face of the absurd have been the means "without which a certain species of life could not live." Consequently, it is not a question of "Truth," or whether a morality is right or wrong per se; as always, the "value for *life* is ultimately decisive"

---

6. Even the strongest cultures that serve as the foundation for Western culture could not affirm life in the face of the absurd. However, Nietzsche envisioned a future in which Western culture might do precisely this.

(WP 493). The master morality of antiquity served to protect cultures from the absurd and at the same time helped them to say yes to the dark face of existence. This morality served "as an illusion of the species, designed to motivate the individual to sacrifice himself to the future" (WP 404).

By contrast, we moderns are the physiological product of two thousand years of slave morality, the fictions of which negate "all that is life-furthering, all that holds a guarantee of the future" (A 43). The "spirit" of early antiquity created "truths" essential to reverence for life in this world. That of modernity inspire flight from this world and sanction whatever contradicts the conditions of life. Hence, the essential distinction Nietzsche makes between healthy and decadent antiquity is not to be understood in terms of " 'truth' in struggle with life," but rather "*one kind of life in struggle with another*" (WP 592).

Since Western culture is the product of slave morality, it has cultivated a "spirituality" appropriate to "the instinct of decadence," through which "the exhausted and disinherited . . . take their revenge and play the master" (WP 401). This revaluation was regarded as "Truth" in the metaphysics of a decadent Greek culture and as "divine Truth" in Christianity. But "centuries of moral interpretation" (WP 5) have rendered the old death wish inherent to decadence unavoidable. Because our morality has preserved everything weak and sick and holds as "Truth" whatever contradicts life, Nietzsche believes modern humanity too debilitated to affirm life in the face of the absence of "Truth"; in the face of the absurd. Now the absurd, instinctively avoided by healthy antiquity, emerges before us with such lucidity that we are driven to despair.

This battle between "Truth" and the absurd represents the eye of the storm that is Nietzsche's philosophy. The former constitutes "everything men have heretofore respected and loved";[7] the latter, everything we have despised, that is, the idea that this world and our existence are the product of blind chaos. The history of "Truth" constitutes all the illusions that protected us from getting "a hold of the *truth too soon*" (B 59; emphasis added). When this history, "upon which a tremendous amount of energy has been lavished," is perceived as a compilation of illusions in the face of the absurd, then "Nihilism stands at the door." This "uncanniest of all guests" awakens "the suspicion that *all* interpretations of the world are false" (WP 1).

Of course all interpretations are "false," but "falsehood" and "error" are essential to life—degenerate or otherwise. Yet if we are "morally"

---

7. Nietzsche to Reinhardt von Seydlitz, February 12, 1888, SPL 106 (BKG III[5]:248).

compelled to deny falsehood in favor of "Truth," we are thereby *compelled to deny life*. This is what Nietzsche means in saying that nihilism is the historical phenomenon wherein we see "*the highest values devaluate themselves*" (WP 2). The best example of this devaluation is his description of the pursuit of "Truth" as a moral imperative. The collapse of this pursuit into the negation of its goal resides in the very sincerity of the pursuit itself. After "centuries of moral interpretation," one of the most powerful "forces cultivated by morality was *truthfulness*" (WP 5): the moral compulsion to pursue "Truth" at all costs. The moral necessity of "Truth" demands its affirmation as the path to the "improvement" of humanity.[8] But for Nietzsche, this is the road to despair.

Beginning with Greek metaphysics and throughout the history of Christianity, the foundation of "Truth" has resided not in this world but in that ideal, "Eternal" world wherein death, "change, age, as well as procreation and growth" were banished (T 4:1). In short, the "True world" of Greek metaphysics and the "heaven" of Christianity are illusions essential to the preservation of everything that wants out of this world. Yet the double legacy of decadent Greek and Christian "Truth" inevitably leads to the realization "that we lack the least right to posit a beyond or an in-itself of things that might be 'divine' or morality incarnate" (WP 3). In all honesty, that is, out of loyalty to the moral dictum to pursue the "Truth," we are forced to acknowledge that our faith in it is "fabricated solely from psychological needs" (WP 12). In short, everything that guarantees our eternal value and meaning is recognized as false. This is the paradox: the serpent eats its tail, the *telos* of "Truth" caves in, and we stand before "the ultimate logical conclusion of our great values and ideals" (WP pref.:4).

It is precisely at this point, Nietzsche says, that the "problem of the value of truth came before us—or was it we who came before the problem? Who of us is Oedipus here? Who the Sphinx? It is a rendezvous, it seems, of questions and question marks" (B 1). It is an extraordinary rendezvous. Suddenly the question emerges; why pursue "Truth" when it commands no moral necessity and reveals the ugliness this illusion was meant to conceal? The moral necessity to pursue "Truth" compels us to admit that the "True world" that sanctions this pursuit is "[u]nattained . . . at any rate. And if unattained also *unknown*. Consequently also no consolation, no redemption, no duty: how could we have a duty towards something unknown?" (T 5:3). Here is the other side of the paradox inherent to the pursuit of "Truth": It leads, on the

---

8. "Improvement" is understood here as making us "virtuous." "Truth" is conceived as the path to happiness, wisdom, and salvation.

one hand, to a recognition of "Truth" as a fiction, and thus we are morally compelled to deny it as falsehood. Yet insofar as it is seen as falsehood, we are morally compelled to *deny* the necessity of illusion "as a condition of life" (B 4).

And it is exactly here that we "discover in ourselves," says Nietzsche, needs "that now appear to us as needs for untruth; on the other hand, the value for which we endure life seems to hinge on these needs" (WP 5). This is the calling card of that "uncanniest of all guests," nihilism. Our moral duty to pursue the "Truth" brings us face to face with the human need "for untruth." Its pursuit has brought us to the point where we realize that the virtue of this pursuit rests on foundations that are fictions and illusions, that is, untruth. Yet we require fictions, those necessary deceptions that enable us to survive and grow. But modernity is schizophrenic with the "antagonism—*not* to esteem what we know, and not to be *allowed* any longer to esteem the lies we should like to tell ourselves" (WP 5).

The Ancient Death Wish

After centuries of believing in "Truth" at all costs, and to the extent that this belief has become an instinctive conviction, modernity finds itself incapable of affirming the necessity of illusion, because it still cleaves to "Truth," that is, the moral obligation to deny falsehood. This incapacity "results in a process of dissolution" (WP 5) that "may become a fatality" (WP 404) because, caught in the undertow of our convictions, the "aim is lacking; 'why?' finds no answer" (WP 2). Appalled at the falsehoods upon which humanity has ever attained real greatness, we are rendered impotent at the prospect of the future. We are, as it were, overwhelmed by our perception that indeed there is no "objective" guarantee of our value from the standpoint of a "real world" or a God "out there." And so this "real world" and the God who guaranteed the virtue, nobility, greatness, and very *telos* of the pursuit of "Truth" dissolve.

With this, the meaning and value of existence in this world becomes dubious. The "Truth" is dead, "God is dead," "Humanity" is dead, and the illusion of Western metaphysics is revealed. Where does one go from here? Why should we go on? God has passed away, and with Him, the "true world" of metaphysics. We are left with this world wherein all that is guaranteed is suffering, death, our insignificance, and our "accidental occurrence in the flux of becoming and passing away" (WP 4). In short, we find ourselves "confused by our split desire for freedom, beauty and greatness on the one hand and our drive toward truth on the other, a drive which asks merely 'And what is life worth, after all?' " (PTA 1:33; M 4:158).

"Truth" demands that we deny illusion as false, but life as will to power demands illusion as the means to its affirmation. Locked in this "spiritual" stalemate, the foundation for "a Yes, a No, a straight line, a *goal*" (A 1), is obliterated. In the age of nihilism everything that promised "freedom, beauty and greatness" has been a deception. And looking into the future, we see "human life . . . sunk deeply in untruth; the individual cannot draw it up out of this well without thereby growing profoundly disillusioned about his own past, without finding his present motives, such as that of honour, absurd, and pouring mockery and contempt on the passions which reach out to the future and promise happiness in it." When we look at the past as a great falsehood while staring into the abyss of truth as chaos, a terrible "question seems to lie heavily on our tongue and yet refuses to be uttered: whether one *could* consciously reside in untruth? or, if one were *obliged* to, whether death would not be preferable?" (HH 1:34).

Millennia of belief in the inherent goodness of "Truth" has, in its very pursuit, revealed "Truth" bereft of virtue and the good. Thus, the old foundation of "Truth" caves in. Everything that conferred meaning on the risk of death, the endurance of pain, great loneliness—in short, "*great* suffering" (B 225), is revealed as false. There is nothing worth living or dying for, and the future promises only falsehood as the basis for any such meaning. In light of this state of affairs, Nietzsche recognizes that the will to "Truth" "might be a concealed will to death" (GS 344).

The death wish inherent to the decadent "spirituality" of the West emerges as a *moral* obligation. The pursuit of "Truth" has led us to the sanctuary of the good and eternal, and we find it empty. Yet we still prefer "Truth" over myth, the "True" over appearance. Do we opt for illusion and myth? Nietzsche sees how this would be next to impossible, since we are too conscious of the fact that a new myth would not be "True." Thus, the desire for "Truth" is poisoned by our awareness of its being only a beautiful illusion. For Nietzsche, it is this *consciousness* that leads us to despair over our history and the future. We see that the past was built on "lies" and that the future requires yet more lies. At least when we still had faith in "Truth," we could go on into the future; but this faith is shattered; we are no longer naive. We have seen through "Truth," and the consciousness of this perception will no longer allow us to believe in the lies and illusions required for the future. With "Truth" destroyed, we ask, What is the meaning and value of existence when "Truth" is gone? Nietzsche expected us to answer, There is no meaning or value to existence without "Truth." Then, out of its self-hatred, *ressentiment*, and despair, he envisioned degenerate modernity lingering for a while in the ruins of "Truth," until inevitably, and for old time's sake, it does the "honorable" thing and self-destructs. This is not only the "logical conclusion of our great values and ideals" (WP pref.:4) but also the physiological requirement through which life as will to power "considerately—kills" (B 69).

This became Nietzsche's tortured vision of the future: a kind of "spiritual" holocaust wherein after centuries of a morality that presupposed revenge and *ressentiment* the ultimate act of revenge would occur as its logical consequence. The secret will to nothingness, like a worm coiled in the heart of Western morality, finally corrupts not only faith in "Truth" but, more important, our ability to create a new vision for the future.

What, in the end, is one to make of this strange reversal wherein "*the highest values devaluate themselves?*" I have shown that, for Nietzsche, illusion is absolutely essential to life. It is not only the means through which we have been able to feel at home in the world but also the path to revering ourselves and the world. He perceives we moderns far removed from the "naive clarity of conscience characteristic of pre-Socratic Greek philosophy" (HH 1:261).[9] Western culture followed every highway and byway to the "True" world and deified it in the guise of Christianity. With the demise of "Truth" comes the simultaneous negation of any transcendent meaning and value to existence. This ignites the secret death wish smoldering in Western morality. And it neither contemplates "the 'in vain!' nor is it merely the belief that everything deserves to perish: one helps to destroy." In the end, nihilists can only follow their creed "that everything deserves to perish," including the future. Their faith rests on the denial of faith in anything. "This is, if you will, illogical; but the nihilist does not believe that one needs to be logical" (WP 24). The nihilist's "Truth" is the necessity for the destruction of any semblance of "Truth."

This is reminiscent of Nietzsche himself, who made "a *grand declaration of war*" (T pref.) upon everything humanity has held dear for two thousand years. In him is a certain intoxication in the destruction of the foundation of the values of the West. Indeed, this is one of the most

---

9. Nietzsche says of the pre-Socratics, "Their attitude towards life is *naive*" (PT 52; M 4:243). Ultimately, the faith in life exhibited in pre-Socratic thought and culture rested on a certain naiveté, as if it were inconceivable that existence is fundamentally absurd. For them, the fictions they embraced were by no means "illusions." Yet the promise of power inherent to the fictions upon which a healthy Greek culture flourished had an intoxicating effect and were, at bottom, irresistible.

spellbinding features of his philosophy. There is a rage here that is directed at the failure of the two thousand years of Western "spirituality" he called "the pathos of 'in vain' " (WP 585). Out of this pathos he walks into the house of everything we have ever held sacred and finds only conceptual mummies. Thus, in the case of nihilism he regarded himself an authority: "the first perfect nihilist of Europe" (WP pref.:3).

The conviction of his expertise in this matter hinged on his having "lived through the whole of nihilism" (WP pref.:3). "I speak," he says, "only of what I have lived through, not merely of what I have thought through; the opposition of thinking and life is lacking in my case."[10] Nietzsche saw that the ground upon which Western culture built its ladder to eternal value and meaning was eroding. But this perception presupposed how he felt this erosion within himself. *The Gay Science* has a section entitled "From the seventh solitude," wherein Nietzsche, "the wanderer," says, "I often look back in wrath at the most beautiful things that could not hold me—*because* they could not hold me" (GS 309). Nihilism is something that happened to Nietzsche; God, "Truth," and "Humanity" had all died in him. And he saw that everything that once allowed individuals a sense of purpose and inspired the courage, bravery, and sacrifice required for culture turned out, in the end, to be nothing but a sham and disease.

Nietzsche once remarked that he and Lou Salomé shared that unique ability "to glean . . . many objective insights from personal experience."[11] His "personal experience" of nihilism forced him to confront the question "to what extent one can endure to live in a meaningless world" (WP 585). The human animal can endure any suffering as long as it can answer "the crying question, '*why* do I suffer?' " The answer has always been the means to avoiding "any kind of suicidal nihilism" (G 3:28). But when Nietzsche realized that the very answers to this question, "our great values and ideals," have all along been leading us into "a fearful *void*" (G 3:28), he anticipated "the history of the next two centuries" (WP pref.:2).

Nietzsche confronted "*the advent of nihilism*" within himself and, in so doing, found his way through the mansions of despair. This does not necessarily mean, however, that he managed to cure himself. Yet whether he did or not, he says he came through the disease of his age before anyone else. This victory led him to take on "the role of *cultural physician*" (PH 121; M 7:31), wherein he confronted nihilism: the sickness driving Western culture "toward a catastrophe, with a tortured

---

10. See note 1 above.
11. Nietzsche to Franz Overbeck, September 1882, SPL 67 (BKG III¹:254).

tension that is growing from decade to decade" (WP pref.:2). That is, Nietzsche sought to cure his culture from a disease it had inherited from infected antiquity. Success in this endeavor would, he hoped, allow for "faith in a tomorrow and the day after tomorrow . . . anticipation of a future, of impending adventures, of seas that are open again, of goals that are permitted again, believed again" (GS pref.:1).

This task indicates that we do an injustice to Nietzsche if we see his philosophical project as one devoted to destruction. In *Being and Time* Heidegger said it was necessary to destroy the history of ontology in order to begin anew, and hence "its aim is *positive*."[12] With regard to the necessity of the destruction of Western metaphysics, Nietzsche is, in this and in other instances, Heidegger's precursor.[13] The rage, despair, and, at times, ardent celebration of destruction in Nietzsche's texts may appeal to those who (whether from lack of nerve, imagination, or opportunity) cannot be "bad" very often and enjoy, therefore, a vicarious thrill when Nietzsche trashes tradition. Others not attracted to philosophical vandalism have rejected Nietzsche's philosophy as nihilism. I think those who get to be "irresponsible" via Nietzsche and those who despise his philosophy as nihilism fail to see the depth of responsibility he possessed, and in this they are bound to misunderstand his thinking. The destructive element in his diagnosis of the sources of modern decadence is only too apparent. But Nietzsche the physician does not stop at diagnosis any more than did his philosophical ancestor, Socrates.

Revaluation of All Values

Suffering and Its Discipline

If, as Nietzsche said, every philosophy is "the personal confession of its author" (B 6), then his task of healing the "spirit" of the West is a simultaneous attempt to heal himself. His battle with nihilism certainly led to a "brooding over the future of mankind,"[14] and this in conditions

---

12. Martin Heidegger, *Being and Time*, trans. John Macquarrie and Edward Robinson (New York: Harper & Row, 1962), 44.
13. Hans-Georg Gadamer said, "Heidegger may have realized . . . only later" that Nietzsche was his "true predecessor" in "going contrary to the whole direction of Western metaphysics" (*Truth and Method* [New York: Crossroad Publishing Co., 1982], 228).
14. Nietzsche to his mother, around July 9, 1881, *Nietzsche: Unpublished Letters*, 83 (BKG III¹:104).

that reveal a man simultaneously fighting for his life. In 1880 he described these conditions to a physician as "constant pain, a feeling much like seasickness several hours each day, a semi-paralysis which makes speaking difficult and . . . furious seizures (the last involved three days and nights of vomiting; I lusted for death)."[15] These afflictions, including serious eye problems, were not as severe in childhood, but he "was *constantly ill in some way after 1873*," his twenty-ninth year.[16] "I seem designed," he once said, "for lengthy torment and skewering over a slow flame."[17] Advancing blindness, and days and nights of headache and vomiting exacerbated by large doses of chloral hydrate,[18] led him to say "I've been, body and soul, more of a battlefield than a human being."[19]

Nietzsche's illness rendered him an invalid, and this only enhanced a sense of loneliness he had felt from "an absurdly early age" (E 2:10). In a letter to his friend Franz Overbeck he said: "If only I could give you some idea of my feeling of *isolation*. Neither among the living nor among the dead is there anyone with whom I feel any kinship. This is inexpressibly horrible; only the experience I've had, ever since I was a child, of living with this growing isolation makes it comprehensible why I haven't already been destroyed by it."[20] Elsewhere he speaks of experiencing "for years not a word of comfort, not a drop of human feeling, not a breath of love."[21] Loneliness was his most constant

---

15. Nietzsche to Dr. Otto Eiser, January 1880, SPL 51 (BKG III¹:3).
16. Karl Jaspers, *Nietzsche: An Introduction to the Understanding of His Philosophical Activity*, trans. Charles F. Wallraff and Frederick J. Schmitz (South Bend, Ind.: Regnery/Gateway, 1979), 89.
17. Nietzsche to Hans von Bülow, December 1882, SPL 69 (BKG III¹:290).
18. Nietzsche's experience as a medical orderly exposed him to the administration of various painkillers. This may have led to his experimentation with "all sorts of medicaments . . . [including] considerable quantities of chloral hydrate" (Jaspers, *Nietzsche: An Introduction*, 109). Nietzsche is said to have consulted over thirty physicians and physiologists in his lifetime (SPL 52n) and to have experimented with various combinations of drugs from 1875 on, in an attempt to treat himself (Jaspers, *Nietzsche: An Introduction*, 109). He even became convinced that atmospheric conditions played a significant role in his maladies. In a letter to Franz Overbeck (September 18, 1881) he said: "What months, what a summer I've had! My physical agonies were as many and various as the changes I have seen in the sky. In every cloud there is some form of electric charge which grips me suddenly and reduces me to complete misery. Five times I have called for Doctor Death, and yesterday I hoped it was the end—in vain" (SLN 179; BKG III¹:128–29). Again to Overbeck (February 10, 1883) he refers to himself as "the victim of a terrestrial and climatic disturbance, to which Europe is exposed. How can I help having an extra sense organ and a new, terrible source of suffering!" (SLN 206; BKG III¹:325).
19. Nietzsche to Peter Gast, July 25, 1882, SPL 64 (BKG III¹:230).
20. Nietzsche to Franz Overbeck, August 5, 1886, SPL 90 (BKG. III³:223).
21. Nietzsche to Reinhardt von Seydlitz, February 12, 1888, SPL 107 (BKG III⁵:249).

companion, and this was perhaps more painful than all of his physical ailments. Sick, alone, and bedridden, he told Overbeck: "I've lost interest in everything. Deep down, an unyielding black melancholy.... The worst of it is, I no longer see why I should live for even half a year more."[22] It is hardly surprising that, at times, Nietzsche found "the barrel of a revolver . . . a source of relatively pleasant thoughts."[23]

Though he was attracted, in the end Nietzsche fought the temptation to commit suicide.[24] He sought a way to endure the perception of his life devoid of meaning, a life wherein God and other "metaphysical comfort[s]" (WP 30) were as useful as the "knowledge of the chemical composition of water must be to the sailor in danger of shipwreck" (HH 1:9). And it was within the storm of constant illness and virtually unbearable loneliness that he saw the inadequacy of these "comforts" not only for himself but also for Western culture. His philosophy is indeed "the personal confession of its author" insofar as he sought to forge out some semblance of meaning in the face of unavoidable pain. The problem of the meaning of suffering fuels the violence of Nietzsche's attack on Greek metaphysics and Christianity. The former's "detestable pretension to happiness" (SSW 132; M 4:112) and the latter's preoccupation with "salvation of the soul" were so bereft of meaning in the midst of his own suffering that his rejection of both is riddled with fury (SSW 144; M 4:117).

On the island of sickness, occasionally tempted to remove himself "with a single stroke,"[25] Nietzsche felt the "Truths" of Western "spirituality" entombed within himself. In the company of these corpses, there could be no question of saying yes to life. But it was in this company that his philosophical task was galvanized. On the one hand was the destruction of the dead "spirituality" of the West, but on the other hand, this only had significance within his search for an interpretation through which he could love life in spite of his suffering. His philosophy

---

22. Nietzsche to Franz Overbeck, March 22, 1883, SPL 73 (BKG III⁵:348). He said this to Overbeck while he was waiting for the publication of book 1 of *Zarathustra*. He goes on to mention being "inexpressibly conscious of having bungled and botched my whole creative life." His prodigious creative powers would finally flame out almost six years later, after writing books 2, 3, and 4 of *Zarathustra*, *Beyond Good and Evil*, book 5 of *The Gay Science*, *The Genealogy of Morals*, *The Case of Wagner*, *Twilight of the Idols*, *The Anti-Christ*, *Ecce Homo*, *Nietzsche Contra Wagner*, as well as a huge quantity of notes (1883–88) never meant for publication but subsequently published by his sister under the title "The Will to Power."

23. Nietzsche to Franz Overbeck, February 10, 1883, SLN 206 (BKG III¹:326).

24. Ronald Hayman suggests that Nietzsche did, in a manner of speaking, commit suicide to the extent that he actually *chose* to go insane. See Hayman's *Nietzsche: A Critical Life* (New York: Penguin, 1984), 11, 341.

25. Nietzsche to his sister, May 7, 1885, BKG. III³:48; my translation.

is not merely an exercise in destruction or an attempt to reduce everything to the "clinical standpoint." Destruction, and its inherent "physiology," only make sense in terms of Nietzsche's confronting the meaning of suffering with a "pride that refused the *conclusions* of pain" (GS pref.:1).

When Western "spirituality" failed to provide him a single fragment of meaning in the midst of his own suffering, Nietzsche realized that this terrible experience was merely a forerunner of that reserved for future generations. "Only the day after tomorrow belongs to me," he said, "Some are born posthumously" (A pref.). His own experience of nihilism became a blueprint for that reserved "for the generation that is now coming" (B 55). In short, some day his own unique encounter with the dissolution of all meaning and purpose would eventually become commonplace.

Albert Camus said that in Nietzsche "nihilism becomes conscious for the first time."[26] Nietzsche saw how the "ice that still supports people today has become very thin; the wind that brings the thaw is blowing" (GS 377). Unlike his contemporaries, Nietzsche foresaw "the disappearance of the primitive foundation of all faith—namely, the belief in life."[27] How "many centuries," he asked, "does a spirit require to be comprehended?" (B 285). Nietzsche knew that his philosophy would find very few "ears listening today" (A pref.). "[M]y ideas," he said, "are so indescribably strange and dangerous that only much later (surely not before 1901) will anybody be ready for them."[28] Elsewhere he says, "[I]t may yet happen that one day whole millennia will make their most solemn vows in my name."[29]

This is the voice of a man who, from time to time, took refuge in living posthumously. Nietzsche's sense of isolation was only enhanced by what, more and more, seemed a philosophical task reserved for himself alone: the monumental challenge of confronting nihilism within both himself and his epoch. Hence, "a philosophy like mine," he said, "is like a tomb—it seals one off from the living."[30] The revaluation of all values[31] is the name of the battle he fought against the "spiritual" disease of nihilism. It rendered him "something decisive and ominous standing between two millennia," and he was "constantly made to pay

26. Albert Camus, *The Rebel*, trans. Anthony Bower (New York: Vintage, 1956), 65.
27. Ibid., 66.
28. Nietzsche to Malwida von Meysenbug, May 12, 1887, SPL 99 (BKG III^5:70).
29. Nietzsche to Malwida von Meysenbug, May 1884, SPL 81 (BKG III^1:510).
30. Nietzsche to Georg Brandes, December 2, 1887, SPL 104 (BKG III^5:207).
31. Hereafter referred to simply as the revaluation.

for such a singular position—with an ever growing, ever more glacial, ever more piercing seclusion."[32]

Out of this haunting isolation and with his eye on nothing less than the future of the human race, Nietzsche conceived the revaluation as a twofold philosophical agenda. First, he set out to *destroy* faith in the values he knew would sustain neither himself nor tomorrow's generations. Second, he sought a means to *restore* the strength humankind would require to once again say a yes to life and recapture the vitality that had been undermined by the instincts of decadence. This twofold task was "the revaluation of all values," which, under the rubric of physiology, would allow the human race to overcome the problem of the meaning of suffering after its traditional reservoirs of meaning had utterly evaporated.

There is no mystery here. The problem of keeping faith in life in the midst of suffering was an urgent one for Nietzsche. He witnessed within himself the decomposition of the traditional foundations through which life had been affirmed for two thousand years. Yet when he saw how the values adhered to by his culture only sanctioned the pleasures promised by "the barrel of a revolver," he revealed great psychological tenacity. That is, he did not kill himself but went in search for the means to sustain faith in life.

Clearly, this faith is not a belief in yet another deity that, handing out eternal rewards and punishments, serves as a transcendent justification for the cosmos and all that takes place therein. No, this is a faith that directly confronts the absence of any such deity or cosmic underpinning through which the human race can affirm meaning, value, and purpose. It is a faith that, no matter how excruciatingly lonely it becomes or how many and intense the sources of suffering are, one will revere and want to be worthy of life. And one will only be worthy when, in the midst of great suffering, life itself is never betrayed by blaming or hating it *because* one suffers and understands that one will continue to suffer. On the contrary, one can laugh with *amor fati* and dance with death; and though one might mock them, there is no hate for those who are unworthy: those who, in seeking merely to preserve themselves, commit the blasphemy of cursing life out of *ressentiment*. In short, such a faith stands firmly on the side of life, which, as will to power, opens up "every feeling of reverence and distance between man and man" (A 43) and, as the path to an order of rank, "makes noble; it separates" (B 270).

---

32. Nietzsche to Reinhardt von Seydlitz, February 12, 1888, SPL 106 (BKG III[5]:248).

Nihilism: A "Spiritual" Disease

But to reestablish faith in life and therewith the possibility of a healthy order of rank, the physician had to clarify the physio-psychological dynamics characteristic of those most infected by the disease he vowed to fight. To this end, Nietzsche looked at himself and saw the type of the nihilist, the poisoned individual who would flourish in the future unless definite measures were taken. Adopting his clinical standpoint, he said we take the first step toward nihilism "as a psychological state . . . when we have sought a 'meaning' in all events that is not there." In the face of this absence it becomes clear that "becoming has no goal," and one is discouraged by the "recognition of the long *waste* of strength, the agony of the 'in vain' . . . as if one had *deceived* oneself all too long." Nihilism "as a psychological state is reached, *secondly*," when we see "that underneath all becoming there is no grand unity in which the individual could immerse himself completely as in an element of supreme value." Here the traditional, transcendent foundation of "Truth" or God, both of which have been essential to our "deep feeling of standing in the context of, and being dependent on, some whole . . . infinitely superior" to ourselves, has evaporated in the very pursuit of "Truth." Upon this dissolution the individual loses the old standard for measuring value and quickly loses "faith in his own value" (WP 12).

Finally, there is "yet a *third* and *last* form" of nihilism. Following the two insights above, "the last form of nihilism comes into being: it includes disbelief in any metaphysical world and forbids itself any belief in a *true* world." Here the individual realizes "justice," the "holy," the "good," as well as the concepts of " 'aim,' 'unity,' 'being' which we used to project some value into the world"; all *"refer to a purely fictitious world"* (WP 12). Now the "Real World" at last becomes a myth (T 5). This is a strange state of affairs. For Nietzsche, the *creation of fictions* is the domain of "spirit." It is that physiological function by means of which the cumulative perspective of our drives falsifies, that is, "interprets" the world in whatever way affirms this perspective. If this perspective is healthy—that is, symptomatic of an order of rank among the drives dominated by powerful life-affirming instincts—then the organism creates the deceptions through which it may grow in strength. If this order of rank is lacking, the fictions created are symptomatic of exhaustion, decadence, and illness.

The disease of nihilism may appear to hinge on our culture's recognition of "Truth" and God as "fictions," that is, as false or meaningless. But this recognition only indicates a threat to culture. The physician will determine whether a culture is infected by the disease of nihilism by looking at how it meets this threat. Other cultures have endured the collapse of "spiritual" paradigms but still had the means to create new deceptions, new interpretations that allowed for cultural transformation and growth. Such means were available, for example, to the pre-Socratics, who emerged after the demise of the mythopoeic tradition. These "spiritual tyrants" had their "truths," the new deceptions that, in the face of a dying "spiritual" paradigm, represented new interpretations as the possible means to growth in the future. Of course, the pre-Socratics were, at best, a remarkable failure. But more important, these philosophers embodied the reserved strength cultivated by a highly disciplined and ruthlessly maintained order of rank. This order is fundamental to "that economy in the law of life" (T 6:6) through which "the acquired and stored-up energies of many generations have not been squandered" (WP 995).

In the case of nihilism, the physiological conditions essential to creating new interpretations for the future have already been seriously jeopardized. Metaphysics and Christianity rely on fictions determined by the perspective of a dominating instinct of preservation in alliance with the instincts of decadence. These fictions draw their creative energy from the power of *ressentiment*, through which everything antagonistic to life has been preserved. Fundamental to this preservation has been the instinctive hatred of anything essential to health, namely, an order of rank, the means of building up the strength that is required when "spiritual" paradigms cave in. The recognition that "Truth" is an illusion constitutes, therefore, only the *threat* of nihilism; the *event* of nihilism as an historical phenomenon resides in the *physiological inability* to meet this danger.

Nihilism is, therefore, a "spiritual" disease in the strictly physiological sense. On the one hand, with the collapse of the great self-preservative fiction of "Truth," the fiction essential to preserving everything degenerate within our culture also dissolves. On the other hand, the maintenance of this fiction has been possible only through negating the physiological pre-condition for creating new fictions, that is, an order of rank. Now, when the function of "spirit" requires the strength to create new interpretations for growth upon the demise of "Truth," it lacks the power that only an order of rank among the instincts of a culture can generate for precisely such an emergency. And so the cultural organism pays the price for having been solely guided by self-preservation—it is ripe for destruction.

The healthy cultures of antiquity met this emergency time and again. But we moderns are the heirs of strictly self-preservative illusions that, when they collapse, leave us nauseated and repulsed at exactly what life as will to power demands of us—the necessity to create the fictions through which we can say yes to life. This yes is not reducible to the instinct of self-preservation, important as it is. We need to *grow*; and this is only possible when the instincts that risk destruction of the organism for the sake of power dominate the instinct of preservation within an order of rank. But precisely these powerful instincts have been systematically undermined for two millennia. Without the perspectives of these drives within the cultural organism, it becomes dysfunctional in exploiting the destruction of "Truth" toward new interpretations that affirm life. And it is here that the dominance of mere preservation finally reaches its physiological conclusion in nihilism.

Life as will to power requires the destruction of whatever is degenerate. A nihilistic culture will affirm the dark side of this ancient law when, "spiritually" paralyzed and exhausted by the demands of growth in power, it takes the final road on its sojourn toward the ultimate stability of death. When "Truth" is seen to be a fiction, the will to power manifest in the physiological function of "spiritualizing" the world via the instincts does not cease. With the collapse of the very fiction through which everything degenerate has survived, the cultural organism is radically destabilized. Lacking the reserved power that only an order of rank can provide, the old instinct of preservation, the first instinct of "spirit," once again draws from the wellsprings of *ressentiment* and typically asserts its perspective in an attempt to regain stability. But this time it creates the illusion essential to the death wish that always emerges when an organism has sought merely to preserve itself. In a state of siege, it must have some new interpretation in order to find some semblance of equilibrium.

Once upon a time, the instinct of preservation created the fiction of timeless, deathless "Truth" or God as the transcendent ground for all values. When this foundation implodes, preservation once again naturally falsifies the world so that the organism can regain its balance. But in such a decadent organism, the instinct of preservation displays the overall exhaustion and weakness it has so efficiently preserved. In the desire for stability, and stimulated by the chaos unleashed by the collapse of "Truth" and the horrible vision of the absurd, it imposes a fiction through which the death of "Truth" can be overcome. And here it resorts to the strength through which it has always maintained its dominance—the *ressentiment* of the instincts of decadence. Now the old hatred of everything fundamental to affirming life is channeled into yet another self-preservative fiction, and it "selects" yet another eternal, transcendent "Truth," namely, that the world is "False in-itself." This fiction is characteristic of an organism only capable of affirming decadence. Naturally, what it "selects" to maintain the hatred of life through which it has flourished will be a deception that is in accord with the negation of life. Yet in selecting this fiction it also affirms the dark face of life as will to power, and the destruction of what is degenerate is at hand.

Now the organism only realizes purpose and meaning by destroying everything that bears the vestiges of the old "Truth." The sheer hatred of life typical of decadence realizes its ultimate goal in the fiction of a world that is devoid of value because there is no "Truth." The ultimate revenge on life is finally sanctioned with the fiction of a world that is inherently false. Here the ancient hatred of life, with all of its "virtues," can be "preserved" only in the righteous duty of slaughtering everything that can even begin to say yes to life. Everywhere there is nothing but falsehood and deception—a world that is "Untruth." And in accord with the new deception, everything becomes a candidate for execution. This is nihilism, the disease that Nietzsche experienced first and foremost. But having found his way through this illness, he was haunted by a future wherein this sickness would reach epidemic proportions.

Plans and Preparations

Nietzsche's experience of the void of nihilism reveals an extremely lonely and remarkably ferocious psychological struggle. Under the banner of his ill-fated revaluation of all values, he dug in for war and attempted a coherent and sustained assault on nihilism. This "gospel of the future" (WP pref.:4) was never completed. There is even some suggestion that it was never actually begun. Nietzsche's joy in writing outlines for works never written has led to some confusion. In a preface (written between November 1887 and March 1888) for *The Will to Power: Attempt at a Revaluation of All Values*, he refers to this projected work as a "countermovement" to nihilism (WP pref.:4). In the fall of 1888, he planned a work, comprising four "books," entitled "Revaluation of All Values." Book 1 he called "The Anti-Christ: Attempt at a Critique of Christianity"; book 2, "The Free Spirit: Critique of Philosophy as a Nihilistic Movement"; book 3, "The Immoralist: Critique of the Most Fatal Kind of Ignorance, Morality"; and book 4, "Dionysus: Philosophy of Eternal Recurrence."[33] In a sketch for a letter to Overbeck (February 3, 1888), he said, "The first draft of my '[Revaluation] of all Values' is finished" (SLN 282n). Elsewhere he refers to *The Anti-Christ* as "the first

---

33. Walter Kaufmann, *Nietzsche: Philosopher, Psychologist, Antichrist* (New York: Vintage, 1968), 113–14. See M 18:358.

volume of the *Revaluation of all Values*."³⁴ Kaufmann regards *The Anti-Christ* as "the first and only finished part of the *Revaluation*."³⁵ Others have said that Nietzsche's "frequently modified plans" during the fall of 1888 "cast doubt on the relationship of . . . [*The Anti-Christ*] to a larger project" (SPL 126n). But if the plan above, as well as his correspondence, is any indicator, it seems only book 1 was written.

Nietzsche's correspondence indicates he conceived of the revaluation between 1887 and 1888 as a definite philosophical task. And his conceptions of eternal recurrence, the overman, and the symbol of Dionysus were integral to the revaluation and his "pressing need . . . to create a coherent structure of thought during the next few years."³⁶ Who knows, perhaps if his creative life had not been destroyed we could have heard more about his "great new tidings."³⁷

Though there are plans for a work entitled "Revaluation of all Values" and he speaks of it in his late correspondence and texts, its roots go back in Nietzsche's thought long before it became a pet project. Its destructive element, for example, the attacks on Socrates and Christianity, go back to his earliest works.³⁸ The constructive side is also anticipated in the early works, but by the time of *Zarathustra*, it is articulated in terms of a new nobility that, as "cultivators and sowers of the future," press their hands "upon millennia as upon wax" (Z 3:12). The revaluation hinges on Nietzsche's concern with the "uncanny preconditions of cultural growth, the extremely questionable relation between what's called 'improvement' of mankind . . . and the elevation of the species Man." This relation is characterized "above all [by] the contradiction between every moral and scientific view of life."³⁹

The "scientific view of life" is Nietzsche's clinical standpoint and the method inherent to determining the physiological dynamics of ascending and descending organisms. The task of creating the conditions in which the "elevation of the species Man" becomes at least possible demands a physiological revaluation of the dynamics of the body and is, in principle, opposed to the very morality essential to the disease of

---

34. Nietzsche to Franz Overbeck, October 18, 1888, SPL 126 (BKG III⁵:453).
35. Kaufmann, *Nietzsche: Philosopher, Psychologist, Antichrist*, 114.
36. Nietzsche to Franz Overbeck, March 24, 1887, SLN 264–65 (BKG III⁵:49).
37. Nietzsche to Jakob Burckhardt, September 22, 1886, SPL 91 (BKG III³:255).
38. *The Birth of Tragedy* is a precursor to the more intense campaign against Socrates found in Nietzsche's later texts. And Christianity, along with virtually everything "German," is assaulted in the *Untimely Meditations*. These texts are also fraught with the more constructive features of the revaluation, especially where the future of culture is concerned.
39. Nietzsche to Jacob Burckhardt, September 22, 1886, SPL 91 (BKG III³:254).

nihilism in the first place. Thanks to the rigor of his clinical standpoint, Nietzsche arrived at his celebrated *"diagnosis of the modern soul."* The diagnosis showed that the values of decadent antiquity poisoned the original health of Western culture to the point where we "have, unconsciously, involuntarily in our bodies values, words, formulas, moralities of *opposite* descent—we are, physiologically considered, *false*" (C epilogue).

To fight the disease is to battle the life-destroying morality fundamental to it. And here the physician must be ever vigilant: he cannot afford to indulge in even the remotest semblance of the morality that has poisoned the patient. In short, he must be as cold-blooded as any warrior confronted with a deadly enemy and destroy with absolutely no pity. "One should not want to be physician to the incurable: thus Zarathustra teaches" (Z 3:12). On the contrary, what is "incurable" must be ruthlessly carved out of the body of culture. Consequently, the revaluation "may well be the most dangerous venture there is, not for the one who dares to express it but for the one to whom it is addressed."[40] In short, talk about a revaluation of all values is cheap; actually carrying out the task is to take the greatest risk. It means that the physician, in his attempt to create the possibility for health in the human species, must stand directly opposed to the values that for two thousand years have defined a truly human being. Here the old dictum to "love thy neighbor" gives way to the "great love for the most distant men: *Do not spare your neighbour!*" (Z 3:12).

As a physician of culture, Nietzsche was condemned to combat within himself everything that marked him as "a child of this time; that is, a decadent" (C pref.). In setting out to destroy the remaining foundations of the values of his age, he made war on every vestige of these within himself and came to "know the truth as something that one has to tear, piece by piece, from one's heart, every victory taking its revenge in a defeat" (see SLN 282n). This is the meaning of becoming "untimely, that word understood in the profoundest sense" (U 3:2). The sickness of nihilism inherent to what Western culture called salvation was revealed to Nietzsche as an illness come to fruition in himself. And like Socrates, "he grasped . . . *his* case, the idiosyncrasy of his case"; and herein lay his prophetic powers. In short, he saw the "same kind of degeneration . . . everywhere silently preparing itself"; the Europe of his forefathers, like Socrates' Athens, "was coming to an end" (T 3:9).

The revaluation, therefore, is the name of Nietzsche's passion to defeat the specter of meaningless pain and death through reestablishing

40. Ibid.

an order of rank (WP 854) for a culture "spiritually" deranged. And one "must have seen the fatality from close up, better still one must have experienced it in oneself, one must have almost perished by it, no longer to find anything funny here" (A 8). In the face of "such a task," Nietzsche says, "I required a special self-discipline: to take sides against everything sick in me." The revaluation is the first rung on the ladder of cruelty, a cruelty Nietzsche directed at "all of modern 'humaneness' " (C pref.) both within himself and his epoch. The pre-Socratics, the finest, healthiest tyrants of the "spirit," were able to pass judgment on individuals and whole cultures. They determined what deserved to live and to die so that their culture might realize new "spiritual" frontiers upon the death of the old. The revaluation is in accord with Nietzsche's view of philosophy as this most "spiritual" will to power, the attempt to cultivate a new "spiritual" homeland for the future. The pre-Socratics were naive by being unconscious of their function as healers. Nietzsche was quite conscious of philosophy in this role, and in contemplating the revaluation he said it "may be a strange and insane task, but it is a *task*—who would deny that?" (B 230). In such a task he found a meaning and purpose within his own suffering beyond nihilism, not only for himself but for the generations to come. Wanting nothing less than to find himself *inter pares* with the first monarchs of philosophy, he waged war against everything degenerate within himself and his epoch. And typical of the pride he identified with the pre-Socratics, the task of the revaluation allowed him a "profound estrangement, cold sobering up . . . [and] an eye that beholds the whole fact of man at a tremendous distance—below." In light of "such a goal," Nietzsche asks, "what sacrifice wouldn't be fitting? what 'self-overcoming'? what 'self-denial'?" (C pref.).

The Risk of Innocence

Is it possible to affirm life devoid of a divine witness to one's pain? Can there be joy in a life shorn of transcendent guarantees that our loneliness and suffering are somehow meaningful? In the midst of his contemporaries, Nietzsche was convinced that, like him, they were infected by the sickness that makes a positive response to these questions virtually impossible. On the contrary, he saw an age in which a yes to these questions was the mark of the damned—especially if it meant carving from ourselves everything that once defined us as human. The idea of preserving himself for relentless physical torment while convinced that at the foundation of all value and meaning for Western culture was a grinning death mask was hardly an inspiring prospect. "I love," Zarathustra says, "those who do not wish to preserve themselves" (Z 3:12), and Nietzsche, choosing the path of self-vivisection in the attempt to cure himself, turned to "what mankind has always hated, feared and despised the most—and precisely out of this I've made my 'gold.' "[41]

The revaluation moves, not away from suffering, but rather straight into its darkest depths. This most profound suffering is the vision of the absurdity of existence, wherein all hope for escape is cut off.[42] Every inclination he found in himself to find solace in what "men have heretofore respected and loved" appeared as the path to despair.[43] Hence, these avenues were closed to him. But rather than remain in the dead world of Western "spirituality," he chose to "live dangerously." He took the risk of stepping into the chaos where all foundations are gone, where all ideas of a transcendent meaning to life are naive. There he sought an unconditional yes to life and exposed himself to what he could least afford: nihilism.

This was the means the physician saw to cure himself. If he remained attached to the values of his age, then he should take his cue from Socrates, "who handed himself the poison cup" (T 3:12). Thus, he only had one option—going through the illness of nihilism. If he was to have a viable cure for sickness, then experience was the best teacher. In short, he had to cure himself before he could cure his culture. And "out there," far from the virtues and convictions of his age, Nietzsche embraced an insight essential to his recovery. It occurred to him that life was neither meaningful nor meaningless. To insist on it one way or the other betrayed a certain *ressentiment*. To demand that life have a meaning in itself is to say no to it, because life is growth and must shed all interpretations of itself within the vortex of becoming. Then again, to insist that it is meaningless in itself is the no of those angry at life for having taken their meaning away.

Humanity broke solidarity with the earth in ardently pursuing the "virtues" of the "True World" and the "Beyond" wherein God resided. In fully experiencing nihilism, one recognizes that the "True World" is

---

41. Nietzsche to Georg Brandes, May 23, 1888, SPL 118 (BKG III^5:318).

42. This is reminiscent of Albert Camus's statement, "For me the sole datum is the absurd" (Camus, *The Myth of Sisyphus*, trans. Justin O'Brien, [Harmondsworth, Middlesex: Penguin, 1977], 34). Camus's works reveal this datum as a "confrontation and unceasing struggle." Henri Peyre says of Camus, "The thinker to whom he owed most of his early training, and even unto the last, was Nietzsche" (Peyre, "Presence of Camus," in *Critical Essays on Albert Camus*, ed. Bettina L. Knapp [Boston: G. K. Hall, 1988], 24). And in his confrontation with the absurd, "Camus's choice is for Nietzsche's everlasting 'yes' " (ibid., 27).

43. Nietzsche to Reinhardt von Seydlitz, February 12, 1888, SPL 106 (BKG III^5:248).

"an idea no longer of any use, not even a duty any longer—an idea grown useless, superfluous, *consequently* a refuted idea: let us abolish it!" (T 5:5). Here, the typical nihilist despairs at finding him- or herself trapped in a world wherein "the character of existence is not 'true,' is *false*" (WP 12). Nietzsche saw, however, that judging this world as false only makes sense insofar as it presupposes the "True World." Thus, nihilists must at least have the courage of their convictions. By insisting that this world is false, one still hankers, at bottom, after the dead world of "Truth." The old opposition, the old sickness, remains, and hence what nihilists "select as an expedient, as a deliverance, is itself only another expression of *décadence*—they *alter* its expression, they do not abolish the thing itself" (T 3:11). But "the first perfect nihilist of Europe" went further. Since the "True World" is abolished, Nietzsche asked, "what world is left? the apparent world perhaps? . . . But no! *with the real world we have also abolished the apparent world!*" (T 5:6).[44]

By pushing the insight of nihilism to its furthest extreme, Nietzsche saw that the destruction of the "True World" undermined all the dichotomies inherent to the physiology "*of the modern soul*" (C epilogue). Through subjecting himself to the worst possible visions of nihilism, he recognized the simple and "astonishing *finesse, that the value of life cannot be estimated*" (T 3:2). The "True World" is no more, and with its demise, comes that of the merely "apparent" and "false" world. In this, Nietzsche glimpsed "the seductive flash of gold on the belly of the serpent *vita*" (WP 577). He saw the human race riding this serpent, calling it good, evil, meaningful, and meaningless in the attempt to command it. But the serpent goes where it will, not for revenge or love of humanity but because it is life—forever on its way to transformations of power in *all* of its forms. And the human creature, so enmeshed in the dynamics of life is "its object, and not judge of it" (T 3:2).

Yet we *must* judge life—that is, create the deceptions necessary for survival and growth. We "spiritualize" our world in the teeth of chaos, thereby creating a "world" within which we can grow in power. In this we live the cosmological law of life as the lust to command all things. But "value judgments concerning life, for or against, can in the last resort never be true: they . . . come into consideration only as symptoms" (T 3:2). They are symptomatic of the treacherous battle between our drive-perspectives and reveal the individual's *rank* within life as will to power. In short, judgments on life, for or against, are symptomatic of the health or sickness of the judge. He or she cannot express the character of life in its totality; "no one could do it; one cannot judge,

---

44. The ellipsis points are Nietzsche's.

measure, compare the whole, to say nothing of denying it! Why not? . . . *because nothing exists besides the whole*" (WP 765). The very possibility of affirming or denying life presupposes it. These judgments express the will to power of either ascending or descending drives. One way or the other, we cannot jump out of our skin; as *living*, we remain a hunger for what is always unnamed in the midst of transformation.

Like all living things, we are the experiment of life on the path of transformation or obliteration. In pushing the vision of the absurd to extremes, Nietzsche saw humanity as a child of becoming and, like the stars, neither justified nor unjustified. We "are *not* the product of an attempt to achieve an ideal 'of perfection' or an 'ideal of happiness' or an 'ideal of virtue.' " On the contrary, there "is no place, no purpose, no meaning, on which we can shift the responsibility for our being" (WP 765). But here, rather than collapse into nihilistic despair, Nietzsche's perception of the twofold destruction of the "True World" and "False World" showed him the path to a "Yes, a sacred Yes" (Z 1:1). Why cast aspersions on life? There is no cosmic conspiracy against us, nor is there a God to confer a meaning to suffering. Why take revenge on life because it lacks a transcendent goal or purpose? And why insist that it possess this transcendent foundation? Is it not enough, more than enough, to suffer, love, and live in the midst of the beauty and horror of "the *innocence of becoming*" (WP 552)?

Nietzsche saw that personal happiness and suffering, including that of the whole history of the human race, do not constitute arguments for or against life. Such arguments betray "the *hyperbolic naiveté* of man: positing himself as the meaning and measure of the value of things." Our interpretations "are, psychologically considered, the results of certain perspectives of utility, designed to maintain and increase human constructs of domination" (WP 12). And trying to stop interpreting our world is like trying to avoid breathing. Our happiness, suffering, and judgments of "life," pro or contra, are nothing within the totality of endless becoming.

The perception of the utter indifference of the cosmos to the human animal can drive this animal to despair and nihilism. But Nietzsche looked upon the turbulent ocean of becoming and found, not a reason for suicide, but a new vision of himself and, indeed, of the whole human race. There was humanity, that unique form of will to power wherein life articulates itself. There was life trying to capture itself within interpretations torn asunder as soon as they were rendered. In this Nietzsche saw himself and his fellow creatures inextricably unified to a terrifying and majestic innocence. We have created values, laws and gods; through these we have created cultures, the sense of cosmos within chaos. In this we have followed the path of all life toward transformation. These "homelands" have sheltered us from the absurd, and even the strongest types of Greek and Hebrew antiquity needed this shelter. Nietzsche saw that these old forms of "spirit," these old deceptions once so necessary, had long ago run their course. The old "virtue" was at an end, and this opened up exhilarating prospects and "a tremendous restorative; this constitutes the innocence of all existence" (WP 765).

The death of God is not a call to despair but a call to "a new beginning" (Z 1:1) and a sign of release from the bondage of values steeped in *ressentiment*. Thus, "the innocence of becoming gives us the *greatest courage* and the *greatest freedom!*" (WP 787). By leaping into the volcano of becoming, we regain the innocence we lost in positing God as our shield from life. We do not need the old code of good and evil, because we find ourselves exactly where we have always been: in the innocence of all creation. In this Nietzsche saw us on the threshold of a freedom terrifying to behold. The old God and code of good and evil are gone. "The sea is stormy," says Zarathustra; "everything is at sea." And if we are to secure a future, then we have to create it without an a priori cosmic blueprint. We must take the side of life and follow its most dangerous pathway, that of experiment—and "[a]las, with what protracted searching and succeeding, and failing and learning and experimenting anew!" (Z 3:12). If we have a future, we have to create, and to create is to experiment. We have to risk destruction and understand that as creators *everything is permitted*.

The innocence of becoming is not, therefore, a sweet vision of humanity surrounded by light, reclining angelically on clouds of perfection. On the contrary, from the standpoint of the old morality, this innocence constitutes evil incarnate. For Nietzsche, if we continue to "crucify the whole human future" (Z 3:12) through the values that have already poisoned us, then evil and the ruthlessness of the Devil himself are the antidote for this poison both within ourselves and our culture. The revaluation is this antidote; it provides no Ten Commandments or step-by-step formula for determining good and evil. But neither is the revaluation "value-free." On the contrary, the intense necessity that Nietzsche identified with it is derived from an appeal to something of value: "the value for life is ultimately decisive." But since life is itself forever on the way to transformation in all of its forms, its value *"cannot be estimated."* The value to which Nietzsche's revaluation of all values is appealing is life, but now liberated from the illness that denies its innocence within constant transformation.

At bottom, the revaluation is an appeal to health—a health manifest in a profound faith in life that does not require a standpoint outside of life from which its value can be measured, a faith that hinges on the capacity to affirm our unity with life and disdains self-preservative guarantees of eternal rewards or punishments. Life is *overcoming:* the transformation and constant experiment with itself toward new expressions of power. As for ourselves, we are enmeshed in the nexus of this experiment and share the destiny of all living things. If we maintain the values through which we have poisoned life, we are doomed to oblivion. But what if we take a chance, risk failure and death, without heed to the decadent, self-preservative fictions through which we have avoided the resistance, suffering, and destruction that life requires? For Nietzsche, life is innocent in these requirements for growth; the question for the physician is, Are we worthy of them, or have we been sick for so long that ours is the fate of cowards? In attempting to eradicate the values of decadence, the revaluation is the means of awakening us to our origins as will to power. It constitutes the experiment of restoring us to the innocence of becoming, thereby liberating us to the will to power we are. In short, it grants us the terrible freedom inherent to all life—to create ourselves "beyond good and evil." By affirming experiment, we affirm our unity with life as overcoming and answer the call of the "conscience behind your 'conscience,' " that with "a prehistory in your instincts" (GS 335).

The revaluation portrays a Nietzsche similar to Zarathustra: "Here I sit and wait, old shattered law-tables around me and also new, half-written law-tables" (Z 3:12). On the one hand, the old laws have been shattered, but those of the future are, as it were, half-written fragments. I noted above that the revaluation is a twofold philosophical task, that is, both destructive and constructive. What require destruction are "the many vain and overly enthusiastic interpretations . . . that have so far been scrawled and painted over that eternal basic text of *homo natura*" (B 230). These interpretations have been, for the most part, determined by the values of decadence. What is to be constructed is a restoration of faith in life. The hallmark of such faith is our capacity to "spiritualize" the world so that we can not only preserve ourselves but grow in power. "Spirit" is the means of saying yes to life and is exemplified in the healthy epochs of the Greek and Hebrew cultures. But since decadence had poisoned the "spirit" of Western culture, Nietzsche had serious doubts that the revaluation could restore its health.

One thing was clear to him: if health was to be cultivated for our culture, certain physiological criteria must be met.

Eternal Recurrence

A Cosmic Therapy

"[I]t's going *very* badly," Nietzsche told his friend Overbeck. "My health is back to where it was three years ago. Everything is wrecked. . . . What a life! And I'm the great affirmer of life!!"[45] These were his words just as *Zarathustra*, the book he later said carried the doctrine of eternal recurrence[46] as its "fundamental conception" (E Z:1), was about to be published. "I do not wish to live *again*," he said in a note while writing *Zarathustra*.[47] Yet in his battle against all that within himself said no to life, Nietzsche took on the burdensome thought of recurrence. "How have I borne life? By creating. What has made me endure? The vision of the Overman who affirms life. I have tried to affirm life *myself*—but ah!"[48]

Nietzsche saw recurrence as a possibility that, if taken to heart, might plant the seeds for the type of the overman, the one who could endure what at times drove Nietzsche to despair. "All this overcoming of self, all this endurance—what good has it ever done me?"[49] This is the voice of a man in pain. But through it all, and under "the pressure of a great passion and a great project" that was, at times, "too enormous,"[50] Nietzsche weighed the possibilities for "a *different* kind of spirit from that likely to appear in this present age" (G 2:24). This "spirit" he described with the "word 'overman,' as the designation of a type of supreme achievement" (E 3:1).

When he embraced recurrence, Nietzsche entered into what I have called a process of dehumanization, that is, a systematic destruction of the insidious infection of nihilism within himself. There were times when he could not affirm life and love it *no matter what*. In the background loomed the remarkable failure of the first great cultural physician, Socrates, who, in the attempt to save his beloved Athens, only promoted the illness of the age. To avoid this great danger and yet maintain his authority as a physician of culture, Nietzsche had to confront his own infection. That is, he had to cut into the "human, all

---

45. Nietzsche to Franz Overbeck, February 22, 1883, SPL 72 (BKG III¹:337).
46. Hereafter referred to simply as recurrence.
47. The translation is from Erich Heller's "Zarathustra's Three Metamorphoses: Facets of Nietzsche's Intellectual Biography and the Apotheosis of Innocence," in his *Importance of Nietzsche: Ten Essays* (Chicago: University of Chicago Press, 1988), 78 (WKG 7:139).
48. Ibid.
49. Nietzsche to Paul Rée, end of January, 1880, SPL 52 (BKG III¹:7).
50. Nietzsche to Carl Von Gersdorff, December 20, 1887, SPL 106 (BKG III⁵:214).

too human," within himself, and he began by carving from his heart whatever marked him as "a child of this time; that is, a decadent" (C pref.). To cleave to the human within himself was to submit to the death wish that was luring his own epoch into the abyss. Nietzsche was therefore driven into taking a stand against anything in himself that whispered, "I do not wish to live *again*." The task of pointing the human race toward the path of health was, he said, fraught with "indescribable sadness."[51] Turning his back on everything "in which formerly we may have found our humanity" (GS pref.:3), he started down a road full of those silent, private dangers of self-doubt and hopelessness. Here Nietzsche said he was lonely "and deeply suspicious of myself" because he had to take "sides *against* myself and *for* anything that happened to hurt me and was hard for me."[52]

For him, recurrence was a process of self-vivisection. The very idea of the hopeless repetition of all he had suffered might well kill him or make him stronger. This was not merely an "academic" exercise but an experiment appropriate to his conviction that a philosopher could only *create* after being "burned, as it were, with green wood" (GS pref.:3). If recurrence could eradicate the "human" and therefore the values of decadence within himself, then perhaps the doctrine might serve Western culture in the same way. In this he saw recurrence having a twofold effect: it "removes degenerate and decaying races to make way for a new order of life" and implants in the degenerate "a longing for the end" (WP 1055). Here again, the old ways of the ancient thinkers, as Nietzsche saw them, come into focus. The pre-Socratics and even Socrates emerged when there was much to be destroyed; the vision of the philosophical type made possible the selection of what must be preserved and what deserved to perish. And this is why Nietzsche saw recurrence as "the great *cultivating* idea" (WP 1056).

Satanic Interlude

Devils, it seems, are not unfamiliar with the idea of recurrence. A second-rate one appears in Dostoevsky's *Brothers Karamazov*, saying:

> "You're thinking of our present earth: why, our present earth has probably repeated itself a billion times. I mean, it has become extinct, frozen, cracked, fallen to pieces, resolved itself into its

---

51. Nietzsche to Franz Overbeck, August 5, 1886, SPL 254 (BKG III³:223).
52. From section 4 of Nietzsche's preface, written in 1886 for the second edition of *Human, All Too Human*. The translation is from Erich Heller's "Zarathustra's Three Metamorphoses," 72 (WKG IV³:7).

> component elements, again the water above the firmament, then again a comet, again a sun, again an earth from the sun—this evolution, you see, has repeated itself an infinite number of times, and all in the same way, over and over again, to the smallest detail. A most indecently tedious business."[53]

And Nietzsche asks:

> What, if some day or night a demon were to steal after you into your loneliest loneliness and say to you: "This life as you now live it and have lived it, you will have to live once more and innumerable times more; and there will be nothing new in it, but every pain and every joy and every thought and sigh and everything unutterably small or great in your life will have to return to you, all in the same succession and sequence—even this spider and this moonlight between the trees, and even this moment and I myself. The eternal hourglass of existence is turned upside down again and again, and you with it, speck of dust!" (GS 341)

The "loneliest loneliness" emerges upon the death of God, the absence of whom leads us to stray "as through an infinite nothing" (GS 125) wherein all value and meaning has vanished and we are confronted with the absurd.

Nietzsche's demon compounds the loneliness by suggesting that pointless suffering, joy, and death will be repeated in exactly the same way into infinity. If this demon were to appear to you, would you "throw yourself down and gnash your teeth and curse the demon who spoke thus? Or have you once experienced a tremendous moment when you would have answered him: 'You are a god and never have I heard anything more divine' " (GS 341). Apparently, Dostoevsky's Ivan Karamazov never experienced the "tremendous moment" that would have allowed him to call his devil a god. On the contrary, Ivan was irritated at the stupidity of this pathetic "flunkey."[54] Nietzsche, on the other hand, saw in his demon a god who offered a vision of redemption, redemption from "all these shadows of God" (GS 109). With recurrence, Nietzsche wants to scorch from the soul of humanity everything reminiscent of the dead God of decadence. The old morality is rooted in sickness and hatred of life, and we have listened to "the siren songs of

---

53. Fyodor Dostoevsky, *The Brothers Karamazov*, trans. David Magarshack (London: Penguin, 1988), 758.
54. Ibid., 763.

old metaphysical bird catchers . . . all too long, 'you are more, you are higher, you are of a different origin!' " (B 230). We are not "more," "higher," or of a "different origin" than life itself. But poisoned by life-negating values, we have become pale shadows of life. Thus, the task is to "translate man back into nature" (B 230) and restore that innocence that has for so long been instinctively denied and despised.

"Scientific" Circles

Recurrence is meant to bring about this restoration. As the "fundamental conception" (E Z:1) of *Zarathustra*, recurrence is articulated, Nietzsche said, within "the mythic style of the book."[55] But he did not want to leave it at that, because of what he called his "terrible antagonism . . . for the whole Zarathustra image."[56] Yet *Zarathustra* constituted "an outline I've made of my 'philosophy.' " Thus, along with the other themes expressed in this book, recurrence required, he said, "filling in." He said that, for him, *Zarathustra* "is 'devotional literature.' For everyone else, it is obscure, mysterious, and ridiculous."[57]

If recurrence was to be "the great *cultivating* idea" (WP 1056), its expression had to be more effective than it was in *Zarathustra*. Nietzsche certainly had plans in this direction, but for the most part, the doctrine is scattered through fragments written after *Zarathustra*. Whether it is expressed "poetically" or not, the idea of recurrence has been obscured both by Nietzsche's attempts to "prove" it as "the most *scientific* of all possible hypotheses" (WP 55) and by the objections to it as such. His tremendous enthusiasm for this "triumphant idea" through which "all other modes of thought will ultimately perish" (WP 1053) is odd, since the *"theoretical* presuppositions and consequences" (WP 1057) of this "scientific" idea have never been seen as particularly compelling.

In the "proof" for recurrence Nietzsche asserts that time is infinite but that the combinations of power that constitute "things" are finite. Within infinite time all possible combinations of power "must pass through a calculable number of combinations" (WP 1066). This means that within infinite time all possible combinations of power have to be realized. But these realizations do not by any means indicate a purpose or end to becoming, because in infinite time this "end" would have been attained. Hence, becoming is without beginning or end; on the contrary, it is now what it has always been and will be. For Nietzsche,

---

55. Nietzsche to Carl Von Gersdorff, June 28, 1883, SPL 74 (BKG III¹:386).
56. Nietzsche to Peter Gast, late August 1883, SPL 76 (BKG III¹:443).
57. Nietzsche to Peter Gast, September 2, 1884, SPL 82 (BKG III¹:525).

the determination of each moment within becoming is already "past" insofar as it has been "selected" as such. When I say "now," it is already past, which is to say I have determined it after it has occurred, that is, in the future that is "now." Thus, within each "now," the past and future are present because the "now" can only be determined after (future) it has occurred (past). Within the flux of becoming, each moment *is* the past and *is* the future. Thus, the determination of past, present, and future presuppose becoming. But saying the "now" is past and future is different from saying it has *always* been—different, that is, from saying the moment is eternal.

The idea of the eternal recurrence follows logically from a simple division of the infinity of time by the finitude of combinations of power. Since within infinite time all possible combinations of power would be realized, and since this realization does not bring all becoming to a grinding halt, the entire process "is realized an infinite number of times." "And since between every combination and its next recurrence all other possible combinations would have to take place, and each of these combinations conditions the entire sequence of combinations in the same series, a circular movement of absolutely identical series is thus demonstrated: the world as a circular movement that has already repeated itself infinitely often and plays its game *in infinitum*" (WP 1066).

Each moment (combination) of power as becoming is repeated *in infinitum*. That is, every form of life has always proceeded toward transformations that have occurred an infinite number of times and will be repeated again into infinity. Consequently, each moment of becoming is the past and future because any particular combination of power is "the entire sequence of combinations in the same series" preceding it—including those occurring after it was realized in the last cycle. Each form of life at any particular moment is what it has always been as becoming throughout infinity and what it will always become throughout the same. Everything returns in exactly the same way, and at each particular moment it is the infinity of all that it has been before that moment as well as what it must become.

In the end, the "scientific" idea of recurrence attempts to articulate the essence of becoming as the ebb and flow of a finite quantity of power within infinite time. The grand multiplicity of combinations of power, that is, all organic and inorganic things, is transformed within a power quantum that remains constant and infinitely repeats itself in exactly the same way. The dynamics of creation and destruction never increases or decreases the cosmos as power.[58] It remains a reservoir of

---

58. In attempting to articulate how this actually happens, Nietzsche resorted to inter-

power throughout all of its transformations. Will to power as a constant becoming is the being of all things. With recurrence Nietzsche attempts to articulate the identity of all things as *the same* throughout all possible transformations. The idea that *"everything recurs"* (WP 617) undermines the traditional division of "pre-Socratic thinking in two halves" (PTA 9:69; M 4:189). Here is the ancient barricade dividing the cosmologies of Heraclitus and Parmenides. The unification of these two standpoints resides in how the Being of Becoming *is the circularity* of everlasting becoming. Thus, within recurrence the Parmenidean "doctrine of Being" is affirmed (PTA 9:69; M 4:189). On the other hand, since the cycle presupposes all the transformations of power that constitute any of its particular points, Heraclitus's doctrine of becoming is affirmed. In this vein Nietzsche says, "That *everything recurs* is the closest *approximation of a world of becoming to a world of being"* (WP 617). Eternal recurrence is his solution to the ancient cosmological riddle of the cosmos as "at the same time one and many" (WP 1067).[59]

Nevertheless, Nietzsche's "scientific" proof for recurrence is wanting. First, there is no scientific validity to the physics of recurrence in its *"theoretical* presuppositions and consequences" (WP 1057).[60] Second, it goes against everything Nietzsche asserts regarding the possibility of interpretation, "scientific" or otherwise. Interpretations are manifestations of the dynamics of power wherein multiple drive-perspectives fictionalize the world in whatever manner allows preservation and growth. This is the activity of "spirit." When Nietzsche speaks of recurrence in terms of the "law of the conservation of energy" (WP 1063) and of the *"shape* of space . . . [as] the cause of eternal movement" (WP 1064), he appeals to interpretations of laws and causality as magically independent of the dynamics of will to power that he affirms to be basic to all interpretation. It is as if he wanted the objectivity of physics for recurrence—laws to provide it a "validity" wholly distinct from the

---

pretations of the law of the conservation of energy that were popular in his own time (WP 1063). For the compatibility of Nietzsche's "scientific" explanation of recurrence with the law of the conservation of energy, see SLN 182n and 244n.

59. Alexander Nehamas points out legitimate doubts that recurrence is a cosmological doctrine (Nehamas, *Nietzsche: Life as Literature* [Cambridge: Harvard University Press, 1985], 142–54). These hinge on (*a*) the difficulty of finding "clear references to cosmology in Nietzsche's published discussions of the recurrence" (ibid., 145) and (*b*) the fact that the significance of recurrence does not reside in its cosmological character. There can be no doubt about both of these points; nevertheless, they are not compelling enough to force Nehamas to abandon the idea of recurrence as such. At bottom, its cosmological expression is so fragmentary that it certainly cannot be considered something Nietzsche was satisfied with.

60. See ibid., 143. See also Arthur C. Danto, *Nietzsche as Philosopher: An Original Study* (New York: Columbia University Press, 1965), 203–9.

self-seeking drive-perspectives that he insists are fundamental to both the creation and destruction of all laws.

Finally, assuming that recurrence is scientifically valid and that time is indeed cyclical, why should it have the tremendous effect on me that Nietzsche hoped for? If his conception of recurrence is true, my embracing it means little, since this has already happened an infinite number of times and will be repeated infinitely. My having lived in exactly the same way an infinite number of times already, and my destiny to repeat my life into infinity, render my existence a matter of utter indifference in virtually every respect.

Psychological Circles

Nietzsche's articulation of recurrence as a "scientific" conception is so lame that its absence in his published works is not surprising.[61] Nevertheless, his genuine conviction of the importance of recurrence within his philosophy never wavered—perhaps because the significance of recurrence lies not in its "scientific proof" but rather in the psychological impact it has on the individual who takes it to heart. It is an invitation to live *as if* this "life as you now live it and have lived it, you will have to live once more and innumerable times more; and there will be nothing new in it, but every pain and every joy and every thought and sigh and everything unutterably small or great in your life will have to return to you, all in the same succession and sequence" (GS 341). As "the most *scientific* of all possible hypotheses," recurrence fails to inspire an eternal affirmation of life. But its psychological significance emerges when applied to the pain of our existence "as it is, without meaning or aim, yet recurring inevitably without any finale of nothingness. . . . This is the most extreme form of nihilism: the nothing ('the meaningless'), eternally!" (WP 55).

Recurrence, the hopelessly absurd and infinite repetition of everything, and devoid of any purpose or meaning whatsoever, is "the most extreme form of nihilism." But within the experiment to reestablish the possibility for health, it is meant to intensify the death wish inherent to the decadence values of Western culture. In short, one of the psychological effects of its being embraced is to help nihilists, those who hate life

---

61. There are echoes of "scientific" expressions of recurrence in *Zarathustra*, for example, in part 3, in the section entitled "Of the Vision and the Riddle." But this work "is poetry, and not a collection of aphorisms" (Nietzsche to Franz Overbeck, received February 11, 1883, SLN 207; BKG. III¹:324); hence, the "scientific hypothesis" of recurrence remained in notes that (unlike many others) did not find expression after *Zarathustra*.

for its innocence and are outraged at the collapse of two thousand years of "Truth," to destroy themselves.

One cannot help thinking of Socrates here. For Nietzsche, his suicide is the only act of nobility open to a decadent. This is why Nietzsche speaks of "the *wisdom* of his courage for death" (T 3:12). But this makes Nietzsche's situation interesting as well. After all, he refers to himself as a decadent. Hence, his statement "[W]hen physicians are required most . . . they are also most in peril" (U 3:2), is appropriate to both himself and Socrates. The difference is that Nietzsche sees Socrates' suicide as the latter's judgment on life, that is, as an act of revenge. Here, when "one *does away with* oneself one does the most estimable thing possible: one thereby almost deserves to live" (T 10:36).

Nietzsche acknowledges there is no a priori meaning and value to existence, and for him suicide was at times a temptation. But unlike Socrates, Nietzsche strove to affirm the innocence of life. This is what hurt him the most; in his view, the "human, all too human," within himself was full of hatred and bitterness because meaning and value, in the midst of his own suffering, were lacking. When Nietzsche "dehumanized" himself, he was attempting to carve *ressentiment* toward life out of his own soul in order to say yes to life in spite of "meaningless" physical and emotional torment. This was his underground war against the no inherent to a nihilistic desire that blames life for one's pain and that, in despair, rage, and hatred attempts an impotent revenge through suicide. It was precisely this battle through which Nietzsche sought, not to condemn, but to affirm life in all its innocence. It was also the means to realizing his intimacy with those he deemed worthy of life. Socrates, the first great cultural physician, was noble in his desire to salvage his culture but only promoted its decline. Nietzsche took on the same task, but strove to outrank Socrates' authority as a cultural physician by fighting every inclination to condemn life.

Nietzsche's inner struggle became the blueprint for the destructive role of recurrence within the revaluation, since it was meant to destroy those incapable of facing nihilism.[62] The "races that cannot bear it," says Nietzsche, "stand condemned; those who find it the greatest benefit are chosen to rule" (WP 1053). Recurrence is a powerful medicine through which the physician attempts to separate the weak from the strong. The former "shall perish" (A 2), and the latter must be preserved. Nietzsche, convinced of the debilitating physiological effects of two thousand years of decadent values, concludes that the generations

---

62. Recurrence has its constructive role as well, and insofar as it does, it shares both the destructive and the constructive features of the revaluation.

to come will be too weak to withstand the disease of nihilism. Hence, recurrence, which magnifies "the nothing (the 'meaningless'), eternally" (WP 55), is meant as a potent drought of poison for those incapable of affirming life as incessant becoming, and neither meaningful nor meaningless in itself. Indeed, this constitutes its innocence, and in this "time of extensive inner decay and disintegration" (WP 57), those who see their innocence within recurrence "are chosen to rule." For Nietzsche, the problem was how to bring those "chosen to rule" into the foreground. Hence, recurrence is "a doctrine that sifts men—driving the weak to decisions, and the strong as well" (WP 56).

The doctrine provides no consolation for those crushed by the death of God, or any promise of meaning and value independent of life. Nietzsche hoped recurrence would actually lead people to say, "[D]eath alone is a physician here" (T 3:12). In this vein, he speaks of the necessity to "create a new responsibility, that of the physician, in all cases in which the highest interest of life, of *ascending* life, demands the most ruthless suppression and sequestration of degenerating life—for example in determining the right to reproduce, the right to be born, the right to live (T 10:36). The degenerate that must be isolated from the healthy are those who hate life for lacking a transcendent meaning or value and who seek revenge. These are precisely the ones who cannot endure the innocence of life and who must be "helped" in every way to destroy themselves. Hence, recurrence has a role within the "first principle of *our* philanthropy." This first principle is that the "weak and ill-constituted shall perish," and the physician "shall help them to do so" (A 2).

Who, on the other hand, are the healthy? To Nietzsche's mind, the highest specimens of health were virtually nonexistent in his "age of decay and declining vitality" (WP 58); the best one could hope for were those capable of enduring "the nothing (the 'meaningless'), eternally." The healthiest type is, of course, the overman. He is the one to be bred out of the "pieces and fragments of man" as he is today. That is, he will be the offspring of those initially capable of enduring recurrence. The "real issue," said Nietzsche, "is the production of the synthetic man" (WP 881). Recurrence is meant, therefore, as a ploughshare tilling the soil of humankind to cultivate the overman. It is the doctrine "powerful enough to work as a breeding agent: strengthening the strong, paralyzing and destructive for the world-weary" (WP 862). This is why recurrence is inextricably linked to the revaluation as a physiological concern with the "uncanny preconditions of cultural growth . . . [and] the extremely questionable relation between what's called 'improvement' of mankind . . . and the elevation of the species Man."[63]

63. Nietzsche to Jakob Burckhardt, September 22, 1886, SPL 91 (BKG III³:254).

Recurrence is meant to effect the preconditions of cultural growth whereby, like a sifting process, the weak and strong are separated. And the latter are an essential precondition for "a genuine culture." But this brings us to another peculiarity of recurrence. If the process of creating a gulf between the strong and the weak is to be successful, then recurrence must be a doctrine compelling *belief*. Why, however, would the sick and decadent be attracted to a doctrine that must strike them as repulsive? Recurrence undermines precisely the values essential to the preservation of "the underprivileged"; hence, they would hardly find the doctrine attractive. Yet it would have to be taken very seriously by the sick if their "perishing takes the form of self-destruction" (WP 55). And though the overman is to be the progeny of the semihealthy, why would his presumably barbaric ancestors embrace recurrence?

Does the absence of a compelling reason to accept recurrence explain Nietzsche's search for a "scientific" confirmation of the doctrine? Did he think that a scientific veneer for it would make it more palatable? as if the authority of science could be used to lure his patient, his culture, into swallowing this strange potion? But why, on the other hand, does Nietzsche seem so full of enthusiasm for its scientific character in his notes? Is this enthusiasm directed at its "genuine" scientific validity, or at its seductive possibilities? If the former, the doctrine remains enigmatic and hardly compelling in its force. If the scientific expression of the doctrine is meant as a deceptive sugarcoating for a bitter pill, then why did Nietzsche not attempt a scientific proof in his published works?[64] The answers to these questions remain a secret of the workshop. One way or the other, there can be little doubt of Nietzsche's passionate desire to provide a vision of innocence and eternity which "compels a faith in the 'eternal recurrence'" (WP 55). Somehow the

---

Nietzsche's conception of the overman, as well as his preoccupation with the conditions making this type possible, is anticipated in his earlier work. For example, in 1873 he wrote, "[I]ndividuals are subordinated to the welfare of the *highest individuals*, to the welfare of the highest specimens" (PH 120; M 7:30 31). For the preconditions making the "highest specimens" possible, see "Schopenhauer as Educator," the third of Nietzsche's *Untimely Meditations*, and notes from the year 1872 in P 5 (M 6:5).

64. As discussed above, Nietzsche seriously sought some kind of "scientific" explanation for the doctrine, and though its inadequacies have been pointed out, one should remember that none of them ever found their way into his published works. In this vein, Nehamas points out that one may argue "the style in which *Zarathustra* is written does not tolerate an attempt at a scientific proof of the theory" (Nehamas, *Nietzsche: Life as Literature*, 143). He then points out, however, that *Twilight of the Idols*, which differs from *Zarathustra* in "style and force" and in which Nietzsche still claims "himself as the teacher of eternal recurrence . . . could easily tolerate a rigorous proof of the cosmological doctrine; nevertheless, Nietzsche chose not to include such a proof in that text either" (ibid., 143).

doctrine had to be taken to heart and held with the same fervent devotion that any Christian ever directed to God.

Socrates, the "pied piper of Athens" (GS 340), did persuade his culture to take his "cure." But from Nietzsche's standpoint, Socrates promised a "happiness" that boiled down to a moral justification for weakness and cowardice. Nietzsche, on the other hand, had to deal with the physiological consequences of this morality in the form of his sick contemporaries. He had the problem of seducing them into a *creative* vision that would open up the possibility for a return to health. Recurrence was supposed to constitute this vision, but Nietzsche never had Socrates' success in having it capture the hearts and minds of his fellow decadents. He was probably well aware that the inspiring, seductive value of the "scientific" conception of recurrence was so minimal that he chose to remain with its mythopoeic expression in *Zarathustra*. In the end he wanted to lure his epoch into the possibility of a new life-affirming faith, and in this he failed.

Despite this failure, Nietzsche was serious when he said: "In place of 'metaphysics' and religion, the theory of eternal recurrence" (WP 462). As the myth for the future, it was meant to "split the history of mankind into two halves."[65] Recurrence was to have its "place in history as a *midpoint*" (WP 1057), just as metaphysics and Christianity were midpoints dividing two "spiritual" epochs within their respective cultures. This new myth was actually a weapon in the "*greatest* of struggles" (WP 1054) to purge Western culture of decadence "for a new order of life" (WP 1055). Though Nietzsche claimed much "is already astir in this most radical revolution that mankind has known,"[66] he admitted to his friend Overbeck that "people are simply deaf to anything I say; *consequently* there is neither a *for* nor an *against*."[67]

He believed recurrence "makes everything *break open*" (WP 1057), bringing forth a "period of catastrophe" (WP 56), "strengthening the strong and destructive for the world-weary." These were the "consequences of its being *believed*" (WP 1057). It is incredible to think of the magnitude of such "an immeasurably difficult and decisive task."[68] With what he called his "physiological turn of mind,"[69] and in accord with his perception of the philosopher as a tyrant of the "spirit," Nietzsche proposed the doctrine of recurrence to create nothing less

---

65. Nietzsche to Paul Deussen, September 14, 1888, SPL 124 (BKG III^5:426).
66. Ibid., SLN 311.
67. Nietzsche to Franz Overbeck, October 18, 1888, SLN 315 (BKG III^5:454).
68. Nietzsche to Paul Deussen, September 14, 1888, SPL 124 (BKG III^5:426).
69. Nietzsche to Franz Overbeck, February 11, 1883, SPL 70–71 (BKG III^1:325).

than a new "spiritual" epoch that would alter the course of human history.

For Nietzsche, no human being could endure recurrence, especially after Christianity reduced the "human" to the status of a sick animal. In many respects, he saw the disease of Western culture to be so advanced that here the "physician says 'incurable' " (A 47). Hence the "human" as defined within the old deceptions of decadent "spirituality" has to be destroyed. Or at least the "physiologist demands *excision* of the degenerating part" (E D:2). If "spirit" is that capacity to create the deceptions necessary for life, recurrence, as a counterdoctrine (WP 862) to the decadent "spirituality" of the West, is meant to destroy the old deceptions and, presumably, those who cleave to them. For what does it affirm? The cycle of becoming without aim or purpose. Who can endure this most extreme form of nihilism? Who can look into this abyss without being nauseated at life? Who can contemplate the profound absence of all transcendent meaning and not only avoid despair but be inspired to *love and revere* the innocence of life? The doctrine of recurrence is meant to separate those who despair from those who can at least endure. If it does not kill us, it will make us stronger. Now the question becomes, "How much truth does a spirit *endure*, how much truth does a spirit *dare*? More and more," says Nietzsche, "that became for me the real measure of value" (E pref.:3).

Experiments and Explosions

"Live in such a way that you desire nothing more than to live this very same life again and again!"[70] This doctrine was meant to intensify the sickness of nihilism within Western culture. It was to function as a kind of powerful vaccine, destroying "the degenerating part" and forcing whatever strength was left to come to the fore. Here again the physician holds fast to his clinical standpoint and thereby to his interpretation of the dynamics of life. I have shown throughout my investigation that life as will to power needs resistance (WP 656) and that the threat of destruction stimulates an organism to draw on whatever resources it has in order to meet the threat. Recurrence is meant to trigger those resources that, if successful, will bring about a transformation of the culture as a whole.

According to a strictly physiological definition, nihilism is a "spiri-

---

70. This is from a note written while Nietzsche was working on *Zarathustra*. The translation is from Erich Heller's "Importance of Nietzsche," in *The Importance of Nietzsche*, 13 (M 14: 173–74).

tual" disease. Self-preservation is not the goal of life. Life as will to power demands growth, but Western culture has been maintained through an instinct of preservation in alliance with the power of *ressentiment*. For Nietzsche, the potent hatred for life peculiar to decadence instincts is the reservoir of *strength* underlying the self-preservative fictions of "Truth" and God—fictions crucial to the disease of nihilism. With the collapse of these fictions, everything essential to maintaining sickness within our culture has fallen apart. The "Real World" has at last became a myth, but the insight precipitated by the advent of nihilism, namely, that *"with the real world we have also abolished the apparent world"* (T 5:6), is simply too horrible for a culture fueled by hatred of life.

The old death wish, its hankering after a transcendental guarantee for meaning and value that negates the value of this world, does not disappear. When confronted with the threat of the collapsing fictions through which our culture has maintained itself, its self-preservative drive attempts to regain stability by imposing a fiction poisoned by *ressentiment*. And it realizes success in positing this world as "false in-itself." Now the life-denying instincts that negated existence via the transcendent, eternal idols of "Truth," "Beauty," and "Goodness" posit "Falsehood," "Ugliness," and "Evil" as the transcendent meaning of this world and this life. Here the ancient hatred of life finally realizes victory in attaining the ultimate goal of decadence: its revenge in the fiction of existence as worthless in-itself.

Ressentiment, hatred, and the unbridled lust for destruction are extremely dangerous sources of strength. Within Nietzsche's analyses, these constitute the cornerstone of Christianity. But within his clinical standpoint, recurrence can be seen as an experimental attempt to exploit precisely this volatile negative energy. He wants to channel it so as to undermine nihilism and simultaneously open up the possibility for cultural health. Such a strange physiological coup can occur only if the strongest, most dangerous individuals come to the fore. Naturally, for Nietzsche, we would not have to wait very long to find an abundance of such individuals. They would be, of course, thoroughgoing nihilists. The manipulation of their strength hinges on how the doctrine of recurrence would affect them, and we learn more about this when Nietzsche speculates on the type of the nihilist.

Nietzsche divides them into two strains. The first is fundamentally overwhelmed at the destruction of the foundation of the old morality and cannot fail to find death attractive. This type is an expression of *"passive* nihilism" (WP 22). The second type is essentially enraged at the destruction mentioned above, but this type possesses a "maximum of relative strength as a violent force of destruction—as active nihilism" (WP 23). It is in this "maximum of relative strength" that Nietzsche sees a certain glimmer of hope.

The passive nihilist constitutes a "recession of the power of the spirit." The active nihilist indicates at least "a sign of increased power of the spirit" (WP 22). The "spiritual" strength of the former is so depleted that the capacity to create the deceptions necessary for life is minimal. That is, this type lacks the "strength to posit for oneself, productively, a goal, a why, a faith." The latter, on the other hand, has the "spiritual" capacity to create a deception that can sustain them. The "faith" of active nihilism is motivated by rage, and it embraces destruction pure and simple because precisely the old " 'convictions,' [and] articles of faith" (WP 23) are no more. Here nihilism "does not only contemplate the 'in vain!' nor is it merely the belief that everything deserves to perish: one helps to destroy" (WP 24). This may very well be illogical, Nietzsche says, "but the nihilist does not believe that one needs to be logical." Logic stands within the nexus of the perspective of preservation,[71] and active nihilism's contradiction of this perspective "is the condition of strong spirits and wills." Active nihilists, Nietzsche says, "do not find it possible to stop with the No of 'judgement': their nature demands the No of the deed." With active nihilism, the "reduction to nothing by judgement is seconded by the reduction to nothing by hand" (WP 24).

The active nihilist is at least still capable of deeds, though these are rooted in the intoxication of destruction. But it is this rage and strength to destroy everything that bespeaks the old "spirituality" that the physician wants to harness. Recurrence is meant to do this insofar as it appeals to active nihilism. And it appeals to active nihilism because (a) it affirms that the old faith is dead, (b) it sanctions the destruction of everything reminiscent of the old "spiritual" paradigm within which this faith flourished, (c) it appeals to the active nihilists' craving for "everything perfect, divine, eternal" (WP 55), the negation of which motivates their desire for revenge.

Nietzsche did not find the health typical of the predecadent Greek and Hebrew cultures in his own age. And looking around for whatever healthy human material was left, he asked, "[W]here are the *barbarians* of the twentieth century?" (WP 868). The active nihilists are these barbarians. They are decadent, but their desire for revenge is something the physician wants to exploit. This means he must somehow tap the

---

71. See Chapter 1, "Combat and the Order of Rank"; Chapter 3, "The Deceptions of Grammar"; and WP 507 and WP 512.

unbridled lust for destruction peculiar to them, as the means to a physiological reversal such that this destructive power can be detonated as a *creative* force. This is essential to the revaluation's task "to reestablish *order of rank*" (WP 854). The "relative strength" of active nihilism must be turned in this direction despite these individual's indifference to cultivating "higher culture."

Self-preservation, recall, is not the goal of life as will to power. Organisms dominated by this drive become debilitated, since its perspective, especially in alliance with decadent drives, is naturally antagonistic to the ascending instincts of life, those drives that are not at all concerned with preservation. Without the affects of the ascending instincts, exhaustion sets in to the point where death is the goal. In Chapter 3, I presented a physiological portrait of advancing cultural decadence. There a degenerate instinct of preservation in alliance with decadence instincts undermined the cultural strength of the Greeks. In Chapter 4, this same drive was fundamental to the poisonous affects of Christian *ressentiment*, which spread into the Western cultural organism.

Since the physiological function of recurrence is a means of harnessing the "strength" of active nihilism and exploiting it creatively, the negative energy of active nihilism is a source of power that, if used properly, might restore cultural health. And it is here that the doctrine of recurrence is most intimately bound with the task of the revaluation. For Nietzsche, the basic precondition for health is some semblance of an order of rank wherein the ascending instincts of life are dominant. The revaluation has the task of reestablishing this order, of re-creating precisely not only what is essential to health but what has also been instinctively denied. The extremely toxic medicine of recurrence is meant to counter the affect of the instinct of preservation dominating Western culture. It has been the affect of this drive, in league with decadent instincts, that has ruthlessly opposed that order of rank wherein the dangerous, ascending instincts of life can come to the fore within our culture. Recurrence is not supposed to destroy preservation, because, after all, as the first instinct of "spirit" it is essential to life. Rather, the doctrine must somehow neutralize or render superfluous the fictions that for the last two millennia have preserved sickness and turned "man into a *sublime miscarriage*" (B 62).

From a physiological point of view, if the doctrine is believed, the deceptions essential to preserving the sick become superfluous *because* one is condemned to the cycles of recurrence. Here the suffering inherent to the collapse of the old fictions of "Truth" and God is magnified. Acceptance of the eternal recurrence of all things means that the death wish, that longing for an end in an eternal and "True" world beyond this one, is denied. Recurrence affirms that what is most hateful to decadence, that being life itself, will never realize the perfect stasis of death—"escape is impossible" (WP 1058). Not only does the "True" world evaporate, but the very *passion* for that world is also revealed to be eternally in vain. In this sense recurrence stands in accord with nihilism by intensifying the absurd. The nihilists understand that the old "spiritual" paradigm is false and yet, with recurrence, they are condemned to a passion for what is false. The doctrine, then, is meant to take advantage of nihilism by exploiting the perception that the old "spiritual" order is gone while making the desire for a new one appear equally meaningless. In this situation, the nihilist is left to burn in the hell of a passion that, on the one hand, will never be sated and, on the other, remains eternally "without meaning or aim, yet recurring inevitably without any finale of nothingness" (WP 55). This is the abyss wherein the weak and exhausted confront the impossibility of attaining the "True" world and are cursed by an inescapable desire for it. Thus, recurrence could drive some to select the Socratic option of suicide.

A Physiological Revaluation of Values

The more creative result of believing in recurrence might be the doctrine's appeal to the ancient and, like all instincts, greedy drive of self-preservation. That is, the doctrine, as a guarantee of eternal power in this world, might be irresistible to the totally self-centered perspective of this instinct. This would render all the fictions antagonistic to life here, that is, those of decadence, interpretations that are no longer advantageous to preservation. Now the quantum of power fueling hatred and destruction and exploited for so long by the instinct of preservation toward stability, has to be channeled toward deceptions appropriate to the recurrence of *its* perspective. "To *endure* the idea of the recurrence," Nietzsche says, "one needs: freedom from morality; new means against the fact of *pain* . . . the enjoyment of all kinds of uncertainty, experimentalism, as a counterweight to this extreme fatalism." This means we must dare a revaluation of all values, destroy the foundations of everything that has passed as "good and evil," and cremate the values inherent to decadence and *ressentiment*. And this requires, Nietzsche says, the "abolition of the concept of necessity; abolition of the 'will'; abolition of 'knowledge-in-itself' " (WP 1060).

Insofar as the instinct of preservation may be seduced by an eternal guarantee of its power in this world, all the fictions antagonistic to life become obstacles to its perspective. This means that somehow a *physiological revaluation* must take place within the body. Now the best interest of preservation resides in the recurrence of its power, and it becomes imperative that the negative energy of nihilism be used to create the deceptions essential to recurrence. These deceptions, these new fictions, Nietzsche says, allow for happiness and joy no longer "in certainty but in uncertainty; no longer 'cause and effect' but the continually creative; no longer will to preservation but to power" (WP 1059), and thereby enable us to endure recurrence. Unfortunately, the perspective of preservation is extremely limited. As "the first instinct of spirituality" (T 9:2), it provides only an initial deception of stability upon which the other instincts can determine the fictions appropriate to themselves.

The cumulative power of the decadent instincts led to a "spiritualization" of the world that negated life in this world. But in that recurrence is an affirmation of life in *this* world, only life-affirming instincts have the perspective appropriate to it. The weakest and most decadent instincts of a culture are not capable of affirming what is now in the best interest of the instinct of preservation. Only the most dangerous instincts, those most willing to sacrifice everything and risk destruction of the whole culture, are capable of recurrence. Just as preservation exploited the power of decadence to maintain its perspective, so it is now compelled, strictly out of self-interest, to ally itself with the most dangerous drives once again. This means, of course, that it will no longer dominate but, intoxicated by the deception through which the power of its perspective is eternally victorious, it will be seduced into life. Now the immortality of every moment becomes yet another fiction essential to life.

With this, the old fictions essential to preserving sickness collapse because they are no longer of any utility and the power of negation is dispersed through the body. The instincts of decadence require fictions antagonistic to life, but they no longer have exclusive rights to this power. They have been betrayed by preservation. The contract has been terminated and the power to create new interpretations based on preservation's intoxicated vision of eternal stability within the flux of chaos allows exactly those instincts, the ascending instincts of life, access to a power that precisely they are most adept at exploiting—that of destruction.

This physiological revaluation is only possible if recurrence is believed. The revaluation means establishing a new order of rank as the foundation for culture in the future. Recurrence is meant to neutralize the perspective of preservation by guaranteeing the eternal validity of its perspective. Insofar as one is "eternal," one thereby acquires the distance necessary to act, not in terms of mere self-preservation but rather with a willingness to sacrifice oneself according to the instincts of ascending life. Recurrence is to serve as the myth through which human material is "sifted" for its strongest specimens. The physiological revaluation suggested above shows how the most dangerous and warlike drives within an individual gain access to an extraordinary destructive power. And since each of us "transports the order of which he is the physiological representative into his relations with other human beings and with things" (T 7:2), the active nihilists are the physiological representatives of these extremely dangerous drives within the cultural organism.

Once the deceptions allowing belief in recurrence become necessary, "a violent force of destruction—as active nihilism" (WP 23)—emerges. Nietzsche says recurrence functions "as a *selective* principle, in the service of strength (and barbarism!!)" (WP 1058). He places recurrence in the service of barbarism because he never abandoned the idea *"that the destiny of humanity depends upon the attainment of its highest type"* (WP 987). However, the "highest type" is the product of a genuine culture. And every such culture originates with "barbarians in every terrible sense of the word" (B 257). Initially these fragments of humanity "will experience the belief in the eternal recurrence as a curse, struck by which one no longer shrinks from any action" (WP 55). And as "a violent force of destruction" (WP 23), all they have in common is the "blind rage at the insight that everything has been for eternities—even this moment of nihilism and lust for destruction" (WP 55).

There is something familiar about these nihilists. They remind us of "the Greeks, the most humane men of ancient times," who possessed that "tigerish lust to annihilate . . . throughout their whole history and mythology" (HC 32–33; WKG 3:277). Again recall that genuine cultures "can grow up only out of terrible and violent beginnings" (WP 868). This has been the path through which "every higher culture on earth so far has *begun*" (B 257). The barbarians of antiquity originally established an order of rank through the ability to inspire terror; recurrence has the same effect. The new "children of Night" (HC 34; WKG 3:279) may be the harbingers of a "period of catastrophe" (WP 56) and impending dark ages, but it is "the value of such a crisis that it purifies" (WP 55). This process of purification is parallel to the physiological revaluation referred to above. Once the most dangerous drives start to use the power of destruction that has fallen to their lot, the battle for supremacy typical of the drives begins. This entails the destruction of the "spiritual" affects of the drives characteristic of exhaustion, decadence, and sickness. In short, the remnants of the "old regime" are purged. This naturally involves the enslavement of the weaker drives within the perspective of the more powerful ones. Nietzsche says this purification "pushes together related elements to perish of each other . . . it assigns common tasks to men who have opposite ways of thinking." In short, it "brings to light the weaker and less secure among them and thus promotes an *order of rank* according to strength" (WP 55; emphasis added).

I will not repeat the contents of Chapter 2 concerning the barbaric origins of culture. But insofar as recurrence is meant to engender the physiological foundation of a new culture, a dark age of barbarism is a precondition. That is, barbarism constitutes the fundamental foundation for the physiological dynamics of culture. And this is what belief in recurrence is meant to effect; once again a ruthlessly violent type emerges, and through terror a rudimentary order of rank is established. The attraction to "everything underlying existence that is frightful, evil, a riddle, destructive, fatal" (BT S:4), emerges. Cruelty, the delight in "*making* suffer," becomes "an enchantment of the first order" (G 2:7). Those most capable of terror and violence, of enduring great pain and of gladly inflicting it, are distinguished above others (D 30). This distinction is the mark of those who will enslave and exploit the weak to their own ends. Among "the *barbarians* of the twentieth century" (WP 868), those "who command are recognized as those who command, those who obey as those who obey. Of course, outside every existing social order" (WP 55).

But why should this primitive order of rank even hold together? After all, these individuals have a hatred of the utter futility of life within recurrence. The only sign of rank among them is the extent to which they will go in cruelty and destruction. They have nothing to lose, not even their lives, since recurrence guarantees life no matter what. But precisely this guarantee, which is most horrible, is at the same time most inspiring: horrible to the extent that they will return eternally as slaves, inspiring to the extent that they have the prospect of taking themselves in hand and earning the eternal right to command. These nihilists need not be concerned with "self-preservation"; now one must *create oneself forever*.

Once again, as with the origins of the Greek and Hebrew cultures, this is a world of smoldering violence. But just as this was only half the story in the creation of the Greek and Hebrew cultures, so it is here; the other half, the "spiritualization of *cruelty*" (B 229), will also be found. This "spiritualization" will be quite different from that exhibited by the Greeks and Hebrews, for the reason that, unlike the ancients, the postmodern children of night will realize their "spiritual" capacity from within the abyss of nihilism. The Greeks and Hebrews could stare into the vortex of becoming but only with eyes dazzled by the morning of the world. They always managed to shield themselves from a vision of existence as meaningless. But in the future, which "speaks even now in a hundred signs" (WP pref.:2), existence will be seen devoid of any transcendental meaning-in-itself. And yet the passion for "a goal, a why, a faith" (WP 23) will burn through the lucid perception that all goals and faiths rest on the fabrications, the illusions, we require. Recurrence only magnifies this nihilistic insight and constitutes "the most paralyzing idea," Nietzsche says, "particularly when one understands that one is being fooled and yet lacks the power not to be fooled" (WP 55). This is the abyss of nihilism: the knowledge that the human animal is condemned to the necessity of illusion. And it is within this abyss that the future of a genuine culture finds its "spiritual" point of departure.

The power of Greek "spirituality" was intimately related to an experience of cruelty and horror. Among the Greeks it was the strongest who had the capacity to create the deceptions necessary for enduring cruelty and suffering; they created the values necessary to the survival of the culture. Their art of tragedy was a deception essential to surviving the terrible idea that an existence devoted to victory and war might be devoid of meaning. The "spiritualizations" with which the Greeks kept horror and suffering at bay ultimately allowed them to affirm the dark faces of life. In this they not only "preserved" themselves but grew in power as a culture. But "for the generation that is now coming up" (B 55), Nietzsche sees a kind of horror beyond that experienced by the Greeks. For unlike the Greeks, whose "attitude towards life [was] naive,"[72] the modern nihilists have exposed the "Truths" essential to the preservation and growth of the ancient cultures as "fabricated solely from psychological needs" (WP 12). Here is a source of suffering never experienced by the Greeks or Hebrews. Could the Greeks of the tragic age or the Hebrews in their most powerful epoch have accepted the art of tragedy or Yaweh as mere self-deceptions? Could they have agreed that these were the lies they told themselves in order to endure the fact that they were as significant as the smallest cloud in the sky?

If such a thing had taken place among the Greeks and Hebrews, their cultures would never have seen the light of day. However, the barbarians who form the order of rank for the culture of the future are confronted with the necessity of deception as a condition of life. In this situation, that "lies are necessary in order to live is itself part of the terrifying and questionable character of existence" (WP 853). This is

72. This is from a "plan" written in the summer of 1872. PT 152; M 4:243.

why the "spiritual" strength of future culture will be realized within the abyss of nihilism. The physiological upheaval of the meaninglessness of the old "spiritual" paradigm and the hatred with which it is annihilated are permeated with nihilistic insight. Now one sees with a terrifying lucidity that "lies are necessary in order to live" (WP 853) and that we "must even *will illusion*" (P 12; M 6:12).

Cruelty and suffering are inherent to the formation of any culture, as is their "spiritualization." For Nietzsche, the suffering and cruelty required for the culture of the future is beyond that of former epochs. It must take sides against everything within itself that seeks to undermine the lucidity of nihilism. It is a generation scorched by a passionate desire for "Truth" while having to carve out of itself anything that would take such "Truths" seriously. In short, it finds itself having to create "Truth" while steadfastly holding that "there is no 'truth' " (WP 616).

The Redeemer

"[A]ll enhancements of man so far" are the result of the "discipline of suffering, of *great* suffering" (B 225). Within the furnace of nihilism Nietzsche saw the possibility of cultivating a strength that would forge a new "spirituality," that is, a vision that no longer recoils from the circle of becoming but somehow allows one to embrace it as deserving love and reverence. But the path leading out of neobarbarism to the culture wherein one craves *"nothing more fervently* than this ultimate eternal confirmation and seal" (GS 341) is not traveled overnight.

The physiological transformation necessary for such a culture is embodied in the idea of the overman. He is the individual capable of uniting within himself the dilemma inherent to nihilism. That is, he will find, perhaps as something holy, precisely what his barbarian ancestors found hideous: that destruction is essential to creation. Nihilism, though it leads to the death of all "Truth," is also the confrontation with the law of life as overcoming. The experience of nihilism is the revelation of how life requires deception—that is, the creation of "Truths" allowing for growth. But insofar as one is conscious of this function of life, the seeds of destruction are contained within any "Truth."

The inherited decadence of the overman's primitive ancestors makes this essential feature of life a thing of horror. Their antagonism to life naturally renders the law of life repulsive. But the overman will find this law within himself as something he instinctively affirms. He will affirm the process of sifting and weeding out the sick via recurrence, eradicating what has gone by the name of "human." "Not 'mankind' but *overman* is the goal!" (WP 1001). The human is, for Nietzsche, simply not equal to the task of affirming the law of all life. Confronted with the task of creating in the face of the necessity for the destruction of all that is created, Nietzsche says, "Nobody yet has had this strength" (GS 285).

The "maximum of relative strength as a violent force of destruction—as active nihilism"—is only the most primitive beginning of the task to bring about the overman. Recurrence is not some spiritual fad that pops up over night. On the contrary, the doctrine meant to cultivate humanity from the human to the superhuman is itself something to be nurtured over thousands of years.

The progeny of neobarbarism is a hitherto unseen type, only possible in a distant future. Nietzsche says, "[M]y metaphor for this type is, as one knows, the word 'overman' " (WP 866). "Overman" is an appellation for a type of person Nietzsche characterizes in multiple ways, but I shall concentrate on only the one that provides the widest scope. In *On the Genealogy of Morals* he says of the overman that some day

> in a stronger age than this . . . he must yet come to us, the *redeeming* man of great love and contempt . . . who will redeem us not only from the hitherto reigning ideal but also from that which was bound to grow out of it, the great nausea, the will to nothingness, nihilism; this bell-stroke of noon and of the great decision that liberates the will again and restores its goal to the earth and his hope to man; this Antichrist and antinihilist; this victor over God and nothingness—*he must come one day*. (G 2:24)

Hundreds of thousands of years ago, the human animal, a form of life as will to power, emerged on the face of the earth. "[I]n man there [was] . . . fragment, excess, clay, dirt, nonsense, chaos." But there was "also creator, formgiver, hammer hardness, spectator divinity, and seventh day." Thus, as Nietzsche says, in us "*creature* and *creator* are united" (B 225). Our instincts, united as they are with the law of life, gradually found expression in a multiplicity of types. Not only the warrior but also the highest "spiritual" types saw the light of day, and in accord with the ascending instincts of life, "the highest types hitherto [e.g., the Greeks] were reared" (WP 979). But when the experiment of life manifest in the Greek culture was on the verge of transformation, "the only statue from which we could have perceived the purpose and meaning of that great preparatory exercise" was smashed (HH 1:261).

Then the lesser powers of that culture came forward in the guise of

Socrates, whose influence "spread over posterity like a shadow . . . growing in the evening sun" (BT 15). His "spiritual" power resided in that of decadence and combined with the "spiritual" power of *ressentiment* so profoundly exploited by Christianity; our age is the physiological heir of an ancient hatred of life. The physician spoke of recurrence as a vaccine through which this physiological degeneration might be reversed. The medicine "requires many thousands of years" before the physiological reversal to health will be realized. This reversal will be manifest in the overman.

In the description of the overman above, he is immersed in reality as creator, Antichrist, antinihilist and liberator. But dominating these characteristics is that of "the *redeeming* man" (G 2:24). The highest, healthiest, most powerful culture that ever existed on earth strove but failed to realize transformation. This failure, united with the disease of Christianity, has led us further and further astray from the goal of life. The overman, in whom the will to power is manifest both as creation and as destruction, will redeem and thereby justify this whole tragedy. The "will to power can manifest itself only against resistances; therefore it seeks that which resists it" (WP 656); sickness serves the role of resistance very well. All healthy organisms require the threat of sickness as a means to health insofar as they are called upon to draw on whatever resources of strength they have to fight and exploit sickness to its advantage.

Nihilism is an illness of profound dimensions, and certainly, as far as Nietzsche is concerned, it constitutes the greatest threat to the health of culture. And just as recurrence is a means for Nietzsche to purge his own nihilism, so is recurrence a means, Nietzsche hopes, for Western culture to purge itself of the same illness. Here the organism confronts its illness. Given the magnitude of the disease, the process of convalescence is subject to vast stretches of time—the hoped-for result of which would be "a stronger species" (WP 866). The overman stands as the pinnacle and heir to the strength cultivated over thousands of years in the battle against nihilism. In this he not only constitutes the redemption from the illness of nihilism, he also justifies its necessity.

In him, life as will to power is affirmed as the creation made possible through precisely what all creation presupposes—*destruction*. "And life itself told me this secret: 'Behold,' it said, 'I am that *which must overcome itself again and again*' " (Z 2:12). Now the terrible "in vain" (WP 55) of everything reminiscent of the "human" is overcome. The horrible truth of nihilism and recurrence in confrontation with the hopelessness of any other worldly justification of existence is overcome. The overman is the name for *victory* over nihilism and every moment in the history of humankind that made nihilism the consequence of everything humanity ever affirmed to be of value. The "human" is appalled at the void into which it is catapulted with the collapse of all otherworldly existential justifications. The overman finds precisely *this* a source of inspiration. For Nietzsche, this kind of health is something the like of which has never existed on earth. It is the strength to create while happily anticipating the destruction of all that is created and knowing that it will *return*.

The *"redemption* of this reality" (G 2:24) is only possible for the overman. He constitutes an instinctive affirmation of the innocence of all life, standing in perfect accord therewith. What will "culture" mean to him? What powers of "spirit," that is, what deceptions will be necessary for him? What orders of rank will he construct in accord with the innocence of all life? And above all, what will life as will to power threaten him with as the means to overcoming itself? These are the questions reserved for the philosophical "spirits" of the future. And "one really has to wait for the advent of a new species of philosophers, such as have somehow another and converse taste and propensity from those we have known so far—philosophers of the dangerous 'maybe' in every sense. . . . And in all seriousness: I see such new philosophers coming up" (B 2).

Dionysus

When Nietzsche refers to himself as "a disciple of the philosopher Dionysus" (E pref.:2), he identifies what will serve as the most profound symbol of the innocence of all life as becoming for this "new species of philosophers." This "god of darkness" (E G) represents

> an urge to unity, a reaching out beyond personality, the everyday, society, reality, across the abyss of transitoriness: a passionate-painful overflowing into darker, fuller, more floating states; an ecstatic affirmation of the total character of life as that which remains the same, just as powerful, just as blissful, through all change; a great pantheistic sharing of joy and sorrow that sanctifies and calls good even the most terrible and questionable qualities of life; the eternal will to procreation, to fruitfulness, to recurrence; the feeling of the necessary unity of creation and destruction. (WP 1050)

In short, Dionysus represents the *unity* of all life within the creation and destruction of all of its forms. This is the god intoxicated with his own transitoriness. In him, the *necessary* "unity of creation and destruction" in every living thing is affirmed throughout the eternities of recurrence, and this unity is *never* denied. His significance to the philosophers of the future resides in how he is destroyed for the sake of life. The philosophers who emerge within and after the dark ages Nietzsche envisions will have to acknowledge this element of life as becoming. Among these individuals there is no need to *preserve* the "human," because with the demise of metaphysics and God, everything fundamental to defining humanity dissolves. The "spirituality" at one time so essential to interpreting humanity will, in the hands of tomorrow's philosophers, fall away like the skin of a serpent to become "spiritual" artifacts. The old deceptions, those "likely stories" we once needed, will be as the myths of the titans were to the Greeks.

The knowledge of recurrence is personified in Dionysus, who knows he "will be eternally reborn and return again from destruction" (WP 1052). This is the path to every and all "spiritual" possibilities, liberated from merely self-preservative perspectives. The philosophers of the future will battle once again for supremacy, and among them, as it was for their ancient ancestors, the equal and infinite value of all individuals will be denied. To believe in recurrence is the guarantee that one will cast one's shadow again *no matter what*. The most daring, most "dangerous" interpretations will emerge as possibilities through which as yet undreamt orders of rank may arise.

With the destruction of metaphysics and Christianity, everything that defined us as human is on the threshold of obliteration. For Nietzsche, those who stand in opposition, that is to say, those who are still dominated by the instincts of *ressentiment*, will be driven like the leaves of autumn before the destructive force of tomorrow's philosophers. With recurrence, the old morality caves in, and for the "spiritual" tyrants of the future, everything is permitted. Standing within the unity of all life, they are Dionysian as harbingers of destruction and creation. The old "spirituality" will be destroyed in a plethora of experiments so that the overman "*shall be* the meaning of the earth" (Z prologue:3).

Such an individual can only emerge after the establishment of a new order of rank that will yield "that tremendous energy of greatness in order to shape the man of the future through breeding" (WP 964). This will entail "the annihilation of millions of failures" (WP 964) so that a "race with its own sphere of life, with an excess of strength for beauty, bravery, culture, manners to the highest peak of the spirit" (WP 898), can be cultivated. Naturally, the origins of such a "master race," rooted in the release of the dangerous forces essential to primitive orders of rank, are terrible and utterly barbaric. The greatest threat to the philosophers cocooned within these orders is perishing of guilt and self-hatred over "the suffering one creates" (WP 964). They must be strong enough to maintain the *"moral code for physicians"* (T 10:36) that demands no sympathy "for the ill-constituted and weak" (A 2). Pity in this case is symptomatic of a dead age—symptomatic, that is, of Christianity, which did all in its power to preserve precisely the sick. The battle against pitying what must be destroyed will, as it was for Nietzsche, be fought in the hearts and minds of tomorrow's philosophers.

"Terribleness is part of greatness: let us not deceive ourselves" (WP 1028). For the philosophers of the future, Dionysus stands in marked contrast to the "god on the cross." As Nietzsche puts it, "Dionysus versus the 'Crucified': there you have the antithesis." The former *"redeems* the contradictions and questionable aspects of existence"; the latter constitutes an objection to existence "as a formula for its condemnation" (WP 1052). The difference, Nietzsche says, between the crucifixion of Christ and the destruction of Dionysus cannot be recognized in terms of their martyrdom. For Nietzsche, Jesus of Nazareth had nothing to do with the *ressentiment* that fueled Christianity. But even if Jesus was everything Christianity made him out to be, the difference between his destruction and that of Dionysus does not lie in the immortality their deaths promised. The difference is found in the meaning of the promise itself. "The god on the cross is a curse on life, a signpost to seek redemption from life." Here *ressentiment* finds its most perfect expression insofar as "redemption" is seen as an absolute repudiation of life. "Dionysus cut to pieces is a *promise* of life: it will be eternally reborn and return again from destruction." Here, all the pain, absurdity, ugliness, and contradiction permeating human existence do not constitute arguments *against* life. Dionysus always returns back to this life and this earth to redeem all "torment, destruction, the will to annihilation," as an essential element to life. "One will see," Nietzsche says, "that the problem is that of the meaning of suffering: whether a Christian meaning or a tragic meaning." The former is "supposed to be the path to a holy existence," whereas Dionysus represents existence as *"holy enough* to justify even a monstrous amount of suffering" (WP 1052).

This is the tragic insight embodied in Dionysus. One does not attain nobility through a merely self-preservative desire to "get through life" with the least resistance—which desire, from the Christian standpoint, represents a virtue to be rewarded in heaven. Dionysus embodies the tragic insight into how the path to genuine nobility is a recognition of the innocence of life, and the ability to sacrifice oneself without *ressentiment* or self-pity in the face of everything one has ever loved.

To live *as if* one's existence will forever return—for Nietzsche, this idea, embodied in the cycles of Dionysus's birth and death, would allow philosophy to create the "spirituality" appropriate to individuals who are both dangerous and beautiful in their ability to face destruction without blinking. They would be the warriors, artists, legislators, and philosophers of a culture that, when it compared itself to us, would have no end of laughter. They would take life extremely seriously, but on the other hand would gamble anything, play and enjoy the most dangerous games; self-preservation among these individuals would never be an honorable motive. Such a culture would have no pangs of conscience in seeing those dominated by self-preservation as ugly, dishonorable, and therefore deserving of slavery.

Conclusion

> Even now my whole philosophy wavers after an hour's friendly conversation with a total stranger.
> —Nietzsche

What, in the end, can one conclude in regard to the foregoing? Does Nietzsche give us a nightmare from which we struggle to awake? Or given his influence on contemporary literature and philosophy, is the physiology inherent to what I have called his clinical standpoint an unfortunate, even embarrassing factor deserving little if any attention? To consider the last question first, the clinical standpoint deserves attention for the access it allows to virtually every facet of his thought. The determination of health and sickness is the standard permeating Nietzsche's philosophy, and my investigation has succeeded in showing this standard's underlying dynamic.

I have at times moved into the realms of violence, suffering and terror. And one may well ask, where is the "sunny side" of his thought, his ideas of dance, laughter, and play? One may wonder whether my investigation takes the clinical standpoint too seriously. Have I obscured Nietzsche's laughter and forgotten the significance of these themes? After all, we are "involved in a gloomy and exceedingly responsible business," and in these circumstances, what, he asks, "could be more necessary than cheerfulness? Nothing succeeds in which high spirits play no part." And he is quite right, because being able to laugh in the midst of dark undertakings and danger "is no inconsiderable art." Such an undertaking is the revaluation of all values. It stands as a "question mark so black, so huge it casts a shadow over him who sets it up" (T foreword). Under this brooding sky is a task so demanding that we are compelled "to run out into the sunshine so as to shake off a seriousness grown all too oppressive." Every expedient for remaining lighthearted "is justified," Nietzsche says. "Above all, *war*. War has always been the grand sagacity of every spirit . . . grown too inward and too profound;

its curative power lies even in the wounds one receives" (T pref.). The themes of dance, laughter, and play presuppose the character of the *agon* (T 3:8). The dance is that of an exuberant warrior along the edge of the abyss; his laughter echoes the thrilling intoxication of potential destruction; and his play is a test of courage to risk one's life in the affirmation of life and its innocence.

These themes, Homeric in character, reveal a scornful, heartfelt laughter at oneself and those who fear death. Such high spirits are appropriate to warriors: they are the sign of courage in a deadly game and in such company inspire respect. Here is a play consisting of the combat fundamental to "projects that would require thousands of years for their completion" (GS 356). I do not deny the "sunny side" of Nietzsche's thought; it consists in singing while destroying and accepting not only our own obliteration but also the potential futility of all our efforts.

Nietzsche's clinical standpoint also reveals how deeply suspicious he was, not only of his own motives but those of others. In this, his rigor equals the severest discipline of the cloistered monk who is ever watchful for the faintest sign of failure to follow the way of the Cross. The difference is that Nietzsche is always alert to the failure to embrace and affirm life. How each perceives "corruption" is something learned not by rote and "taking courses" but rather through exacting, ruthless self-examination. They are both quite adept at marking within themselves precisely the point where they mask their own weakness and cowardice on the path they have chosen. For the monk, deception is "false," and catching himself in the act, he seeks forgiveness and grace. For Nietzsche, deception is necessary for life, and the only question is whether it is symptomatic of health or sickness. If its creator is healthy, there is a "spiritual" ability to select danger, uncertainty, and suffering so that they are loved—the capacity to see beauty in the fact that life can only be genuinely affirmed when we are willing to be destroyed. Our capacity for nobility, honor, and love is revealed in our daring to lose even our lives in the service of life. The healthy ones are always tragic, and tragedy has a thousand faces. Without this "spiritual" ability, Nietzsche anticipated sick and mediocre "spirituality" and the paralysis of self-preservative deceptions like the "infinite value" and "equal rights" of everyone.

The topic of deception raises many interesting questions. For example, if Nietzsche saw deception as essential to life as power, then is not his philosophy itself a deception? Nietzsche would answer yes but would surely add, "That does not mean I am a liar!" And he would be right. After all, "deception" has a meaning for Nietzsche that is beyond good and evil. "Truths" are the fictions with which we have sheltered ourselves from the chaos of becoming. Nietzsche does not avoid confronting this chaos, his vision of the cosmos bereft of gods, "Truth," reason, and *telos*. Yes, his philosophy is a deception, not only as a means for him to endure "the death of God" but also, he hoped, as an example of new deceptions, the new interpretations necessary for a future devoid of God or metaphysical guarantees of meaning and purpose.

I have been speaking of deception here within the confines of its significance from the clinical standpoint. Hence, my question, Is not Nietzsche's philosophy itself a deception? is addressed in terms of physiology and therefore in terms of deception as a condition of life. But what of the "physiology" itself? Is it yet another deception? Perhaps only a metaphor? And if it is a deception, a wonderfully complicated metaphor, what does it conceal and simultaneously point to?

In 1873 Nietzsche asked, "What then is truth?" And he responded by saying it is a "movable host of metaphors." Our "Truths," he said, "are illusions which we have forgotten are illusions . . . metaphors that have become worn out . . . coins which have lost their embossing and are now considered as metal and no longer as coins" (TL 84; M 6:81). Then in 1886 he reiterates, "Alas, what are you after all, my written and painted thoughts! It was not long ago that you were still so colorful, young, and malicious . . . and now? You have already taken off your novelty, and . . . are ready, I fear, to become truths: they already look so immortal, so pathetically decent, so dull! . . . but nobody will guess . . . how you looked in your morning, you sudden sparks and wonders of my solitude" (B 296). Given these observations, that extraordinary creation that goes by the name of "Nietzsche's philosophy" cannot be regarded as something he believed to be a firm and eternal "Truth." And the physiology pervading his thought is, I think, a metaphor designating the helter-skelter play and combat that is concealed in any interpretation.

Every interpretation has, in Nietzsche's language, an order of rank. Its apparent "unity," or "cohesion," presupposes a great deal of coercion. The creation of an interpretation, be it political, philosophical, religious, and so on, hinges on the violence through which a multiplicity of other perspectives, other interpretations, are exploited to the point of a whisper or are ruthlessly silenced. Apollo is the voice of the sun, and his lucidity is only possible when Dionysus's chaotic howls are exploited and killed. Every interpretation, then, is a tragedy that, within the nexus of life, is by no means avoided by insisting on egalitarian interpretations of "justice." "There is *only* a perspective seeing, *only* a perspective 'knowing,' " Nietzsche says, and "the *more* affects we allow to speak about one thing, the *more* eyes, different eyes, we can use to observe one thing, the more complete will our 'concept' of this thing, our 'objectivity' be" (G 3:12). Every interpretation, then, has a thousand eyes; it consists of that "contract" which is provisionally arrived at after the fight among the "one-sided views," the affects of many drive-perspectives. Each is allowed its say, and they "assert their rights against each other" (GS 333) within the hierarchy dominated by the most powerful instincts. This is the physiological microcosm that, for Nietzsche, constitutes not only interpretation but culture as well. Any "truth," any interpretation, masks the violence through which it is sustained. Nietzsche recognizes how each interpretation conceals a multiplicity of masks, and in this he is among the foremost precursors of what now goes by the name deconstruction in contemporary philosophy. Deconstruction, as one commentator puts it, "seeks to indicate those assumptions and motifs which a text acknowledges but must suppress in order to function."[1] In this regard, I think the physiology in Nietzsche's thinking is the metaphor for the violence and deception through which various assumptions and motifs are exploited or silenced within any interpretation. An interpretation is like any physiological function; it operates through the exploitation and shutting down of others according to an order of rank essential to the preservation and growth of the body. All that is used or "shouted down" within any interpretation stands in an order of rank among perspectives that, like musical notes, including the silence between them, give us a symphony, give us an interpretation. The "play" of interpretations in deconstruction reveals an intoxication with the little fugues and all the multiple notes within notes that have been "disciplined" within any interpretation.

On the other hand, I think the role of physiology in Nietzsche's thought has a character quite unlike the abstraction of deconstruction. In spite of the fact that physiology is a metaphor for the dynamics of interpretation, Nietzsche began intensely to identify these dynamics with the existence of the body. Within the descriptions through which he destroys the foundations for "Truth," the body remains central as an indisputable fact; and Nietzsche came more and more to identify the certitude of this fact with what I have called his clinical standpoint. The indubitable existence of the body provides him an epistemological point of departure that, not only allows him to diagnose the disease of

---

1. Alan D. Schrift, *Nietzsche and the Question of Interpretation: Between Hermeneutics and Deconstruction* (New York: Routledge, 1990), 104.

nihilism but also serves as a means to cure the illness. In this regard, Nietzsche's "destruction" of the foundations of metaphysics and all possible transcendent standpoints for knowledge hinges on a Cartesian interpretation of method that, rather than attain its "validity" in the indubitable activity of a "thinking substance," finds it, as Heidegger has shown, in the physiological activity of a biosubstance.

The certitude of the clinical standpoint rests on the "knowledge" of our body as the locus of life's "essence" pulsating through bones, muscles, cells, and the perspectives of the instincts, whose order of rank is a cumulative "affect" mirrored in consciousness. "As regards the animals," Nietzsche says, "Descartes was the first who, with a boldness worthy of reverence, ventured to think of the animal as a *machine*: our whole science of physiology is devoted to proving this proposition" (A 14). Unlike Descartes, Nietzsche does not exclude man from the animal world. This inclusion of the human within what he called animal physiology exemplifies his "destruction" of the metaphysics that elevated us above the merely animal. But this "destruction" remains within the tradition he attempts to dismantle. Nietzsche is celebrated for undermining our "Rational" essence and therewith our access to the extraworldly existence of "Truth," "Knowledge," and "Being." But in the very process of demonstrating that these are mere fictions, he ends up positing precisely another essence, another metaphysical foundation, as the origin of these fictions. He takes the extraworldly "Truths" of metaphysics and places them, not "out there," but within the human animal, whose essence is *physis* governed by the physiological dynamics of preservation and growth.

Physiology can stand as a metaphor, a kind of coat-of-arms emblazoned on his perception of the possibilities for myriad interpretations, that is, perspectivism. But it is more than that: Nietzsche also saw it as a concrete event, in individuals and cultures, that, if properly understood, could be manipulated. Hence, he is dogmatic with regard to the sickness permeating modern culture. This sickness is no metaphor; it is a *physical* phenomenon of the body that must be confronted by the "physicians for modern mankind" (U 3:2). Nietzsche was dogmatic on "the doctrines of sovereign becoming," doctrines, he said, "I consider true but deadly" (U 2:9). He was convinced that the revaluation was essential to facing the *truth* of these doctrines and that facing this *truth* was essential to the courage to step into the chaos within us and harness it as the means to our transformation as a species. "My task is enormous," he said, his "determination no less so. . . . This much is certain: I wish to force mankind to decisions which will determine its entire future."[2] Nietzsche

2. Nietzsche to Malwida von Meysenbug, May 1884, SPL 81 (BKG III[1]:509–10).

had the courage of his convictions, and we would underestimate him if we thought he did not mean what he said in speaking of the suffering that may be required to force mankind to these decisions.

In the end, the physiology in Nietzsche's thinking certainly allowed him to deconstruct the intellectual history of Western culture. But beyond the physiology permeating the standpoint of this clinician par excellence, physiology is also a *technique* through which Nietzsche thought he might engineer a reversal, a revaluation within the body of culture so that a cure might be found for its illness. And like so many who, to this day, still believe they have a method by which to make the world and humanity somehow "better," Nietzsche was willing to experiment and apply the knife now here, now there. And it is in his conviction of the necessity actually to apply the knife that he is most tormented. The idea that individuals would have to be sacrificed, destroyed in order to create a better tomorrow, filled him with dread.

Nietzsche was no lover of violence. But he seems to have been deeply suspicious of his repulsion toward it, as if this antagonism would somehow compromise his "task." The project of undermining the "human" was an act of violence upon himself, something essential to his world-historical responsibility. The "weak and ill-constituted shall perish," and there is no doubt that he was quite willing to sacrifice himself on the altar of the future. But at times the mask of the physician cracked: "[M]y whole philosophy wavers after an hour's friendly conversation with a total stranger. It seems so silly to want to be right at the expense of love—and at the same time to be unable to impart what's most valuable in oneself, for fear of destroying affection."[3] This tension moves throughout Nietzsche's texts. Ultimately, he saw his desire for affection as a dangerous distraction from what he considered "most valuable" in himself—his philosophical destiny to reestablish the health fundamental to an *Überkultur* for the future. And for this reason, when reading Nietzsche, we, as Kazantzakis did, "feel his heart ripping in two."[4]

Nietzsche certainly had occasion to doubt himself, but at bottom he clung to his "destiny." He saw the "human" permeated with illness, and in order to go into the future, it had to be eradicated. He volunteered himself for this experiment, and between a vision of the self-preservative cowardice marking "modernity" and the self-sacrifice peculiar to the bravery essential for saying yes to life, he crucified himself.

Shall we follow him? After all, "it is a painful and dangerous under-

3. Nietzsche to Peter Gast, August 20, 1880, SPL 54 (BKG III¹:37).
4. Nikos Kazantzakis, *Report to Greco*, trans. P. A. Bein (New York: Bantam, 1971), 318.

taking . . . to tunnel into oneself and to force one's way down into the shaft of one's being by the nearest path" (U 3:1). At what point do *we* set up the fictions *we* require to endure a lucid perception of the limits of our honesty? These questions can seduce us into a certain idolatry of Nietzsche's bravery as a model for proving our own. That is, we can rush headlong into an "affirmation" of the necessity of self-destruction with an eye to self- "re-creation." "Take care," Zarathustra warns, that a "statue does not strike you dead" (Z 1:22). In the end, we must ask ourselves whether Nietzsche really is the epitome of courage. Is he the model for us? Can we recognize ourselves in him to the extent that we affirm his convictions and thereby make his risks our own? In short, is he yet another idol before which we pay homage? No. To do such a thing is simply too easy, and therefore a betrayal.

Nietzsche captures our hearts and minds in his experiments with and exploration of the "spiritual" landscapes of Western culture, and we can show our respect for him by bearing in mind that exploration and experiment cannot be conducted for their own sake—this would be repugnant to him. The exploratory and experimental features of his thinking are motivated not only by a desire for "knowledge" but by a passionate desire to realize his ambitious goal to secure a future wherein our progeny would not be ashamed of themselves or of us, their ancestors. When a people is ashamed, "no one should be surprised if . . . [it] perishes of petty egoism, of ossification and greed . . . and ceases to be a people; in its place systems of individual egoism, brotherhoods for the rapacious exploitation of non-brothers, and similar creations of utilitarian vulgarity may . . . appear in the arena of the future" (U 2:9).

Nietzsche believed "the next two centuries" would see humankind coming to terms with the death of everything that ever affirmed the value of life. With his eye resting beyond the next few centuries, he attempted to provide the possibility for faith in life and a love for the earth. And like Kierkegaard, he was just as concerned to keep the reader from identifying this possibility with himself. For Nietzsche, then, exploration and experiment are what Rilke called "heart-work."[5] This is the task of creating light within the darkness of a world without hope of redemption, a final purpose, or cosmic payoff after death, but a world that nevertheless is never hated or allowed to twist us into bitterness at our lot. This work lies at the center of Nietzsche's philosophical project. "I speak only of what I have lived through," he said,

---

5. Rainer Maria Rilke, "Turning-Point," in *The Selected Poetry of Rainer Maria Rilke*, ed. and trans. Stephen Mitchell (New York: Random House, 1982), 133.

and we believe him. His dedication to the task at hand, and the courage it required, is an example of what we must do for ourselves: take on "a painful and dangerous undertaking" providing no "Truths."

Nietzsche presents a clear-eyed and unashamed vision of ourselves far into the future, but we must draw a line at what he recommends as the path to it. He might call us cowards in our unwillingness to go "over" the human, but perhaps his very willingness to so indicates the limits of his own courage. This is not to condemn or "demythologize" Nietzsche; we all have our limits. As an old sailor once said:

> One is always afraid. One may talk but. . . . I have known brave men . . . I say each of them, if he were an honest man . . . would confess . . . there is somewhere a point when you let everything go. . . . And even for those who do not believe this truth there is fear all the same—the fear of themselves. . . . Trust me. . . . At my age one knows what one is talking about—*que diable*! Man is born a coward (*L'homme est né poltron*). It is a difficulty—*parbleu*! It would be too easy otherwise.[6]

It was not easy for Nietzsche, and we respect his confronting a world devoid of a transcendent meaning or value. But in the end, perhaps he "let everything go." He pushed himself to the limits of his strength and found *he* could not believe in *our* ability to endure a world drained of eternal meaning and value. "No human being has yet had this strength," he says. Only someone "over" man can endure; only someone beyond all the old definitions of the "human" can affirm life when the old faith crumbles, love life in the face of its sublime indifference to love, and bear the knowledge of the death of God. When Nietzsche says his "entire philosophy wavers after an hour's friendly conversation with a total stranger," he is saying that the "stranger," for all of his small talk and Christianity, allowed him to feel kinship and some semblance of intimacy. But precisely such moments were the source of a deep feeling of shame for him; for a brief span of time he forgot the clean, cold showers of his ascetic task and actually enjoyed the company of one of those filthy human animals that, in principle, should be despised (E 4:6).

Ultimately we have to ask ourselves whether Nietzsche's "cure" is any more effective than the Socratic one he hated. We have to grant him the point that without some sense of purpose we and our future are doomed. Unless we have something to suffer *for*, or, as he put it, "a

---

6. Joseph Conrad, *Lord Jim* (New York: Modern Library, 1931), 146–47.

goal," then we will degenerate into "self-seeking cattle and mob" (WP 752). On the other hand, his conviction that the human race is incapable of dealing with the death of God, of faith, is naive. He was so terrified at his own incapacity to believe in anything that when he contemplated a race of individuals with the same incapacity, he panicked (and with good reason). But why should he have been so quick to extrapolate our condition from his own? It is true that, for the most part, one has to look long and hard to find something noble about human beings, but Nietzsche seems to have despaired entirely.

I think he underestimated the tenacity of human beings, their capacity for generosity and courage. He believed these would eventually be undermined, so he "jumped ship," went *AWOL* on humanity. He preferred to throw in his chips with some ideal man who would save us if only we went to work now and tore out of ourselves "everything men have heretofore respected and loved."[7] It is a genuinely human experience to find the foundations of one's faith lying in ruins. The darkest suffering is occasioned by the destruction of everything we have ever loved, and this pain is not uncommon. When Nietzsche experienced it, he was overwhelmed. He could not find in himself the strength to say yes to it; the only way he managed to hold himself together was to dream of life in a transfigured state.

This is Nietzsche's no to life; he could only say yes to a life wherein the possibility of nobility would be restored in the future. He could not see himself rising above the pain of his shattered faith in this existence. He dreamt of his overman with the same passion he said Christ felt in dreaming of "his rainbow and his ladder to heaven" (GS 137). Nietzsche is a virtuoso in his self-analysis of faith destroyed. This experience is the source of the passion and suffering that permeates his work. He transforms his experience of the death of metaphysics and Christianity into his prophecy for the next few centuries. In this, we owe him a great deal: what artist or philosopher today is not somehow indebted to him? But in trying to cope with this death, he turns his back on us; not only does he rightly extrapolate our experience of terror from his own, he similarly extrapolates our weakness as well.

Was it so inconceivable to Nietzsche that there were people who could experience the death of God and "Truth" and still not degenerate into hatred? Why should we even speak of the "death of God" and other such world-historical events? Are there not individuals around us everywhere who are crushed by the loss of everything they ever loved and who still manage to rise again? This kind of courage is around us if we

---

7. Nietzsche to Reinhart von Seydlitz, February 12, 1888, SPL 106 (BKG III[5]:248).

only look. Did Nietzsche look? How many times a day all over the world do the most horrible events take place? Nietzsche speaks of the ugly faces of existence, and we see them served up in the media all the time: women, beaten and raped, then burned alive with their children; the old, sick, and insane drifting through the rubble, garbage, and corpses of bombed-out cities, scratching, like crows in the snow, for firewood and food—the horror is endless. Nietzsche is correct: if we ever lose faith in the future, then none of this will touch us. But in the midst of this ugliness, we can find the extremely rare individuals who are still capable of courage, compassion, and love for the earth. As Camus saw, among we humans there are always rebels, those who would *actually risk* being smashed and murdered rather than be intimidated into accepting the destruction of the innocent according to grand schemes promising greatness in the future. Was Nietzsche's Europe so bereft of examples of courage in the face of great suffering? No. One may rest assured that humans, being humans, have everywhere and at all times created hell on earth, and among them there were those who would not submit to it.

Did he think the humanity of the future would be entirely incapable of enduring the disaster of having their love shattered again and again? Yes. And so he wanted to cultivate the type of man who could endure. Nietzsche did not look at his contemporaries enough; perhaps he was a little too self-absorbed with his "task." He did not seem to see the examples of courage and heroism that take place everyday—courage and heroism here understood as the ability to endure the greatest suffering without collapsing into hatred of others and of life on this earth. Nietzsche could only say yes to a humanity transformed after millennia; he could not say it to those around him.

Perhaps, in the end, Nietzsche was the coward; he could not stand beside us, feel any solidarity with us; and in many respects, he had a very good perception of just how ugly we can be. It was exactly this ugliness, within both himself and us, that nauseated him, and the "man of the future" became a pathetic consolation. He speaks about how he felt no solidarity with anyone living or dead;[8] he asks for love, compassion, and understanding (his letters are full of such requests), yet he cut himself off from his own kind—precisely the source of love, compassion, and understanding. This timid and shy man only felt at ease with people through the distance of letters, or when his "task" was acknowledged. But he was happy once, when he was part of the warmth and daily routine of the Wagner household. But looking into

---

8. Nietzsche to Franz Overbeck, August 5, 1886, SPL 90 (BKG. III³:223).

the eyes of his contemporaries, he shuddered, and never exposed himself to the pain of love, never made himself vulnerable through trusting someone in love, and only experienced the suffering of the absence of genuine human contact. Nietzsche acknowledged his reclusiveness and timidity, and we do not doubt his sincerity; we doubt only his courage to *rebel* against his own perception of our cowardice.

Nietzsche is right to point out how much human frailty and weakness lies behind all we have valued for centuries. But he was naive to think that enhancing our capacity to confront the destruction of the human, lies in manipulating our eternal essence as a physiological datum or substance toward interpretations that would allow us to go "overman." Descartes reduced us to thinking substances, and Nietzsche saw us as power quanta that, like the tides of a bay, can be dammed up, then channeled toward the *virtues* he truly loved and rightly identified with genuine nobility. He thought that mastering this energy would allow us to go over the human via new interpretations that could forge a new culture, one that centuries from now would make the Renaissance look like barbarism.

As I noted above, in spite of his battle against all the essences through which metaphysics sustained an interpretation of the human, Nietzsche did not win the war. He destroyed the human only to embrace it transformed according to the dynamics of its original essence as will to power. He went beyond the code of "good and evil" only to find it again, transformed and embodied in the overman's clear-eyed and innocent gaze. In his role as a physician of culture, he could see that, as Foucault says, with the dissolution of God comes the dissolution of the human.[9] He saw physiology as a technique through which the interpretations that allow us to overcome the death of humanity could be squeezed out of a concentrated glycerin drop of will to power. But we will not accept yet another interpretation of ourselves in terms of some metaphysical/cosmological essence, including Nietzsche's offering of a transformed *physis*—as if by affirming ourselves as will to power, we could stand within its cosmic nexus and, guided by its natural dynamic, cultivate ourselves to a higher plateau of existence. Having reduced the possibility of interpretation to the perspectives of the instincts, Nietzsche thought he had found not only access to the "degenerate" interpretations fundamental to the sickness of nihilism but also the cosmic source for overcoming it. But our capacity to endure suffering and loneliness and the courage to face a world unprotected by

---

9. Michel Foucault, *The Order of Things*, (New York: Random House, 1973), 342.

the hand of God cannot, like the color of a rose or the speed of a horse, be bred into us. If it were only that easy.

Perhaps the most important feature of Nietzsche's philosophy is the conception of physiology as a metaphor. With the collapse of metaphysics and the death of God is that of humanity. Nietzsche's physiology throws us back upon ourselves as a great mystery once again. The physiology is the method inherent to his revaluation; it points to the task of revaluation, reinterpreting ourselves without recourse to metaphysical "Truth" or God. Nietzsche's task of "applying the knife" to humanity becomes our task. He saw that new interpretations of right and wrong, just and unjust, would become necessary for the culture of the future. The multiplicity of interpretations unleashed by Nietzsche are perhaps most at home in what goes by the name deconstruction in contemporary philosophy. What also remains, however, as his legacy to us is still the exacting, indeed painful surgery of establishing an order of rank for interpretations within this multiplicity. This is not the place to go into deconstruction's ability, or lack thereof, to determine the value of interpretations, but I think that, at least as far as Nietzsche was concerned, we will have to look at the old conception of humanity and endure the pain of deciding what to take and what to leave behind. The loneliness of his project is now our own.

Nietzsche was right: with the death of God comes the death of the human, but in coming to terms with this event, there is no easy biological fix. Nietzsche still wanted to hold on to a transcendent essence through which, upon the death of God, we would still have a metaphysical ticket for the ride over the abyss. This is where he turns his back on us. Metaphysics does not find its last domicile in Nietzsche's philosophy; it remains alive and well in the dreams of genetic technology.

He went to war against metaphysical "essences" and "substances" but, in the end, posited yet another substance that, if properly understood, could engineer our "redemption" from the shame at the failure of humanity. But we can be grateful to him for many things. In spite of its metaphysical "cure," his revaluation still seeks precisely the values that were, for him, the epitome of a once healthy humanity. We can be grateful that he consistently speaks of the things that have always, and often foolishly, given us pride in ourselves: bravery, honesty, integrity, leadership, self-sacrifice, a sense of honor. These are the old virtues of nobility, characteristics that Nietzsche embraced and so compellingly demanded of himself and of us within the *deed* of his philosophy.

We cannot accept Nietzsche's metaphysical conception for creating the interpretations meant to excavate our nobility. But he has shown us that nobility has always been required in creating new meanings and visions of ourselves in the midst of collapsing, worn-out interpretations. We can be grateful for the responsibility that, in the midst of his "play," reveals Nietzsche's firm seriousness in advancing what he knew were mere "deceptions." He tried to find a way to look into a windy future with a light heart full of daring. For ourselves, the shadowy backstreet and boardroom affairs continue, and terror is rarely so gauche as to lack an exquisite precision. Now, when all the innocence of the earth and of children everywhere is offended as we gaze, seemingly paralyzed, at their rape, starvation, and murder, we will need the interpretations that provide, as Nietzsche says, "a Yes, a No, a straight line, a *goal*."

He teaches us that unless we try to find our way, we will be unworthy of the innocence of life. Nietzsche asks us to play with interpretations, not for interpretations' sake, but for the sake of a revaluation of humanity. This revaluation might, he thought, allow us to cultivate everything he identified with what has always been called noble. In this sense, his is a philosophy for the rare ones who feel the gift of the sun and therefore all the tragedy reserved for standard-bearers and heroes. And what of us? The insight that humanity lies in a grave beside its God by no means eradicates the necessity for a revaluation of values; Nietzsche was right: we can no more stop "interpreting" than we can stop breathing. But we do not have his physiological blueprint. Neither do we have, as he saw, the hand of God, or a built-in historical *telos* to protect us as we look upon the horizon of the future. Will we end up as starving pigeons cooing over multiple "interpretations of interpretations?" Or will we somehow find the ability to play while keeping our balance in the sky of our interpretations? We can take Nietzsche's conception of physiology as the metaphor for the necessity of our learning once again when to say yes and when to say no and, like the eagle, dare to lift off into a gale, protect our young, and, high over the graves of God and humanity, remain vigilant.

Bibliography

Primary Sources

Nietzsche, Friedrich. *Briefwechsel: Kritische Gesamtausgabe.* 16 vols. Edited by Giorgio Colli and Mazzino Montinari. Berlin: Walter de Gruyter, 1972–84.
———. *Friedrich Nietzsches Werke des Zusammenbruchs.* Edited by Erich F. Podach. Heidelberg: Wolfgang Rothe, 1961.
———. *Gesammelte Werke: Musarionausgabe.* 23 vols. Munich: Musarion, 1920–29.
———. *Werke: Kritische Gesamtausgabe.* 22 vols. Edited by Giorgio Colli and Mazzino Montinari. Berlin: Walter de Gruyter, 1967–84.

Translations of Nietzsche's Published Works

Beyond Good and Evil. Translated by Walter Kaufmann. New York: Vintage, 1966.
The Birth of Tragedy. Translated, with an introduction, by Walter Kaufmann. New York: Vintage, 1967. (*The Case of Wagner* shares this volume.)
Daybreak: Thoughts on the Prejudices of Morality. Translated by R. J. Hollingdale, with an introduction by Michael Tanner. Cambridge: Cambridge University Press, 1982.
The Gay Science. Translated, with an introduction, by Walter Kaufmann. New York: Vintage, 1974.
Human, All Too Human: A Book for Free Spirits. Translated by R. J. Hollingdale, with an introduction by Erich Heller. London: Cambridge University Press, 1986.
On the Genealogy of Morals. Translated by Walter Kaufmann, with R. J. Hollingdale, and with an introduction by Walter Kaufmann. New York: Vintage, 1966. (*Ecce Homo* shares this volume.)
Thus Spoke Zarathustra. Translated, with an introduction, by R. J. Hollingdale. Harmondsworth, Middlesex: Penguin, 1975.
Twilight of the Idols. Translated, with an introduction by R. J. Hollingdale.

Harmondsworth, Middlesex: Penguin, 1972. (*The Anti-Christ* shares this volume.)

Untimely Meditations. Translated by R. J. Hollingdale, with an introduction by J. P. Stern. Cambridge: Cambridge University Press, 1983.

Translations of Nietzsche's Unpublished Works

"Homer's Contest." In *The Portable Nietzsche*, translated by Walter Kaufmann. New York: Penguin, 1984.

"The Last Philosopher; the Philosopher; Reflections on the Struggle Between Art and Knowledge." In *Philosophy and Truth: Selections from Nietzsche's Notebooks of the Early 1870's*, edited and translated by David Breazeale, with an introduction by Walter Kaufmann. Atlantic Highlands, N.J.: Humanities Press, 1979.

"On Truth and Lies in a Nonmoral Sense." In *Philosophy and Truth*.

"The Philosopher as Cultural Physician." In *Philosophy and Truth*.

"Philosophy in the Tragic Age of the Greeks." In *Philosophy in the Tragic Age of the Greeks*, translated, with an introduction, by Marianne Cowan. Chicago: Regnery/Gateway, 1962.

"The Struggle Between Science and Wisdom." In *Philosophy and Truth*.

"Thoughts on the Meditation: Philosophy in Hard Times." In *Philosophy and Truth*.

"The Will to Power." In *The Will to Power*, translated by Walter Kaufmann and R. J. Hollingdale, with an introduction by Walter Kaufmann. New York: Vintage, 1968.

Translations of Nietzsche's Correspondence

Nietzsche: A Self-Portrait from His Letters. Edited and translated by Peter Fuss and Henry Shapiro. Cambridge: Harvard University Press, 1971.

Nietzsche: Unpublished Letters. Edited and translated by Karl F. Leidecker. London: Peter Owen, 1960.

Selected Letters of Friedrich Nietzsche. Edited and translated by Christopher Middleton. Chicago: University of Chicago Press, 1969.

Secondary Sources

Alexander, Michael, trans. *The Earliest English Poems.* Harmondsworth, Middlesex: Penguin, 1977.

Bertram, Ernst. *Nietzsche: Versuch einer Mythologie.* Berlin: Bondi, 1918.

Brinton, Crane. *Nietzsche.* Cambridge: Harvard University Press, 1941.

Camus, Albert. *The Myth of Sisyphus.* Translated by Justin O'Brien. Harmondsworth, Middlesex: Penguin, 1977.

---. *The Rebel: An Essay on Man in Revolt*. Translated by Anthony Bower. New York: Vintage, 1956.
Cicero. *De Fato*. Loeb edition. Translated by H. Rackham. London: William Heinemann, 1942.
---. *Tusculan Disputations*. Loeb edition. Translated by J. E. King. London: William Heinemann, 1927.
Conrad, Joseph. *Lord Jim*. New York: Modern Library, 1931.
Crawford, Claudia. "Nietzsche's Physiology of Ideological Criticism." In *Nietzsche as Postmodernist: Essays Pro and Contra*, edited, and with an introduction, by Clayton Koelb. Albany: State University of New York Press, 1990.
Dannhauser, Werner. *Nietzsche's View of Socrates*. Ithaca: Cornell University Press, 1974.
Danto, Arthur C. *Nietzsche as Philosopher: An Original Study*. New York: Columbia University Press, 1965.
Derrida, Jacques. *Positions*. Translated by Alan Blas. Chicago: University of Chicago Press, 1981.
Dostoevsky, Fyodor. *The Brothers Karamazov*. Translated, with an introduction, by David Magarshack. London: Penguin, 1988.
---. *Selected Letters of Fyodor Dostoevsky*. Edited by Joseph Frank and David I. Goldstein. Translated by A. R. MacAndrew. New Brunswick, N.J.: Rutgers University Press, 1987.
Foucault, Michel. *The Order of Things*. New York: Random House, 1973.
Gadamer, Hans-Georg. *Truth and Method*. New York: Crossroad Publishing Co., 1982.
Hayman, Ronald. *Nietzsche: A Critical Life*. New York: Penguin, 1984.
Heidegger, Martin. "The Anaximander Fragment." In *Early Greek Thinking*, translated by David F. Krell and Frank A. Capuzzi. New York: Harper & Row, 1975.
---. *Being and Time*. Translated by John Macquarrie and Edward Robinson. New York: Harper & Row, 1962.
---. *An Introduction to Metaphysics*. Translated by Ralph Mannheim. New Haven: Yale University Press, 1980.
---. *Nietzsche*. Vol. 1, *The Will to Power as Art*, edited and translated by David F. Krell. San Francisco: Harper & Row, 1979.
---. *Nietzsche*. Vol. 4, *Nihilism*, edited by David F. Krell, translated by Frank A. Capuzzi. San Francisco: Harper & Row, 1982.
Heller, Erich. *The Importance of Nietzsche: Ten Essays*. Chicago: University of Chicago Press, 1988.
Jaspers, Karl. *Nietzsche: An Introduction to the Understanding of His Philosophical Activity*. Translated by Charles F. Wallraff and Frederick J. Schmitz. Tucson: University of Arizona Press, 1965; South Bend, Ind.: Regnery/Gateway, 1979.
Kaufmann, Walter. *Nietzsche: Philosopher, Psychologist, Antichrist*. 3d ed. New York: Vintage, 1968.
Kazantzakis, Nikos. *Report to Greco*. Translated by P. A. Bien. New York: Bantam, 1971.
Knight, A.H.J. *Some Aspects of the Life and Work of Nietzsche, and Particularly of His Connection with Greek Literature and Thought*. New York: Russell & Russell, 1967.

Lewis, C. S. *Mere Christianity*. London: Fontana, 1975.
Mann, Thomas. *The Magic Mountain*. Translated, with an introduction, by H. T. Lowe-Porter. New York: Knopf, 1968.
Megill, Allan. *Prophets of Extremity: Nietzsche, Heidegger, Foucault, Derrida*. Berkeley and Los Angeles: University of California Press, 1985.
Mochulsky, Konstantin. *Dostoevsky: His Life and Work*. Translated, with an introduction, by M. A. Minihan. Princeton: Princeton University Press, 1967.
Nehamas, Alexander. *Nietzsche: Life as Literature*. Cambridge: Harvard University Press, 1985.
Oehler, Richard. *Nietzsche und die Vorsokratiker*. Leipzig: Dürr'schen Buchhandlung, 1904.
Peyre, Henri. "Presence of Camus." In *Critical Essays on Albert Camus*, edited by Bettina L. Knapp. Boston: G. K. Hall, 1988.
Plato. *Phaedo*. In *Great Dialogues of Plato*, translated by W.H.D. Rouse. New York: Mentor, 1956.
Rilke, Rainer Maria. *Duino Elegies*. Translated, with an introduction, by J. B. Leishman and Stephen Spender. New York: W. W. Norton, 1939.
———. *Selected Poetry of Rainer Maria Rilke*. Edited and translated by Stephen Mitchell, with an introduction by Robert Hass. New York: Random House, 1982.
Sandvoss, E. *Sokrates und Nietzsche*. Leiden: E. J. Brill, 1966.
Schmidt, Hermann-Josef. *Nietzsche und Sokrates: Philosophische Untersuchungen zu Nietzsches Sokratesbild*. Meisenheim am Glan: Hain, 1969.
Schrift, Alan D. *Nietzsche and the Question of Interpretation: Between Hermeneutics and Deconstruction*. New York: Routledge, 1990.
Strong, Tracy. *Friedrich Nietzsche and the Politics of Transfiguration*. Berkeley and Los Angeles: University of California Press, 1975.
Thomas, Dylan. *Dylan Thomas Collected Poems: 1934–1953*. Edited by W. Davies and R. Maud. London: J. M. Dent & Sons, 1988.

Index

absurd, 39–41, 118, 131, 135–37, 140, 150, 157, 158, 162, 166, 175
agon, 76, 83, 188. *See also* contest
  agonal instinct, 33, 37, 55, 76, 104
altruism, 30, 80
Amor Fati, 41, 147
Anaxagoras, 55, 78
Anaximander, 55, 78
Apollo, 189
arché, 11–13, 15, 55
aristocracy, 45, 63, 86, 87, 90, 130, 96. *See also* nobility
  Greek, 71–73, 76, 79
  Jewish, 92, 93
  origins of, 28, 29, 31, 42
Aristotle, 40
art, 35, 42, 46, 73–75, 94, 104, 108, 187, 135. *See also* tragedy
artist, 40, 136, 195
ascetic, 52n, 194
asceticism, 109, 116, 127
Asclepius, 81
Assyrian, 92
Athens, 63, 70, 72, 76, 81, 153, 160, 170
authority, 32, 47, 52, 67, 71, 87, 142, 160, 167, 169
  hatred of, 95, 115, 120

barbarian(s), 29, 30, 173, 177–80
barbarism, 42, 118, 169, 177, 178, 184, 197
becoming, 12, 13, 41, 43, 47, 60, 66, 83, 104, 148, 155, 168, 179, 184, 189, 191
  as eternal recurrence, 163–65, 171, 180
  as flux, 44, 101, 110, 139
  innocence of, 157–59, 183
being (Being), 2, 43, 44n, 54, 55, 67, 89, 94, 96, 98, 101, 116, 148, 191
  and stability, 60, 65, 66, 69, 80, 91
  and will to power, 11, 13, 44, 165. *See also* fiction(s)
Bertram, Ernst, 62n.8
biology, 1, 2, 16, 17, 74, 198
body, 1, 2, 15, 18, 20, 21, 24, 25, 30, 36, 47, 60, 66, 69, 70, 75, 109, 110, 144, 152, 175, 176, 190, 191
  of culture, 31, 39, 98, 153, 192
  as political entity, 24n, 28, 29, 42, 45, 129
  as will to power, 4, 16, 17
breeding, 2, 30, 31, 100, 128–30, 168, 184, 198
Buddhism, 42, 107n, 109

Camus, 15, 146, 155n.42, 196
caste(s), 29, 30, 33, 89, 92–98 passim, 114n.14, 115–17, 120. *See also* class(es)
Cervantes, Miguel de, *Don Quixote*, 111
child(ren), 32, 85, 103, 104–7, 110–13, 117, 118, 129, 144, 153, 161, 177, 178, 196, 199
Chinese, 106
Christ, 6, 10, 85, 86, 98–119 passim, 128, 151, 152, 185, 195. *See also* Jesus
Christian(ity), 106, 113, 114, 132, 137, 151, 171, 172, 174, 185, 194

and Greek philosophy, 6, 10, 79, 123,
126–31 passim, 133, 134, 138, 141, 145,
149, 152, 170, 182, 184, 195
origins of, 85, 86, 98, 107, 110, 115–17,
119–21
Cicero, 63–64n.12
class(es), 29, 31, 87, 89, 91, 94, 96, 116, 117,
120, 127, 128, 136. *See also* caste(s)
combat, 4, 16, 32, 34, 42, 56, 71, 76, 84, 87,
153, 188, 189
and instincts, 18, 19, 21–23, 25, 37, 65,
66, 73–75, 103. *See also* war; warrior
Conrad, Joseph, *Lord Jim*, 194
consciousness, 13, 16–18, 20, 21, 51, 58–61,
66, 69, 91, 99, 140, 191
contest, 15, 23, 33, 34. See also *agon*
cosmology, 10–12, 19, 21, 54, 56, 156, 165,
169n, 197
Cowan, Marianne, 62n.8
Crane, Brinton, 62n.11
Crawford, Claudia, 3n.5
cruel(ty), 29, 37, 48, 106, 124. *See also* spiritualization
and suffering, 32–34, 52, 134, 154, 178–80
culture, 1, 11, 13, 15, 16, 18, 34, 38, 49, 74,
75, 82–84, 103, 106, 129, 131, 134,
141–43, 145, 147, 148, 154, 155, 157,
158–61, 167, 169, 171–73, 176–80,
182–84, 186, 190, 192, 193, 197, 198. *See
also* body; organism; survival
decadent, 3, 6, 29, 39, 47, 48, 71, 92–94,
126–28, 130, 166, 170, 174
Greek, 10, 27, 32, 37, 39–41, 44–47, 50,
52, 53, 56–58, 61, 62, 67, 68, 72, 73,
77–80, 86, 87, 92, 93, 127, 132, 137,
141n, 181
healthy, 5, 27–30, 32, 35, 47, 56, 57, 61,
69, 86, 87, 127, 133, 136, 149
Hebrew, 6, 86, 91, 123
Jewish, 86, 90–101 passim, 108, 114n,
115, 116, 118, 120, 121. *See also* survival

dance, 20, 43, 147, 187, 188
danger, 50, 45, 53, 68, 89, 123, 135, 145,
155, 160, 161, 187, 188
challenge of, 33, 34, 37, 41, 149, 192
dangerous individuals, 29, 32, 86, 172,
186

Dannhauser, Werner, *Nietzsche's View of
Socrates*, 62
Danto, Arthur C., 165n.60
death, 1, 5, 6, 12, 25, 32, 37, 41, 42, 61, 67,
70, 74, 79, 82, 83, 102, 111, 116–18, 126,
129, 130, 132, 134, 135, 138, 144, 147,
153, 159, 167, 175, 180, 185, 186, 188,
193
death wish, 10, 24, 73, 78, 80, 81, 101,
110, 116, 119, 124, 128, 132, 137,
139–41, 150, 161, 166, 172, 174
of God, 91, 158, 162, 168, 189, 194, 195,
198
decadence, 64, 66, 74, 77, 79, 83, 95, 109,
114, 123, 129, 131, 136, 143, 151, 156,
159, 161, 162, 175, 180, 182
formula for, 22–24, 43, 65, 90, 101, 108,
112, 133
instincts of, 39, 51, 70, 102, 119, 121, 126,
137, 147, 149, 150, 172, 174, 176. *See
also* culture; symptom(s)
and sickness, 25, 39, 48, 76, 82, 90, 112,
116, 130, 132, 148, 169, 177
deception, 14, 36, 43, 52, 56, 60, 66, 68, 73,
74, 92, 125, 128, 132, 134, 140, 148, 169,
175, 184, 185, 190. *See also* spirit
necessity for, 3, 40, 42, 44, 45, 139, 156,
158, 171, 173, 174, 176, 177, 179, 180,
183, 188, 189
self-deception, 41, 133, 134, 136, 179
deconstruction, 3–6, 43, 190, 192, 198
democracy, 4, 130, 131, 136
Democritus, 55, 78
denaturalization, 68, 97, 100, 120, 126, 127
Derrida, Jacques, *Positions*, 3–5
Descartes, René, 12n, 191, 197
devil, 111, 158, 161, 162
diagnoses (sis), 3, 6, 10, 15, 58, 62, 84, 123,
131, 143, 153
dialectic(s), 38, 104, 126. *See also* Socrates
Dickens, Charles, *Pickwick Papers*, 111
différance, 4
Dionysus, 1, 7, 12, 129, 151, 152, 183–86,
189
disease, 7, 66, 72, 75, 79, 81, 82, 142, 143,
149, 152, 171, 182. *See also* nihilism
distance, 21, 31, 36, 48, 52, 63, 74, 93, 98,
130, 147, 154, 176, 196. *See also* order
of rank

Dostoevsky, Fyodor, 105, 111, 112, 161, 162
    The Brothers Karamazov, 117, 161, 162
    The Idiot, 105, 111
    Selected Letters of Dostoevsky, 111
drives. *See* instinct

economics, 18, 25, 30, 31, 39, 48, 109, 133, 134, 149
Empedocles, 55, 78
enemy(ies), 33, 42, 69, 84, 94, 95, 98, 101, 112, 115, 117, 118, 153
equal(ity), 4, 14, 20, 21, 30, 36–38, 73, 80, 84, 118, 130, 131, 133, 134, 184, 188, 189
error, 12, 44, 68, 69, 75, 76, 82, 103, 107, 108, 126, 128, 129, 136, 137
eternal recurrence. *See* recurrence
exhaustion, 22, 24, 39, 48, 64, 70, 78, 79, 86, 93, 101, 103, 110, 132, 148, 174, 177
    and weakness, 6, 21, 72, 109, 112, 116, 119, 130, 137, 150, 175
existence, 3, 17, 29, 34, 38, 43, 46, 56, 57, 59, 64, 66, 80, 81, 88, 90, 91, 94, 98–104 passim, 107, 110, 116, 118, 126, 155, 156, 158, 162, 166, 172, 182, 190, 191, 195, 197
    threats to, 33, 36, 41, 89, 108, 135, 137, 178, 179, 185, 196
    value of, 12, 13, 37, 39, 136, 139–41, 167
experiment, 34, 46, 48, 125, 129, 157, 158, 161, 166, 171, 172, 175, 181, 184, 192, 193
    as will to power, 38, 45, 77, 159
exploitation, 10, 14, 18, 19, 41, 43, 46, 47, 50, 52, 56, 172, 173, 182, 190, 193
    and strength, 17, 23, 29, 38, 45, 53, 87, 88
    of the weak, 29, 30, 63, 87, 93, 178

faith, 67, 76, 87, 103, 104, 114, 117, 119, 138, 140, 141, 143, 169, 173, 179, 194–96
    in life, 134, 146–48, 159, 170, 193
fiction(s), 37, 54, 65, 67, 75, 97, 106–8, 110, 112, 114, 151, 175, 191, 193. *See also* illusion
    of preservation, 69, 90, 101, 103, 104, 113, 130, 132, 135, 149, 150, 159, 165, 172, 176. *See also* spirit
    of stability, 43, 66, 91. *See also* being
    of truth, 5n.9, 139, 149, 150, 172, 174, 189

force(s), 12–15, 17, 19, 25, 28, 29, 31, 38, 44, 45, 48, 49, 54, 62, 79, 83, 120, 174
    of destruction, 77, 173, 177, 181, 184. *See also* power; strength; will to power
Foucault, Michel, 197
Francis, Saint, 105

Gadamer, Hans-Georg, 143n.13
Goethe, Johann Wolfgang, 75
Greek(s), 3, 12, 33, 34, 38, 42, 49, 54, 63, 69, 70, 74, 75, 81, 91, 97, 98, 130, 133, 136, 158, 159, 173, 174, 178, 179, 184. *See also* aristocracy; Hellene(s)
    antiquity, 35, 67, 73, 134
    metaphysics, 6, 123, 126, 127, 131, 134, 138, 145
    philosophy, 15n.6, 40, 51, 55, 121, 128. *See also* culture; Christianity

happiness, 10, 12, 68, 69, 72–74, 76–78, 81, 88, 89, 107, 109, 110, 116, 119, 126, 140, 145, 157, 170, 176
hatred, 42, 48, 100, 101, 106, 130, 131, 141, 149, 167, 175, 180, 185, 195, 196. *See also* authority
    of life, 119, 136, 147, 150, 151, 162, 166, 168, 172, 178, 182
    and *ressentiment*, 89, 90, 94, 95, 99, 113, 150
Hayman, Ronald, 145n.24
heal(ing), 41, 50, 56, 72, 77, 78, 80, 81, 83, 125, 129, 143
health(y), 31, 36, 41, 43, 50, 54, 58, 65, 66, 73, 77, 80, 93, 97, 120, 132, 134, 137, 148, 153, 160, 161, 166, 168, 170, 172–74, 183, 192, 198
    culture, 5, 27–30, 32, 35, 47, 56, 57, 61, 69, 86, 87, 127, 133, 136, 149
    individual(s), 15–25 passim, 28, 30, 38, 40, 46, 52, 53, 69, 70, 86, 87, 168, 173
    profound, 11, 20, 34, 38, 44–47, 61, 130, 154, 159, 182
    and sickness, 1, 2, 4, 5, 6, 11, 19, 28, 38, 39, 40, 82, 99, 102, 123, 156, 187, 188
Hebrew(s), 90, 127, 130, 133, 135, 136, 158, 159, 173, 178, 179. *See also* culture
Heidegger, Martin, 1, 2, 12n, 43–44, 54, 55, 143, 191
    An Introduction to Metaphysics, 54

Being and Time, 143
Early Greek Thinking, 54
Nietzsche, Vol. 4 Nihilism, 2
Hellene(s), 32, 33, 37, 40–42, 55, 57, 69, 74–76, 79, 83, 86, 97, 127, 134, 135. *See also* Greek(s)
Heraclitus, 55, 78, 165
herd, 23, 24n, 36, 37, 59–61, 71, 78, 94
hero(ic), 10, 42, 57, 58, 67, 71, 82, 83, 114, 117, 196
Homer, 42, 75
  The Iliad, 42
Hugo, Victor, 111

illness. *See* sick(ness); health
illusions, 3, 24, 27, 41–43, 67, 69, 90, 134–41, 149, 150, 179, 180, 189. *See also* fiction(s)
Indian, 91
inherit(ance), 30, 99–101, 114n.14, 120, 131, 132, 134, 143, 180
instinct, 1, 4, 5, 19n.11, 21, 31, 33, 34, 36, 39, 41, 44, 48, 50, 52, 54, 55, 57, 61, 64n, 77–79, 81–83, 116, 119, 127, 140, 157, 159, 160, 184, 190, 191, 197
  ascending, 74, 75, 87, 104, 108, 112, 114, 174, 176
  Jewish, 93, 98, 100, 101, 106
  of life, 32, 69, 73–76, 87, 88, 92, 102, 103, 112, 114, 128, 174, 176, 181
  of strength, 17–20, 22–24, 29
  of weakness, 17, 24, 29, 30, 35, 36, 39, 63, 64, 71, 87, 92–94, 102, 103, 115, 126, 132, 176, 177. *See also* agon; combat; decadence; order of rank; preservation; war
interpretation(s), 3, 5, 11, 15, 17–19, 35, 44n, 46, 49, 52–55, 60, 71, 82, 97, 112, 117, 118, 123, 137, 138, 145, 148, 157, 171, 175, 190, 197
  multiplicity of, 4, 6, 21, 43, 47, 50, 149, 150, 159, 176, 184, 189, 191, 198, 199
  as will to power, 44, 67, 155, 157, 165. *See also* perspective(ism)
intoxication, 32, 55, 141, 173, 176, 183, 188, 190
Israel, 90, 91, 96, 97, 117

Jaspers, Karl, 2, 62n.11, 144
  Nietzsche: An Introduction, 2, 144

Jehovah, 99, 107
Jesus, 10, 85, 86, 98, 99, 102, 105–7, 111, 113–15, 117, 118, 120, 185. *See also* Christ
Jews, 3, 106, 117. *See also* aristocracy; culture; Hebrew(s); instinct; survival
Judaism, 117, 118, 128

Kaufmann, Walter, 2, 62, 105, 152
  Nietzsche, 105, 151, 152
Kazantzakis, Nikos, 9, 192
  Report to Greco, 9, 192
Kierkegaard, Sören, 113, 114, 193
  Philosophical Fragments, 113
Knight, A.H.J., 62n.8

language, 1, 3, 43, 61, 66, 97, 120, 189. *See also* sign
Lao-tse, 106
Lewis, C. S., *Mere Christianity*, 111
logic, 16, 60, 61, 65–67, 75, 91, 128, 136, 138, 141, 173
loneliness, 124, 140, 144, 145, 147, 151, 154, 161, 162, 197, 198
love, 5, 31, 33, 45, 48, 70, 76, 99, 101, 107, 109–10, 112, 117n, 119, 123, 144, 153, 154, 156, 157, 180, 181, 192, 193, 196, 197
  of life, 41, 100, 108, 145, 160, 171, 188, 194

Mann, Thomas, *The Magic Mountain*, 132, 133
master(s), 14, 20, 29, 30, 39, 45, 71, 76, 78, 79, 89, 96, 103, 112, 116, 121, 197
  morality, 86, 87, 90, 91, 135, 137
  race, 46, 184
  self-mastery, 64–66, 72
Megill, Alan, *Prophets of Extremity*, 3
metaphor, 18, 28, 103, 105, 136, 181, 189. *See also* physiology
metaphysics, 4, 11, 12, 54, 80, 82, 139, 148, 163, 197
  and Christianity, 128, 129, 137, 149, 170, 189
  destruction of, 5, 6, 143, 184, 191, 195, 198
  tradition of, 3, 43, 55, 84. *See also* Greek
method, 152, 191, 192, 198
Mithras, 127
modern(ity), 11, 16, 134, 136, 137, 139, 141, 143, 149, 156, 191, 192

and nihilism, 3, 16, 82, 124, 179
and sickness, 4, 6, 10, 82–84, 86, 125, 128, 129, 130, 142, 153, 154, 160, 170–72, 197
morality, 3, 13, 41, 42, 58, 67–69, 70, 75, 76, 80, 92, 97, 101, 127, 128, 130–33, 136, 141, 151–53, 158, 162, 170, 172, 175, 184
code(s), 12, 88, 138–40, 185
interpretation of, 5, 6, 137. *See also* master; slave
myth(s), 41, 53, 75, 140, 148, 170, 172, 177, 184

naive(té), 12, 13, 43, 74, 90, 100, 140, 155, 157, 179, 195, 197
of the pre-Socratics, 56, 58, 77, 141, 154
Nazi, 2
negation, 20, 24, 41, 42, 43, 65, 67, 69, 70, 88, 90, 95, 96, 98, 100, 102, 104, 106, 108, 112, 114, 116, 138, 141, 173, 174
of life, 12, 39, 81, 101, 120, 121, 137, 151, 163, 172, 176
Nehamas, Alexander, 165n.59, 169n.64
New Testament, 113
nihilism, 10, 15, 88, 126, 128, 130–33, 137–40, 141, 142, 143, 149, 150, 154–57, 160, 166, 167, 171, 173–83 passim, 197. *See also* modern(ity)
disease of, 3, 6, 83, 123–25, 146, 148, 151, 153, 168, 172, 191
nobility, 10, 29, 30, 31, 36, 37, 70, 78, 81, 88, 95, 115, 116, 127, 139, 147, 152, 167, 185, 188, 195, 197–99
ancient, 33, 42, 48, 63, 67, 68, 71, 73, 75, 86, 87, 92, 93, 96, 98. *See also* aristocracy
nothingness, 13, 119, 121, 141, 166, 175, 181

Occidental, 128
Oehler, Richard, 62n.8
Old Testament, 91
ontology, 60, 143
order of rank, 1, 5, 14, 16, 21, 33, 35, 38, 45, 47–49, 52, 63, 69, 77, 80, 87, 91–94, 98, 101, 109, 115, 116, 120, 130–32, 136, 147, 154, 176–79, 184, 189–91, 198. *See also* distance
among instincts, 17–19, 28–30, 36, 39, 53, 60, 64, 86, 95, 99, 109, 133, 135, 148–50, 174
organic, 3, 6, 11, 13–15, 17–19, 23, 28, 29, 31, 34–37, 39, 41, 44, 59, 66, 79, 83, 86, 164
function, 16, 27, 30, 42
organism, 13, 15–17, 22–25, 34, 36–39, 41, 43, 49, 57, 64, 65, 70, 74, 77, 80, 92, 93, 96, 99, 101–3, 105, 109, 110, 114, 127, 132, 133, 136, 148, 151, 152, 171, 182
cultural, 27–31, 42, 45–48, 52, 56, 63, 71, 90, 91, 95, 149, 150, 174, 177
Osiris, 127
Overbeck, Franz, 144, 145, 151, 160, 170
overcoming, 33, 36, 37, 39, 41, 47, 52, 68, 69, 125, 128, 147, 150, 154, 160, 197
life as, 34, 77, 159, 180, 182, 183
overman, 1, 7, 11, 12n, 18, 19, 21, 43–44n, 124, 129, 152, 160, 168, 169, 180–84, 195, 197

pain. *See* suffering
paradigm, 50, 80, 82, 149, 173, 175, 180
paralysis, 6, 70, 144, 188
Parmenides, 55, 78, 165
passion(s). *See* instinct
perspective(ism), 1, 28, 36, 41, 44, 53, 61, 78, 69, 87, 109, 136, 156, 165, 166, 178, 191. *See also* spirit
and interpretation, 6, 17, 18, 21, 35, 43, 148, 157
multiple perspectives, 4, 5, 19, 60, 69, 102, 114, 115, 189, 190, 197
and preservation, 2, 22, 24, 37, 59, 65, 66, 96, 103, 111, 112, 119, 132–34, 149, 150, 173–76, 184
Peyre, Henri, 155n.42
philosopher, 55, 75, 76, 84, 109, 124, 126, 129, 149, 170, 183–86, 195
type, 6, 28, 47, 49–54, 56, 58, 62, 66, 72–74, 77–80, 83, 98, 125, 161
philosophy, 1–3, 9, 11, 12, 16, 27, 61, 68, 69, 76, 82, 84, 88, 102, 105, 131, 124, 126, 127, 129, 137, 142, 143, 147, 151, 154, 163, 166, 183, 186–90, 192, 193, 194, 198, 199. *See also* Greek
task of, 78, 131, 145, 146, 152, 159
physician, 9, 31, 38, 71, 80, 128, 143, 144, 148, 153, 155, 159, 168, 171, 173, 182, 185, 191, 192
cultural, 1, 3, 6, 10, 16, 40n.5, 55, 56, 58, 73, 79, 129, 142, 197

Socrates as, 72, 73, 76–78, 81, 83, 84, 123, 125, 160, 167
physiology, 1–3, 6, 10, 11, 13, 16, 22, 27–30, 35, 39, 40, 42, 51, 58, 59, 62, 74, 80, 82, 85, 86, 105, 108, 113, 114, 123, 128, 146, 147, 156, 187, 189, 192, 197
  as metaphor, 5, 190, 191, 198, 199
physiological, 7, 15, 18, 19, 21, 23, 24, 34, 64, 65, 70, 71, 75, 90, 91, 93, 95, 98–100, 103, 104, 107, 109–12, 116, 119, 126, 130, 131, 133, 135–37, 141, 153, 159, 167, 170–72, 180, 182
  conditions, 20, 39, 73, 92, 108, 149
  dynamics, 2, 17, 19, 20, 27, 30, 31, 37, 40, 47, 59, 86, 113, 152, 178, 191
  function, 63, 148, 150, 174, 190
  phenomenon, 33, 36, 115, 134
  revaluation, 25, 67, 101, 152, 168, 175–77
Plato, 5, 12n, 29, 78, 79, 81–83, 126–28
  Crito, 81
  Phaedo, 81
  The Republic, 29
post-Socratic, 12, 15, 121
power, 1, 24, 33, 36, 37, 42, 48, 57, 60, 63, 64, 72, 84, 91–94, 97, 115, 120, 121, 132, 149, 153, 163, 164, 173, 175–79, 185, 188. *See also* force; strength; will to power
preservation, 18, 34, 44, 54, 56, 58, 73, 75, 77, 108, 116, 138, 147, 155, 169, 178, 185, 186, 188, 192
  and growth, 4, 19, 60, 130, 165, 179, 190, 191. *See also* fiction(s); perspective(ism)
  instinct of, 2, 14, 15, 22–25, 36, 37, 39, 42, 43, 53, 59, 64–69 passim, 71, 74, 80, 88–91, 93–104 passim, 106–12 passim, 114, 120, 132–34, 136, 149, 150, 172, 174–76
pre-Socratic(s), 11–13, 28, 50–55 passim, 57, 61, 62, 72, 74, 80, 92, 125, 130, 149, 161, 165. *See also* naive(té)
priest(s), 52, 53, 93–98, 106, 114n.14, 115–18, 120
Protagoras, 12n, 43n
psychology, 11, 21, 103, 104, 107, 111, 113, 116, 138, 147, 148, 151, 166, 179
  of the redeemer, 98, 99, 105, 112, 114

rational(ity), 42, 57, 58, 66, 67, 69, 70, 73, 75, 76, 78, 80, 81, 110, 112, 191

reason, 31, 41, 60, 61, 65–69, 70, 71–76 passim, 78, 80, 81, 103, 108, 126, 135, 189
recurrence, 1, 7, 124, 129, 151, 152, 160–84 passim
redeem(er), 97, 104, 107, 108, 110, 113, 115, 180, 181, 182, 185. *See also* psychology
religion, 52, 53, 86–88, 91, 97, 103, 107n, 116, 118, 120, 127, 170, 189
Renan, Ernest, 114, 115
resist(ance), 4, 16, 17, 22, 30, 32, 36, 37, 38, 47, 88, 95, 96, 99, 119
  desire for, 14, 15, 46, 68, 108, 112, 171, 182
  nonresistance, 69, 80, 100, 101, 103, 104, 108, 109, 159, 185
ressentiment, 86, 88, 96, 98, 103, 106–10, 112, 114–17 passim, 120, 121, 126, 128, 130, 134, 147, 149, 155, 158, 174, 175, 182, 184, 185. *See also* hatred
  and revenge, 90, 94, 100–102, 118, 119, 141, 167, 172
revaluation, 1, 7, 25, 67, 68, 73, 84, 92, 94, 101, 124, 126, 127, 129, 130, 137, 143, 146, 147, 151–55 passim, 158, 159, 167, 168, 174, 175, 187, 191, 192, 198, 199. *See also* physiological
Rilke, Rainer Maria, 9, 193
  Duino Elegies, 9
  Selected Poetry, 193

Salomé, Lou, 142
Sandvoss, Ernst, 61n
Schmidt, Hermann-Josef, 61n
Schrift, Alan, D., 62n.11, 190
  Nietzsche, 190
sickness, 5, 20, 22, 24, 36, 37, 42, 47, 51, 72, 74, 77, 80, 85, 89, 95, 101, 103, 109, 111, 115, 119, 120, 121, 124, 126, 127, 131, 133, 134, 137, 145, 155, 158, 159, 162, 168, 169, 174, 176, 180, 182, 185, 191, 192, 196. *See also* decadence; health(y); modern(ity); Socrates; symptom(s)
sign, 118, 120, 158, 178, 179
  and language, 4, 60, 67, 87, 103, 105, 106, 135
  as symptom, 28, 30, 46, 48, 51, 63, 71, 87, 173, 185, 188
slave, 28, 29, 35, 42, 86, 116, 121, 136, 178, 186
  morality, 87–91, 94, 95, 135n, 137

Socrates, 5, 6, 10–12, 16, 27, 40n.5, 41, 62–66, 74, 79, 82, 86, 90, 101–4, 108, 109, 111, 114, 115, 121, 126–29, 143, 152, 153, 155, 170, 175, 182, 194. *See also* physician
  and dialectics, 51, 61, 67, 68, 70–73, 75, 76, 78, 80, 83, 110, 112
  and pre-Socratics, 50, 51, 58–58, 61, 77–80, 125, 161
  and sickness, 58, 61, 73, 76, 78, 81, 83, 84, 125
species, 21, 23, 30, 34, 36, 44, 47, 68, 87, 129, 136, 137, 152, 153, 168, 182, 183, 191
spirit, 5, 10, 27, 28, 32, 34, 46, 50, 54, 55, 57, 75, 85, 93, 116, 121, 143, 154, 159, 160, 170, 187
  and deception, 39, 44, 49, 61, 64, 65, 90, 135, 136, 139, 149, 151, 158, 174, 183
  fictions of, 38, 41, 52, 60, 87, 88, 89, 94, 95, 102, 133, 134, 137, 148
  and perspective(ism), 35, 53, 103, 150, 165
spirituality, 13, 36, 40, 43, 45, 47, 63, 87, 104, 120, 130, 132–34, 137, 155, 176, 179, 184, 186, 188. *See also* strength
  Western, 128, 140, 142, 145, 146, 171
spiritualization, 37, 91, 126, 131, 133, 176, 180
  of cruelty, 31, 35, 42, 134, 178
strength, 5, 6, 28, 33, 34, 37, 40, 42, 53, 57, 59, 69, 70, 74, 79, 86, 90, 91, 93, 94, 101, 108, 110, 120, 121, 129, 136, 147, 150, 167, 171, 177, 178, 183, 185, 194, 195. *See also* force; exploitation; instinct, power; will to power
  accumulated, 22, 30–32, 39, 45, 47, 49, 52, 56, 66, 92, 109, 133, 149, 172–74, 181, 182
  enhanced, 15, 31, 36, 46, 48, 65, 89, 148, 149, 168, 170, 180, 182, 184
  spiritual, 38, 95, 131, 173, 180
  wasted, 23, 30, 39, 48, 102, 148
Strong, Tracy, 62n.9, 84
  Nietzsche, 84
suffering, 5, 10, 83, 88, 93, 95, 115, 119, 126, 136, 143, 144, 153, 159, 160, 161, 174, 175, 183, 187, 188, 192, 197, 198
  enduring, 37, 107, 108, 142, 197
  from life, 81, 90, 99, 100–103, 112
  meaning of, 57, 124, 125, 134, 135, 139, 142, 145–47, 154, 157, 162, 167, 185, 194, 195. *See also* cruel(ty)
  profound, 37, 38, 124, 125, 140, 155, 180, 196
suicide, 10, 81, 82, 124, 142, 145, 157, 167, 175
survival, 3, 14, 15, 18, 22, 29, 33, 36, 52, 53, 67, 88, 107, 108, 119, 139, 156
  of culture, 37, 40, 150, 179
  of Jewish culture, 93–96, 98, 100, 103, 120
symptom(s), 16, 23, 27, 88, 92, 108, 110, 120, 148, 156, 185
  of decadence, 62–64, 70, 74, 76, 81, 83, 90, 101, 112, 127
  of sickness, 4, 6, 20, 36, 58, 74, 76, 82, 86, 125, 129, 188. *See also* sign

Tacitus, 90
telos, 20, 69, 135, 138, 139, 189, 199
Thomas, Dylan, *Collected Poems*, 14
tragedy, 39–41, 58, 179, 134

unity, 10, 11, 17, 46, 58, 60, 74, 87, 118, 148, 189
  cosmic, 11, 13, 16, 41, 55, 68, 69, 80, 157, 159, 183, 184
utilitarian, 193
utility, 59, 74, 87, 88, 90, 157, 176

value(s), 3, 5, 10, 11, 18, 20, 21, 24, 30, 31, 37, 42, 43, 51, 68, 69, 70, 71–73, 74, 85, 87, 88, 90, 91, 94, 95, 96, 103, 109, 136, 147, 154, 155, 157, 159, 161, 166, 169, 170–72, 177, 179, 183, 194, 198. *See also* revaluation
  highest, 44, 128, 130, 131, 133, 134, 138, 141, 142, 148, 184, 188, 192, 199
  of life, 15, 39, 61, 66, 82, 98, 151, 156, 158, 162, 163, 168, 193. *See also* existence

Wagner, 196
war, 41, 48, 55, 66, 76, 95, 100, 102, 112, 115, 117, 130, 133, 135, 141, 151, 154, 167, 177, 179, 187, 197, 198. *See also* combat
  and instincts, 18, 24, 29, 31, 91, 96, 100, 102, 177
warrior, 1, 52, 53, 90, 93, 94, 96, 118, 135n, 153, 181, 188

elite, 30, 33, 37, 39, 42, 67, 68, 87, 90–92, 94. *See also* combat
weak(ness), 46, 52, 59, 67, 73, 74, 89, 90, 104, 108, 120, 131, 133, 134, 167–69, 170, 178, 185, 188, 192, 195, 197
  individual, 20, 22, 23, 28–30, 35, 42, 87, 88, 103. *See also* exhaustion; exploitation; instinct
will to power, 1, 2, 10, 12, 14, 15n.6, 19, 21, 22, 29, 32, 34, 44n, 46, 47, 51–55, 66, 68, 71, 73, 74, 154, 197
  dynamics of, 6, 20, 59, 82, 165

life as, 6, 9, 15, 16, 18, 23, 25, 27, 28, 30, 31, 38, 45, 49, 50, 56, 61, 65, 67, 69, 77–79, 83, 87, 95, 96, 98, 101, 104, 108, 112, 130, 133–36, 140, 141, 147, 150, 151, 156, 171, 172, 174, 181–83. *See also* being; body; experiment; force; interpretation; power; strength

Yaweh, 91, 96, 97, 106, 179

Ziegler, T., 62n.8
Zopyrus, 63–65